GAYLORD S

Books by Robert Alter

Rogue's Progress: Studies in the Picaresque Novel
Fielding and the Nature of the Novel
After the Tradition
Modern Hebrew Literature
Partial Magic: The Novel as a Self-Conscious Genre
Defenses of the Imagination
A Lion for Love: A Critical Biography of Stendhal
The Art of Biblical Narrative
Motives for Fiction
The Art of Biblical Poetry
The Invention of Hebrew Prose
The Literary Guide to the Bible (coedited with Frank Kermode)

The Pleasures of Reading

IN AN IDEOLOGICAL AGE

ROBERT ALTER

Simon and Schuster

New York   London   Toronto   Sydney   Tokyo

Simon and Schuster
Simon & Schuster Building
Rockefeller Center
1230 Avenue of the Americas
New York, New York 10020

Designed by Irving Perkins Associates
Manufactured in the United States of America
3   5   7   9   10   8   6   4   2

Library of Congress Cataloging in Publication Data

Alter, Robert.
    The pleasures of reading : in an ideological age / Robert Alter.
        p.   cm.
    Includes index.
    1. Books and reading.   2. Canon (Literature)   3. Literature—
History and criticism—Theory, etc.   I. Title.
Z1003.A567   1989
028'.9—dc19   88-36590
                                                                CIP
ISBN 0-671-62783-X

For Tom Rosenmeyer
a kind of personal Festschrift,
with affection and diffidence

Acknowledgments

The first spark for the idea of this book was struck in a delightful luncheon conversation with Jane Isay in the fall of 1985. I am deeply grateful to Jane Isay, who a number of years previous had also been unusually helpful as my editor for *The Art of Biblical Narrative*; and I regret that circumstances made it impossible for us to work together on the present book. Part or all of the manuscript was read by Ziva Ben-Porat, Michael Bernstein, Seymour Chatman, Carol Cosman, Marilyn Fabe, Benjamin Harshav, and Thomas Schmidt, and I thank them all for their suggestions, which at least had the effect of saving me from my more egregious imprudences. Some of the ideas and texts expounded have been tested on my students in comparative literature at Berkeley, and, as always, I have learned from the vigor of their questioning and the astuteness of their comments. The typescript was prepared with unflagging patience and precision by Janet Livingstone. The first two chapters were written during a sabbatical semester made possible by a sabbatical salary supplement from the Humanities Research Council of the University of California at Berkeley. Secretarial assistance and incidental research expenses were covered through special funds made available by the chancellor of the University of California at Berkeley.

Contents

INTRODUCTION

The Disappearance of Reading

Peculiar things have clearly been happening in the academic study of literature. This book is in part a response to that tide of peculiarity, though it is meant to be a good deal more than a polemic, for I am convinced that there are more interesting and more important things for a critic to do than merely to expose fashionable absurdities. It may nevertheless be helpful to the reader for me to devote some attention at the outset to the oppositional impulse of my undertaking.

A good many of the most influential currents in criticism and literary theory today can be traced back to the late 1960s. That was a time which seemed to many full of promise and intellectual excitement. In France, where most of the new trends began, the stodginess of academic criticism in that country was dramatically displaced by a bold enterprise of systematic analysis, drawing on linguistics and anthropology, that sought to situate literary studies among the *sciences humaines;* by a radical questioning of Western philosophic premises undertaken through the combined investigation of literary and philosophic texts; by scrutinizing literature through the lens of a drastically revised Freudianism or

Marxism or a "discourse"-based historicism that at once incorporated both and transcended both. In England and America, where literary criticism has by and large been meager on conceptual matters and not much interested in the systematic aspects of literature, these innovative lines of thought seemed to augur the dawning of a new era. The discussion of literature would no longer be the province of the proverbial English professor with comfortable tweed jacket and pipe luxuriating in his chatty, complacent learning. Literature at last would be studied with intellectual rigor, against the background of philosophy, psychology, anthropology, and linguistics; and the most urgent issues of politics, history, personal and gender identity, would be boldly exposed through the analysis of literary texts.

All this ferment was understandable, and, at least at the beginning, had its commendable side. Anglo-American literary studies, as several observers have noted, were in fact "underconceptualized," and they also tended to be geographically parochial in their intellectual purview. Again, the intrinsic value of the literary work was generally taken as a matter of unexamined faith—in one way, by the followers of F. R. Leavis in England, in other ways, by the New York critics and the New Critics in the United States. There was surely something to be gained by looking at literature with the apparatus of different systems of abstract thought, by tracing literature's own systematic operations, and by exercising a higher degree of skepticism about the claims literature made for itself. Of these three broad modes of awareness, the one that has led to the most palpable gains is the concentration on literature as a system. Here, foreign influences have been especially fruitful: Russian Formalism, French narratology, German reader-response theory, Soviet semiotics, and the Tel Aviv School of Poetics. In many respects, however, the great promise of twenty years ago has turned to bitter ashes. The most central failure, I think, is that so many among a whole generation of professional students of literature have turned away from reading. In part, I mean simply that the sundry versions of what Paul Ricoeur has called in connection with Freud "the hermeneutics of suspicion" have led beyond skepticism to an attitude sometimes approaching disdain for literature. In both criticism and in debates over curriculum, one encounters an insistence that daily newspapers, pulp fiction, private diaries, clinical case studies, and imaginative literature belong on one level, that any distinctions among them are dictated chiefly by ideology. One need not argue for an attitude of unreserved adulation toward literature, but without some form of passionate engagement in literary works, without a sense of deep pleasure in the experience of reading, the whole enterprise of teaching and writing about literature quickly becomes pointless.

In fact, for many of the new trends in literary studies, the object of the preposition "about" is often no longer literature. The great prefix of the day is *meta-*: metalanguage, metatext, metadiscourse. To be sure, a discussion of the premises of discussion, talk about how we talk about literature, is necessary for the maintenance of methodological scrupulosity. What is distressing is that such discussion to the second degree should in many instances come to displace the discussion of literature itself. One can read article after article, hear lecture after lecture, in which no literary work is ever quoted, and no real reading experience is registered. Although no one has done a precise quantitative study of current curricula, I strongly suspect that many young people now earning undergraduate degrees in English or French at our most prestigious institutions have read two or three pages of Lacan, Derrida, Foucault, and Kristeva for every page of George Eliot or Stendhal.

This is not to suggest that students should be turned back to some imagined idyllic age when literature and only literature was read. By this point in time, the value of large intellectual overviews and interdisciplinary perspectives should be self-evident. What is at issue is a matter of proportion: with the finite time granted to anyone for reading, whether in or out of the university, should a person drawn to literature be encouraged to devote more attention to Lacan than to Poe, to Barthes than to Balzac? One might further question whether the best guidance is provided by this particular cluster of speculative thinkers, who as Luc Ferry and Alain Renaut have shrewdly argued,[1] represent a reductive French rhetorical radicalization of German thought—Nietzsche, Marx, Freud, and Heidegger—that may lead to an intellectual dead end.

Not long ago, a young woman enrolled in one of my undergraduate courses in comparative literature came up to me to tell me how much she had enjoyed reading *Moby-Dick,* to which the class had just devoted three weeks. Oddly and interestingly, what she particularly liked was the book's grotesque humor, which, despite the bleakness of Melville's sense of life, seemed to her quite hilarious. She went on to say that she was surprised at her own response to the novel because in the previous semester two different professors of English, her major field, had told her that *Moby-Dick* was a bore and scarcely worth the effort of reading. It is hard not to construe this as a discouraging sign of the times, a confirmation of the suspicion that literature faculties may be increasingly populated with scholars who don't particularly care for literature. I am not in the least proposing that one must be regularly reverential toward the literary work, or that it is never appropriate to question the so-called "canon" (I will have something to say about the problematic nature of that notion in my first chapter). There are arguable objections that can be leveled against *Moby-Dick*—that it is sometimes bombastic, that it is top-heavy with whaling lore, that its narrator is inconsistent or even unconvincing, that as a microcosm of human life it is drastically unbalanced because it is a world without women. It is also, warts and all, one of the stupendous achievements of American prose, a work that, even if it may have its irritating side, haunts the imagination, is repeatedly stirring, troubling, exciting, and, as my student testifies, sometimes amusing as well. One may legitimately want to contend with *Moby-Dick*, but a teacher of literature who dismisses it as too much of a bore to read might be better off teaching computer science or selling insurance.

Or perhaps, to give the new academic trends their due, such a person might be better off teaching sociology or history, psychology or political science, whatever the departmental aegis. That is to say, there is real intellectual interest in using literary texts for the investigation of social, cultural, philosophic, or economic issues, and though one may have serious qualms about the ideological tendentiousness with which these issues are sometimes now pursued, such investigation surely has a legitimate place in the university. To examine literature as a symptom of something else—say, high feudalism or late capitalism—requires neither a special liking for literature nor an ability to discriminate between derivative and original, second-rate and first-rate writers. Analysis of this sort may have its own compelling character, but it is disquieting to contemplate the prospect of literature programs in which such analysis is proffered not as a complementary alternative but as the predominant, or even the "correct," approach. The neo-Marxist critic Terry Eagleton shows admirable candor and consistency in proposing that a curricular move be made from literature to "discourse studies," so that instructors would be free to teach Shakespeare, television scripts, government memoranda, comic books, and advertising copy in a single program as instances of the language of power. What is regrettable, though also characteristic of a certain prevalent ideological coerciveness, is that Eagleton also proposes the abolition of departments of literature, having demonstrated, at least to his own satisfaction, that there is no coherent phenomenon that can be called literature.

I will have a good deal to say about this last proposition in my first chapter, but let me emphasize here that the burden of this whole book is that there is a great deal in the intrinsic operations of literature vitally calling for our attention, however much we may also want to look beyond the literary text to its multifarious contexts. Attention of this sort, moreover, by no means implies a commitment either to "monumentalize" the texts under consideration or to regard them as pure aesthetic objects. On the contrary, many— perhaps even most— original works of literature, as I hope more than a few of my examples will show, are themselves powerful vehicles of subversion, variously directed against prevalent beliefs and ideologies, received social and moral attitudes, literary tradition, against the very conception of what literature is. The minute attention to how literature speaks through its own complex and distinctive language is an indispensable step in the process of fully realizing the subversive power of the text, and one could scarcely find a better example than *Moby-Dick*, with its extraordinary deployment of imagery, symbol, allusion, scene, and even rhythmic movement to effect a radical redefinition of nature, historical time, meaning, and value.

The failure of the promise of the late 1960s manifests itself in two principal ways. One is the distancing—in the more extreme cases, an actual estrangement—from the experience of reading literature that I have just indicated. The other is the division of the academic study of literature, especially in the United States, into competing sectarian groups, each with its own dogmas and its own arcane language. Sectarianism has a perennial appeal, at least as much for intellectuals as for others, because it offers to the initiate a reassuring sense of certainty as well as a sense of superiority in relation to the unredeemed masses. The new academic

sectarianism may well be a direct consequence of the unprec-
edented expansion of the American university system that
took place during the sixties. With scores of thousands of
people teaching literature at thousands of institutions of
higher learning, with academic journals and books multiplying
like rabbits, a young scholar may achieve a certain calming
elevation over the madding crowd by following one master,
adopting one "advanced" methodology, and proving fealty on
both those counts by speaking one hieratic language.

The question of language is one of the most acute and
revealing symptoms of this general intellectual disorder in
literary studies. The decline of stylistic standards in critical
writing, though lamentable in itself, is, as an aesthetic matter,
a secondary concern—I refer to the fact that in some circles it
is now regarded as an intellectual virtue to write badly or
obscurely, with at least one prominent literary scholar having
raised the banner of "difficulty" as the very aim and emblem
of critical prose. What is more pertinent to the disturbing
prospect of the disappearance of reading is that the language
of criticism now often reflects an emotional alienation from
the imaginative life of the text under discussion, often seems
in its bristling conceptuality empty of an experiential ground
in reading.

Abstraction, to be sure, is a necessary instrument of
thought, but the stylistic habits of much current criticism
reflect a disquieting tendency to pitch critical discussion at
one or two removes of abstraction from what actually addresses readers in the literary text. One symptom of this
trend is the wild proliferation of verbs with the -ize suffix:
these days, almost everything in a poem or novel is problem-
atized, thematized, narrativized, totalized, historicized, fet-
ishized. In certain frameworks, technical terms may have
their value, but the promiscuous use of intellectual jargon all
too frequently introduces real imprecision or serves as a cover
for the lack of original thought, as one may readily see by

scanning the current academic journals, whose pages are clotted with "discourse," "discursive strategy," "erotics of textuality," "diagesis," "foregrounding," "signifieds," "aporia," and much more of the same.

Let me offer three examples of the way so many academic writers have come to discuss literature. The examples are taken from articles published in the last year or two; for reasons of simple decency, I will not cite the sources or the authors' names.

The first excerpt is from an article on Kafka:

> Everywhere there are moving barriers and a-signifying elements which point to desiring production outside the oedipal domain and rend apart repressive totalities, a testament to Kafka's experimental machine.

It goes without saying that the proverbial common reader would be able to make little of this, and as we shall see in a moment, even less of our next two examples, but perhaps unintelligibility is the least grave of the charges that can be directed against this mode of critical writing. After all, a small lexicon of technical terms can be mastered in a couple of hours' industrious reading, and adherents would argue that a new precision is gained thereby. The sentence may be repellent, but what is baffling about it is not hard to unscramble. "Moving" in "moving barriers" is a participle whereas the "desiring" of "desiring production" has a gerundive force and seems to mean "the production of desire." The concept behind our writer's phrase is a hybrid of Freud and Marx, and the wording also reflects a fashionable fondness for mechanistic metaphors (like the designation of Kafka's iconoclastic fiction as an "experimental machine") about which I will have more to say in Chapter Two. Lurking behind all the forbidding language is a perception about Kafka that has been often stated not only more elegantly but also more instructively by critics who do not use this jargon of the new literary techno-crats: that Kafka invents a mode of enigmatic fiction which taps an inchoate realm of the unconscious and defies conven-tional habits of interpretation. One wonders, moreover, whether the liberationist language ("rend apart repressive totalities") is strictly appropriate to the motive and feel of Kafka's imaginative enterprise, or whether, as happens too often in contemporary criticism, the text has been popped into a premade ideological cubbyhole that in some ways distorts its actual contours.

My next example is from a discussion of Stephen Crane:

> The becoming-visible of writing must be considered in terms of a programmatic equation or identification that, I want to suggest, underwrites realist discourse. This equa-tion involves the perfect "fit" between the ontology of writing and the specific material—the historically specific subject-matter— of the social body-machine complex, the perfect "fit" between the (apparently nonhistoricizable) ontology of writing and a historically specific biome-chanics.

In this writer, the common machine metaphor is entirely explicit and, indeed, a conscious element in the conceptual argument. Whether this neat correspondence between nineteenth-century biomechanics and realist fiction actually exists is a question that lies beyond our present concerns, but the sweeping departure from literary text to large historical context is surely facilitated by this ponderous language so utterly removed from the fiction. One suspects an influence of Heidegger, perhaps mediated by Sartre ("the becoming-visible of writing") in the rebarbative style. The syntactic collapse and terminological tangle of the second sentence are so egregious that one wonders what its author could possibly make of the prose of Stephen Crane. Realism is swollen into "realist discourse" perhaps under the influence of Foucault, for whom devious and oppressive discourse determines most of what happens in culture, and it should be observed that "discourse" is a prominent general offender in contemporary criticism. As a binary opposite to narration (*récit*), "discourse" has a definite utility, but nowadays one finds it used instead of style, rhetoric, speech, diction, narrative technique, narrative structure, fictional representation, language as a formal system, and a good deal else.

My final example is from an essay on J. L. Borges:

> What seems to me important are the correspondences between Borges and midrash in the idea of intertextuality, in the concept of reading not as lineality but as a configuration of textual space, in the notion of the destructurization of the text as a condition for deciphering it, and in the arch principle, as I have said, of interpretative metatextuality as the basis of decentralization.

This single sprawling sentence is a veritable anthology of jargon and voguish imprecisions. In this instance, the addiction to sectarian cant leads to something close to nonsense. It is a loose and misleading approximation to say that the reading experience of, say, "Death by the Compass" or "The Garden of Forking Paths" is "a configuration of textual space," and that peculiar metaphor simply doesn't apply to midrash, the early rabbinic homiletic commentary on the Bible. "Interpretative metatextuality," once the lingo is deciphered, is in fact a preoccupation of Borges, though not at all of midrash, but even in the case of the Argentine writer, it has very little to do with the destructurization or the decentralization of the text (the fondness for the -*ize* suffix, it will be seen, is often complemented by an attachment to the prefix *de-*, with its presumably salutary suggestion of taking things apart). This observation, in sum, on Borges and the rabbis, like the ones on Kafka and Crane we considered before it, is a symptom of the disappearance of reading, for it reflects an inclination not to engage the literary work in its subtle and compelling specificity but rather to use it as a prooftext for preconceived, and all too general, views.

What I try to do, then, in the chapters that follow, is not merely to question a few of the fundamentally misleading dogmas of the new critical sectarians but to propose a set of concepts that will point toward a return to reading. I argue that the language of literature is distinct from the use of language elsewhere in its resources and in its possibilities of expression (Chapter One); that literature is not just a self-referential closed circuit but is connected in meaningful and revelatory ways with the world of experience outside the text (Chapter Two); that there are modalities of literary expression accessible to analytic attention that can give readers clearer insight into the text (Chapters Three through Six); and that there is a crucial difference between interpretive pluralism, which I espouse, and interpretive anarchy (Chapter Seven). The core of the book, Chapters Three through Six, which is also the part most free from polemic, works on the assumption that there are actually certain transmissible skills of reading. This is not to say that there is ever one correct way of reading a literary text but that there are formal resources of literary expression, susceptible to analysis and to critical definition, worth attending to, for the attention may actually sharpen our perception and heighten our pleasure as readers. In contrast to the various critical trends that presume the time has come to move on from literature to some form of politics or metaphysics or politics and metaphysics combined, my argument is that there remain many challenging and useful things to do in the actual study of imaginative literature, both in the classroom and in critical writing.

Since the title I have chosen may sound excessively general, I want to emphasize two basic ways in which this is a study that is intended to be kept within modest limits. In the course of highlighting the various pleasures of reading, I have not tried to provide a comprehensive lexicon of the language of literature. One could readily conceive chapters on rhetoric, genre, convention, tone, and other topics; and I actually contemplated including a chapter on imagery but decided against it after devoting a good deal of space to figurative language in my discussion of style. Any attempt at comprehensiveness would produce a volume three or four times the length of this one, which would inevitably be a reference work rather than a book readers might be likely to read from beginning to end, as I hope they will do in the present case. In order to convey a coherent general sense of what is involved in reading literary texts, it seemed to me sufficient to try to throw a little light on some, but by no means all, of the major aspects of literary expression.

The other self-imposed limitation on the scope of this study is more far-reaching. I in no way claim that the perspective I offer here is the only one warranted for the study of literature. This is a book about the *language* of literature and how it provides rich pleasures for readers, not about the origins of that language, its sundry contexts, its precise relation to other languages. Thus, I make no attempt to deal with the roots of the literary work in the psychology of the writer, or with the ways the reader's response may be dictated by the reader's own psychology, though those seem to me compelling questions that have so far eluded satisfactory answers. Similarly, I do not address the complex anchorage of the literary work in its historical setting, though the neglect of history, or, at best, the eccentric and at times tendentious use of history, is one of the principal weaknesses of contemporary criticism. I do not in the least assume that the literary text is autonomous, absolute, divorced from its specific cultural contexts; but one can't very well talk about everything that needs to be talked about all at once, and it seemed enough to grapple with in one book to try to parse the inflections and syntax of literature's intrinsic language, leaving aside at least for the time being the questions of where that language comes from and where it is directed in historical and psychological space.

Especially because of my conviction that all study of literature must emerge from and return to reading, I have made my case throughout this book by the analysis of examples of literary texts. I have drawn most of the illustrations from English and American writers, despite my own keen interest in other national literatures, in order to avoid the difficulties of dealing with translations when precise discriminations had to be made about features of language, and also because I assumed these texts were likely to be more familiar to readers than works composed in other languages. Choosing examples I knew intimately from teaching and rereading, I have ended up scanting dramatic literature, which I enjoy without professional involvement, and have not represented the medieval period, for which I have no competence. I did make some conscious effort to include a variety of different styles, sensibilities, historical eras, and formal orientations from the many works that have given me pleasure, but I have in no way sought to strike any numerical balance in regard to the period, the politics, the gender, the beliefs, the sexual orientation of the writers. Affirmative-action quotas do not strike me as the most useful point of departure for a study of the language of literature. And since all that is at issue here is the convenience of illustration, no inferences are warranted about my viewing any writer not included as "extracanonical." I could have used the wonderfully resourceful Argentine novelist Manuel Puig in my discussion of allusion instead of Faulkner or Virginia Woolf, but that would have involved a problem of translation; I could have used the brilliant Anglo-Indian writer Salman Rushdie instead of Dickens in the chapter on style, but he would have been unfamiliar to many readers.

In proposing a critical account of some of the principal aspects of literary expression, this study aspires to a certain systematic descriptive character. At the same time, through the abundant discussions of illustrative texts, I have tried to stay in touch with reading as a lively experience, a source of complex pleasure and insight. As readers, we live in constant unfathomable intercourse with the written word—that mere artifice which ensconces itself in the inner sanctum of our imagination, delights us in odd and unpredictable ways, even affects our perception of the world. "I have measured out my life with coffee spoons," Eliot's Prufrock says in the midst of confessing the tedium, the triviality, the timidity of his existence. The image itself is a borrowing from the French poet Jules Laforgue, but in its achieved formulation as a line in an English poetic monologue, what is it about these words that arrests our attention, suggests multiple implications, binds the rhythm (a regular iambic pentameter with an extra initial syllable) with the meaning of the image? Prufrock is a sad character in a sad fix, but a reader may find something quite pleasurable in the coffee spoon metaphor, the rhyme of "spoons" with "afternoons" at the end of the preceding line, the subtle and elusive interplay between coffee spoons and toast and tea, pins, butt-ends of days, the pipes of lonely men in shirt-sleeves, and other concrete elements in the poem. Literary language is an intricate, inventively designed vehicle for setting the mind in restless pleasing motion, which in the best of cases may give us a kind of experiential knowledge relevant to our lives outside reading. In all that follows I will try to explain what it is about the properties of the language of literature that enables it to involve us in this endless, fascinating process.

CHAPTER ONE

The Difference of Literature

Are the kinds of attention we bring to bear on literature, the skills we use to read it, different from those we exercise in reading other sorts of texts? A generation ago, most critical circles in Europe and America would have answered the question unhesitatingly with a fervent yes. Behind that affirmation stood a long tradition of ideas about literature as a unique repository of values and a uniquely rich vehicle of expression that went back at least to the early nineteenth century, or perhaps further still, to Renaissance apologies for literature like Sir Philip Sidney's *Defense of Poetry*. Over the past two decades, however, all such "privileging" of literature over other kinds of discourse has come to seem radically suspect. We read literature, the new wave critics have argued on various grounds, with the same set of complex skills we use to read newspapers, legal rulings, menus, advertisements, sex manuals; and it is only cultural prejudice or ideological conviction that allows us to claim a special truth for literature. For the moment, I would like to concentrate on the issue of how literature is read, leaving the question of truth for separate consideration.

It is obvious that there are usually strong continuities between the ways we read literary texts and the ways we read other kinds of texts. If this were not so, we would all need elaborate specialized training, like taking courses in Sanskrit or calculus, in order to make sense of the simplest story or poem. In fact, this sort of sharp split between literary and ordinary language does occasionally occur in the evolution of literary history. Thus, the poetry of medieval Spain in both Arabic and Hebrew was written in a "classical" literary language entirely different from the vernacular of Andalusian Arabs and Jews, and was composed, moreover, according to the most intricate literary conventions that had little connection with how people wrote and spoke in everyday circumstances. In our own century, certain radical literary experiments, like Joyce's in *Finnegans Wake* or those of the French New Novelists of the fifties and sixties, have so strenuously deformed or reformed the shape of words and sentences, the sequence of verbs and units of syntax, the conventional patterns of narrative continuity, that they have to some degree created their own special languages and may well require some specialized training to read. These exceptions to the general rule suggest that there could be an inherent momentum in the literary use of language that swerves away from the norms of ordinary language, but the manifold connections between the two can scarcely be ignored. When we read a novel or poem, our eyes scan the printed page, left to right, up to down, and our minds identify grammatical forms, syntactical patterns, word choices (often with a subliminal awareness of choices rejected by the writer) with the same cultural reflexes—the same competence, as linguists say—that we use to decipher nonliterary texts. The shared ground of expression is what enables us to put down an issue of *Newsweek* or *The National Geographic* and begin a story by Eudora Welty or a novel by John le Carré without undergoing some sort of mental disorientation.

But the new wave of literary theory has led many to insist not merely on this obvious continuity but on a leveling of literature with other kinds of discourse, and it is worth looking closely at what goes on in literary texts to see whether such leveling is analytically defensible. The denial of the distinctiveness of literature has been made from two general standpoints, one linguistic and the other ideological. Since it may be easier to proceed from large overviews to the close inspection of textual details, let me begin with the ideological argument.

Literature, it has often been claimed over the past quarter century, is neither a stable nor a coherent entity. One way you can tell this is by the shifting nature of the literary canon. As cultural fashions change and new values come to the fore, writers once deemed peripheral or uncanonical are brought into the canon, others once thought central being displaced to the margins. More drastically, books that were not originally imagined to belong to the category of literature, like Augustine's *Confessions*, Nietzsche's *The Birth of Tragedy*, Freud's *The Interpretation of Dreams*, are read into the canon and discussed in the same breath—or in the same course—with novels and poems. The pronounced tendency of our own time has been toward a new inclusiveness, a taking into the canon of philosophers and theorists of culture, previously neglected women writers, unrecognized minority writers, practitioners of folk poetry, and other forms of expression once held to be subliterary.

This movement of inclusion in itself suggests to many that there may be something arbitrary, and, indeed, slanted, about the canon. Literature, then, according to this line of reasoning, is not a fixed entity but a reflection in any society of the values of the ruling class, abetted by a learned or priestly elite. The poems, plays, stories, and discursive texts of a culture may variously delight or stir its members, but they are admitted to the canon chiefly because of their consonance with the distribution of power in the society, their effectiveness in reassuring or training or lulling people so that they will better perform their given social roles. Literature, in this view, is ultimately an arm of politics and as such it can be anything that politics decrees; its status as a specially valued kind of writing—"privileged," presumably, like the privileged classes with their undeserved wealth—is conferred by the values that regulate the flow of power in a society. This position has been stated with uncompromising clarity by the British neo-Marxist Terry Eagleton, who has no difficulty in imagining a future society in which Shakespeare would no longer make sense as literature, "would be no more valuable than much present-day graffiti."[1]

"Damn braces, bless relaxes," William Blake once observed, and it is surely bracing to be reminded that the canon of Western literature was not given for all time from Sinai or Olympus, that its contours have often reflected ideological pressures. On the other hand, the reduction of literature purely to considerations of ideology overlooks a good deal of the historical evidence. For all the changes through the ages in values, and the changes in political arrangements behind them, the literary tradition exhibits a surprising degree of stability. It might be imagined as a large and variegated corpus with a relatively stable center and intermittently shifting borders. We have gone through a dizzying variety of societies over the past two millennia, but none has seriously questioned the status as literature of Homer, Sophocles, Sappho, Virgil, Horace. The significance of the major writers is of course constantly redefined as values shift, but not their connection to literature. Shakespeare has been presented in every conceivable mode from neoclassical stateliness to raucous punk, but even on the basis of a mere four centuries, one would have to say that a society in which Shakespeare's plays were no more than graffiti would have to be a science-fiction construct in which people moved on conveyor belts instead of legs and sorted out reality with microchip implants instead of brains.

One reason for the cohesiveness of literary tradition over a stretch of almost three thousand years is its powerful impulse of self-recapitulation. Writers repeatedly work under the influence of a founding model, whether happily or not; they repeatedly return to origins, seeking to emulate, extend, transpose, or outdo some founder (but not merely to outdo— hence the limitation of the idea of oedipal rebellion as the chief mechanism of literary production). Unless we keep this principle in mind, it will seem bizarre that a seventeenth-century Puritan poet like Milton and an eighteenth-century Catholic-born Deist poet like Pope should devote such energy to the emulation of pagan Homer and Virgil as the great models for their enterprise. On a briefer time scale, it would otherwise be strange that Stendhal and Flaubert, as worldly novelists of post-Napoleonic France, should revert to the model of Cervantes, a writer who flourished two and a half centuries earlier in the aftermath of feudalism that was monarchic Spain.

There is a backward-looking aspect of literature that cuts across political systems; writers, whatever their tacit and explicit ideological commitments, are often extraordinarily preoccupied with literature as an internally coherent, self-propelling set of models and norms. Cromwell was a powerful consideration for Milton but in the end far less compelling than Virgil and the author or authors of Genesis. Again, there is more involved here than the relation, rebellious or other-wise, of literary son to father. The founding instance of every genre, subgenre, or cogent literary mode at once establishes a vocabulary others can abundantly use and constitutes an achievement they may well envy. The achievement elicits competition, or perhaps rebellion, but the vocabulary encourages receptivity, the shared use of valuable common property. The peculiar orientation of literature toward such models

Arnoldian

needs to be understood as one of the conditions for the distinctiveness of the language of literature. Aeschylus and Sophocles invent tragedy; virtually everything that follows in the genre at least indirectly exploits the resources they made available and is gauged by the benchmark they set—at any rate, until Shakespeare, who, blowing the life of genius into an Elizabethan hybrid dramatic form, creates a new model, a new benchmark.

To think of any piece of writing as literature, it has been argued, is to attribute special value to it without in the end being able to specify the nature of the class of textual objects to which it has been attached. The act of classification, then, has to be a reflection of cultural or political values not intrinsic to the writing. It would be foolish not to recognize that literary works are often esteemed at least partly because they express values deemed important by the culture at large: the courtly romance and feudal society are a particularly clear instance of the general principle. But the force of this whole argument will be considerably weakened if we can identify intrinsically literary values, and I believe that to be the case. If any purposeful ordering of language implies some intention of communication, literature is remarkable for its densely layered communication, its capacity to open up multifarious connections and multiple interpretations to the recipient of the communication, and for the pleasure it produces in making the instrument of communication a satisfying aesthetic object— or more precisely, the pleasure it gives us as we experience the nice interplay between the verbal aesthetic form and the complex meanings conveyed. It is on these grounds that it is valued as literature. To call *King Lear* literature and categorically to deny that classification to the most cleverly spray-painted inscription on a wall is to recognize that two drastically different orders of communication are going on in the two "texts" in question, that of *Lear* being not only infinitely richer, infinitely more complicated and more pleasurable, but also recognizably allied with the order of communication that takes place in a very large and variegated body of texts we confidently identify as literature.

It may not be altogether fair to compare the literary act of communication to that of graffiti, or laundry lists, or telephone directories, since there are, after all, works of philosophy, history, psychological theory, and social analysis that exhibit the most formidable complexities. I do not mean to claim that literature is more precise or more profound than these other kinds of discourse, only that it is different in the way it plays with multiple meanings and in the centrality of aesthetic pleasure to the act of communication. (And there are, of course, intriguing borderline cases in which the ostensibly nonliterary text achieves literary force or uses literary techniques, as in Gibbon's history, Plato's philosophy, Freud's psychological theory; but fuzzy borders do not imply that a phenomenon lacks distinctive character.) Spinoza's *Ethics* might arguably offer more probing perceptions of human nature than *Tom Jones* or *War and Peace*, but, even with the essayistic elements in both those novels, the how and what of communication in them are very different from Spinoza's, and the range of aesthetic delights they offer is far removed from any chaste (and purely secondary) pleasure a reader may experience in the logical form of the *Ethics*.

In Chapter 24 of Genesis, Abraham sends his servant from Canaan to the family home in Mesopotamia to find a bride for Isaac, and the servant encounters at the well exactly the girl he is looking for, the lovely, nubile, and generous Rebekah. He loads her with precious ornaments and she hastens home to bring her family the news of the stranger's arrival. At this point, her brother Laban, who will play an important role later in the story of Jacob, is introduced in the following terms: "And it came to pass, when he saw the nose-ring, and the bracelets upon his sister's arms, and when he heard the words of Rebekah his sister, saying, Thus spake the man unto me, that he came unto the man; and behold, he stood by the camels at the well. And he said, Come in, thou blessed of the Lord; wherefore standest thou without? for I have prepared the house, and room for the camels" (Genesis 24:30–31).[2] The remarkable speed of characterization here is in part dictated by the extraordinary economy of means employed by biblical narrative, but the kind of communication that takes place is also characteristically literary. All we know about Laban when he appears on the scene is his name (it means "white one," which later will become thematically significant), his family relationship, and, most strikingly, his eye for the glittering jewels with which his sister appears suddenly bedecked. The eyeing of the jewels is tucked into an introductory subordinate clause, and what it means as a narrative datum is left in delicate suspension. Perhaps, because the seeing is coupled syntactically with the hearing of Rebekah's report, it merely indicates a recognition that the stranger has good connections and honorable intentions, and therefore may be welcomed into the household. But the strategic reticence with which the information is conveyed opens the strong suspicion that Laban's Oriental professions of hospitality are mere hypocrisy, and triggered by the profit motive. The suspicion will be confirmed a quarter of a century later in narrated time through Laban's struggles with Jacob over property and compensation; for the moment, we are invited to set his somewhat ambiguous reception of a guest against quite different hospitality scenes represented earlier in the narrative.

What I would stress about the literary character of this communication is not only the avoidance of semantic closure, the encouraging of a balancing act between different possible construals, but also what might be called the high fun of the act of communication. As receivers of this potentially ambiguous message, we are meant, I think, to take pleasure in the very economy with which it is conveyed (in other kinds of texts, profusion or ornamentation rather than economy might be the source of pleasure), in the syntactic subordination of the information, which has the teasing effect of disguising it but disguising it transparently. In this way we are invited to join actively in a game for which the rules are indicated by the text, imaginatively beginning to build a picture of Laban's character that will have to be augmented and revised if and when we are given more narrative data about him. This open-ended process of pleasurable discovery is literary reading par excellence.

The deep and abiding attractions of this literary experience both for writers and their audiences help explain a curious aspect of literary history—that the literary canon, for all its supposed attachment to ideological values, often incorporates texts that run counter to the dominant ideology of the culture. The novel, for example, is clearly associated through its subject matter, its language, the economic conditions in which it flourishes, with the rise to power of the middle classes and the large movement of urbanization that goes hand in hand with the Industrial Revolution. Thus an older generation of Marxist criticism was encouraged to think of the novel as "the epic of bourgeois life." But if among the principal bourgeois values are acquisitiveness, belief in material progress, disciplined social behavior, sobriety, dedication to family, patriotism, and boosterism, one must conclude that some of the most central figures in the canon of the nineteenth-century novel—Stendhal, Flaubert, Dostoyevsky, Melville, even Balzac—radically subvert these values or vehemently spurn them in their fiction.

The Bible, as the model from which the concept of canon was drawn for application to secular literature, is an especially instructive case in point. Recently, some critics have taken pains to remind us what everyone has always known, that the Hebrew Bible in particular is a preeminently patriarchal document. There are hardly grounds for debate on the subject, but one wonders why the male makers of this patriarchal canon included the story of Tamar and Judah (Genesis 38), Ruth, Esther, the portrait of female shrewdness and male malleability in Rebekah and Jacob, the satire of muscle-bound concupiscent male gullibility in the Samson story. Still more drastically, how did Job, with its radical rejection of an anthropocentric creation and of retributive justice, Ecclesiastes, with its sense of futile, meaningless cycles, the Song of Songs, with its exuberantly playful eroticism, get into the Bible? What happens here, in one of the two ancient matrices of Western literature, is what happens again, repeatedly and characteristically, in the evolution of literary tradition: the literary imagination develops a momentum of its own, in indifference or in actual contravention to reigning ideology; the pleasures of collaborative play we glimpsed in Laban's eyeing of the jewels are exercised far more complexly in the revelatory power of Job's poetry, in the haunting cadences of Ecclesiastes, in the delightfully suggestive imagery of the Song of Songs, and through this collaborative play a silent compact is created between writer and reader, against certain dominant trends of the culture.

But since any statement made with words involves some degree of collaboration between the person who puts the words together and the one who interprets them, we still need to understand more precisely how the collaborative play of literature may differ.[3] In fact, a good many linguistic critics, as I intimated earlier, have contended that there is no real difference. The linguistic argument against difference runs as follows: Every verbal communication involves selecting from the shared system of language certain elements, certain structures, that impose a particular perspective as the message is conveyed. If an American politician chooses to refer to the Soviet Union as a "rival," and not, let us say, as an "adversary" or actually an "enemy," he necessarily communicates to his audience by that choice certain assumptions about the nature of the Soviet Union and its foreign policy and the relations between the superpowers. The devices of expressive manipulation of language that we may associate with literature—like strategic selection of vocabulary, shifts in levels of diction, juggling of syntax, repetition, metaphorical substitution—abound everywhere that language is used. At best, it could be said that these are deployed more spectacularly in certain kinds of literary texts. Thus, the British linguist Roger Fowler quotes a famous couplet from *The Rape of the Lock* which describes the extreme dismay of the fair Belinda when her lock of hair is cut off by the Baron:

> Not louder Shrieks to pitying Heav'n are cast,
> When Husbands or when Lap-dogs breathe their last.
> (III:157–158)

Fowler notes with approval, as most readers would, the striking compression with which Pope succeeds in conveying a deformation of values in the society he represents by the bracketing of Husbands and Lap-dogs. Then he goes on to examine the treatment of an action of a national student organization in the headlines of three different British newspapers, and concludes that the same process of *encoding* (a magic word for linguistic critics) operates in them as in the lines from Pope. "The constructive mode of the newspaper headlines is not essentially different from the 'creativity' of the extract from Pope. . . . Perhaps we load too great a responsibility upon literature by demanding it should be 'creative' if what is encoded in 'creative' is no more than an ordinary capacity of language."[4] It is surely possible to talk about the distinctive language of literature without invoking, as Fowler seems to think inevitable, an effusive cant term like *creative*. More seriously, it is a glaring flaw in reasoning to conclude from the evident continuity between literature and other uses of language that they must be "not essentially different," that what happens in a great poem "is no more than an ordinary capacity of language" such as one might find exercised in the most hackneyed headline. In order to see why this claim ignores much of the relevant evidence, let us look more closely at the couplet from *The Rape of the Lock.*

The syntactic bracketing of Husbands and Lap-dogs achieves its special satiric force partly because it occurs within the tight symmetrical box of the heroic-couplet form, ten syllables to the line, every tenth syllable a rhyme. This form has the effect of sharply *focusing* individual terms, especially when they are metrically equivalent and syntactically parallel. Literary language in general may be usefully thought of as an intricate set of intermeshed focusing devices that give certain chosen terms, phrases, images, and ideas a density of meaning and a range of implication they would not have in ordinary language. To be fair to Roger Fowler, in a later chapter he recognizes the effect of poetic form and poetic context, speaking, somewhat awkwardly, of a "stylistic code [that] is an extra over and above the regular code of the language"—"a stylistic code which is built up in the poem as a whole, Pope's verse as a whole, Pope's predecessors in the heroic couplet verse form."[5] This sensible remark actually quite subverts the previous claim that Pope and the headlines come down to the same exercise of an ordinary capacity of language, for what ordinary language lacks is these concentric sets of elaborately formalized contexts—specific poetic form and genre, the intricate patterning of the work in question, the poet's own body of writings, his predecessors, and the background of literary allusions invoked—that produce the complex meanings of the literary text. A newspaper can, of course, allude to Shakespeare or T. S. Eliot, and it will necessarily refer to certain journalistic conventions, but these analogies to the process of literary communication are intermittent, attenuated, reflect a much thinner order of textual organization, and participate in a kind of communication that has different aims.

The couplet that follows the one already quoted from *The Rape of the Lock* extends the evocation of domestic disasters that elicit anguished female response:

> Or when rich *China* Vessels, fal'n from high,
> In glittering Dust and painted Fragments lie!

Now we have a sequence of treasured things lost: the lock of hair (which has itself been interinvolved through metaphor and double entendre with Belinda's honor, her virginity, her narcissistic sense of self), Husbands, Lap-dogs, *China*. There is more expressed here than the simple distortion of values of the society in which Belinda moves. The couplet about the broken china, like much of the poem, is mock epic but does not just mock. The eighteenth-century convention of capitalizing significant nouns, together with the more general meanings of "Vessels," allows Pope playfully to insinuate into an image of broken cups and vases the suggestion of fallen empires—"when rich *China* Vessels, fal'n from high." The exquisite visualization of the broken pieces in the next line, the "glittering Dust and painted Fragments," is a kind of citation (rather than burlesque) of the epic poetry of once great things in ruins, and with all the sweep of satiric verve, it has an odd plangency: the assignment of value in this mannered society may be arbitrary and even absurd, but once value is conferred upon a fragile object, its irrevocable loss is a source of real pain; in a kind of optical illusion, the yawning gap between empires and vases flickers closed, then quickly opens again. The couplet, or rather the sequence of couplets, is a preeminent instance of the high fun of literary reading which does not allow us to settle on stable ground that offers a single unambiguous perspective, like the political slant of newspaper headlines.

As with most literary texts, there are formal patterns within patterns that complicate our perception of the local

statement. The yoking together of two disparate terms in a
single syntactical structure, Husbands and Lap-dogs, is a
traditional rhetorical device called zeugma, as Pope with his
classical training was surely aware, and zeugma is used so
abundantly in *The Rape of the Lock* that it becomes a defining
rhetorical correlative of the society's wobbly vision of reality.
Zeugma confronts two terms symmetrically; in the poem, it is
repeatedly associated with another formal device, the catalog,
which by giving us a whole series of items invites us to
contemplate in a different way the skewing of moral hierarchies that is one of the chief concerns of the poem. Thus, one
couplet from the splendid catalog of the contents of Belinda's
dressing table:

> Here Files of Pins extend their shining Rows,
> Puffs, Powders, Patches, Bibles, Billet-doux.
> (I:137–138)

The artful patterning of sound within the limits of the iambic
line wonderfully reinforces the satiric force of the catalog. The
cosmetic implements form one phonetic cluster strongly
marked by the triple alliteration of *p*'s (again, conveniently
capitalized, and so made visually prominent, by eighteenth-
century typographic convention). The series then switches to
a pair of alliterated *b*'s, "Bibles, Billet-doux," which thus
constitute a zeugma within the catalog; and "Bibles" works
nicely both ways: following "Puffs, Powders, Patches," it is
Holy Scripture reduced to an appurtenance of beauty (a
dainty little volume Belinda will carry along with her after
patching and powdering); bracketed with "Billet-doux," it is
an instance of writing scarcely different for Belinda from the
lovers' notes she keeps in piles. And the satiric interaction
among the five nouns that make up the line, if reinforced by
alliteration, is doubly reinforced by stress, the line beginning
not with an iamb but a spondee (two stresses in a row), so that

we read through the line stressing the initial accented syllable of each noun instead of following the iambic metrical units. Everyday language, of course, can also make use of expressive rhythm, alliteration, and catalogs containing disparate items, but the point is that the formal grid of the couplet makes possible an extraordinary degree of concentration in the expressive effect of these devices that would scarcely be feasible elsewhere.

The semantic range, moreover, that Pope establishes for the catalog as a central organizing device in *The Rape of the Lock* is greater than this brief instance suggests. Here is a sequence of eight lines at the beginning of Canto IV, just a little after the loss of the lock that was our point of departure:

> Not youthful Kings in Battel seiz'd alive,
> Not scornful Virgins who their Charms survive,
> Not ardent Lovers robb'd of all their Bliss,
> Not ancient Ladies when refus'd a Kiss,
> Not Tyrants fierce that unrepenting die,
> Not *Cynthia* when her *Manteau*'s pinn'd awry,
> E'er felt such Rage, Resentment, and Despair,
> As Thou, sad Virgin! for thy ravish'd Hair.
>
> (IV:3–10)

Any abstract summary of the effect of such a catalog, like deformation of values or skewing of moral hierarchies, drains it of its almost dizzying richness. An obvious satiric point is driven home in the last item of the catalog, Cynthia's rage and despair over her badly fastened cloak, but after what has preceded in the list, that detail has the sort of painful power that we experience in Proust in the Duchess de Guermantes' concern over her red shoes when her old friend Swann is dying. The catalog begins with a properly epic item, the fate of young kings fallen in captivity, and that is complemented by the penultimate item, the death of unrepentant tyrants.

Within this epic or political frame, the scornful virgins and their later embodiment, the ancient ladies, are of course a target of social satire, but the barbed wit is accompanied by a kind of double take of compassion, or at any rate, enough space is opened up in the rapid-fire sequence of vignettes so that we can ponder the possibility of real tragedy in a virgin outliving her charms, an old woman deemed unkissable by society's cruel law of erotic egotism. (The cliché rhyme of "bliss" and "kiss" strengthens this reading, for bliss, in the elegant coded language of the eighteenth century, especially when it is the object of an "ardent lover," means sexual consummation, and so its introduction here "physically" underscores the ancient ladies' plight of neglect in the next line.) Reading such passages, one may relish the wit of individual lines, but, more fundamentally, the mind is teased into a dance of possibilities, society itself being glimpsed in a kaleidoscopic vision where values are confused, men and women deluded and frustrated, and the surface comedy of social pretense and selfishness opens into an abyss of fates too sad for words.

Literary texts, as the instance of *The Rape of the Lock* vividly shows, invite a special mode of attentiveness. The strength of this invitation may be most evident in the way we are led to perceive how the many components of the individual work interact with one another—recurrent rhetorical devices, like zeugma and catalogs, recurrent or related images, thematic key words, parallel scenes and narrative situations. Now, it is conspicuously true of nonliterary texts as well that if they are to be more than jumbles of words and phrases, they necessarily marshal all kinds of techniques to establish internal links, create transitions, and produce meaningful movement from sentence to sentence and segment to segment. But this general quality of *cohesion*, as some linguists call it, is heightened to such a degree in literary texts that it becomes a difference in kind.

Let me propose as a measure of this difference the recurrence in many literary texts of thematically marked single words. In nonliterary texts, though there always exists the possibility of backward reference to previously used terms, virtually any term is in principle expendable, may be replaced by a synonym or a paraphrase or the merest pronoun, because the language is oriented toward its referent. By contrast, in literature, because we are made so conscious of the verbal medium, any thematically marked term is in principle reusable, and often becomes part of an internal feedback system in which as we read we will observe it appearing in new contexts, generating new meanings that double back on the earlier ones. The literary text may indeed be thought of as a formally structured catalyst of memory, even when, in an amnesiac age like our own in which few retain poetry by heart anymore, the memory operates subliminally.

The poetic argument of the Book of Job begins in Chapter 3 with an awesome death-wish poem that features wombs closing, darkness blotting out light. When, thirty-five chapters later, God answers Job out of the whirlwind by evoking the vital power of creation, "womb," "darkness," "light," and even a peculiar verb, "hedge in," all recur, but with the meaning of the cluster of words turned all the way around from death to life. In *The Rape of the Lock*, some 140 lines after the striking zeugma of Husbands and Lap-dogs, which is likely to have been deeply impressed in the imagination of most attentive readers, Belinda's friend Thalestris concludes a solemn oath expressing her outrage over Belinda's fall from grace in the following couplet:

> Sooner let Earth, Air, Sea to *Chaos* fall,
> Men, Monkeys, Lap-dogs, Parrots, perish all!
> (IV:119–120)

The lines are a brief anticipation of the comic apocalyptic mode that Pope would cultivate much later in his career in

The Dunciad. As such, they suggest how the device of the catalog could be moved from an expression of disjointed moral hierarchies to an intimation of all sustaining order going to pieces. In the initial instance, Lap-dogs were symmetrically yoked with Husbands to make a clear-cut, devastating satiric point. (Still earlier, at I:115, Belinda was awakened by her lap-dog.) Here, the Husbands have been replaced by the generic Men—the ambiguous context prevents us from deciding with assurance whether the reference is to male humans or to all humanity—which stands at the head of the series of household pets. Men and Monkeys are bracketed by alliteration, as are Parrots and perish (even though the latter is, of course, a verb that retroactively governs all four nouns). This sound pattern isolates Lap-dogs for special attention at the center of the line, a pampered domestic animal sandwiched in between two jungle creatures removed from their native habitat for the amusement of polite society. The earlier satiric vision of distorted values is recirculated in this brief catalog, but at a higher level of imaginative vehemence: the cosseted canines already equated with husbands are now the pivotal term in a series that points toward the dissolution of all human distinction and that is coupled with a mock-Miltonic enactment of all things plunging back to universal chaos. A single word of two syllables thus illustrates the mnemonic power of the literary text, its fecund production of internal links that qualify each other and dynamically complicate the network of meanings conveyed.

The metaphor of linkages that I have been using is helpful up to a point, but in the end its connotations are too mechanical for what goes on in a work of literature. Linkages are what is eminently analyzable in the cohesion of most nonliterary texts; in the literary work, they are often so multifarious, involve so many different aspects and levels of language, that they resist anything like full analysis. Indeed, despite the sense of exhaustion of some contemporary critics, that is why there is always more work for criticism to perform. For this dynamic system of multiple and often ambiguous connections within the literary work, the metaphor of a world, often invoked impressionistically by critics and also used more rigorously by some theorists,[6] may be the most adequate one. The poet A. R. Ammons states the implication of the world metaphor with nice precision: in every work of literature, he says, "a world [comes] into being about which any statement, however revelatory, is a lessening."[7] In all intellectual humility, a critic should always keep in mind the lessening, though it may be a price often worth paying for the sake of the revelation. This notion of a world should also make us feel unabashed about using the term "literary work," though contemporary practice has preferred the more renunciatory "literary text," which stresses the status of the writing as a weave of words. All literature is that, so the insistence on text may often be perfectly appropriate, but we are also well advised to remember that something is built out of the words (a work) which in the mind of the reader becomes a world.

The evocation of a world through the interplay of elements of language in various ways slipped by the writer out of their conventional grooves is not a quantitative matter: it can happen equally, though differently, in the seventeen syllables of a haiku or in a novel the length of *Middlemarch*. Integral illustration from poetry is obviously more feasible, so let me offer as a prooftext a 1926 poem by Robert Frost, "Once by the Pacific."

> The shattered water made a misty din.
> Great waves looked over others coming in,
> And thought of doing something to the shore
> That water never did to land before.
> The clouds were low and hairy in the skies,
> Like locks blown forward in the gleam of eyes.
> You could not tell, and yet it looked as if

The shore was lucky in being backed by cliff,
The cliff in being backed by continent;
It looked as if a night of dark intent
Was coming, and not only a night, an age.
Someone had better be prepared for rage.
There would be more than ocean-water broken
Before God's last *Put out the Light* was spoken.[8]

I will begin with what would be in Ammons' terms the most drastic kind of lessening, a thumbnail paraphrase that is in no way revelatory: the speaker in the poem stands by the Pacific shore watching the waves pounding and thinks apprehensively of the destruction of all things. The paraphrase in a way does no more than describe the stimulus for the poem, since it seems safe to assume that Robert Frost was actually moved to this somber musing by looking at the Pacific breakers. How do such thoughts generate a world in which as readers we powerfully experience a sustained moment of highly distinctive menace, waves raging and apocalypse impending? I say highly distinctive recognizing that each of us will bring to the reading of the poem his or her own literary and personal associations but also assuming that the elaborate structuring of language in these fourteen lines makes them quite different from any other modern apocalyptic poem (Yeats' "Second Coming," the end of T. S. Eliot's "The Hollow Men," and so forth), whatever the vagaries of our individual readings.

Frost's use of rhyming iambic pentameter in a fourteen-line piece indicates that the poem is meant to be taken as a variant of the sonnet. But the rhymes are a sequence of couplets (AA, BB, and so forth), producing no divisions into quatrains or octet and sestet as in the traditional sonnet form. The sense of neat containment, then, generated by the structure of the traditional sonnet is blurred. There may be an underlying tension between the prosodic form of the poem, whether we call it quasisonnet or heroic couplets, and the

conspicuously colloquial diction preserved consistently
throughout, reflected in the avoidance of the subjunctive after
"it looked as if" (using "was," not "were"), and flaunted in
phrases like "You could not tell," "the shore was lucky,"
"someone had better. . . ." The only word in the entire poem
that points toward a more literary diction is "intent," a choice
dictated not merely by the rhyme but by the need to suggest
something vast, vague, and ominous as the spelling out of the
apocalypse moves to a climax—moves, moreover, through the
only very pronounced enjambement in the poem: "a night of
dark intent / Was coming." The colloquial diction is the matrix
for a peculiar quality of Frost's poetry here and elsewhere that
might be called expressive vagueness, and that is felt, as
several critics have observed, in his general fondness for
words like "something" and "someone." The use of these
words provides an instructive instance of how ordinary language is transmuted as it participates in the world-building of
the poem. The source in spoken English for this usage would
be an idiom employed in a situation like the following: an
angry child says to another child, "Somebody better watch
out"—meaning, of course, *you*— or, "I'm going to do something to you"—meaning, whatever I will do will be so terrible
that I would rather not say exactly what. The extraordinary
effectiveness of the poem is in part the result of transferring
these locutions, with their associations of colloquial vehemence, to a cosmic scale while never committing the sin of
pretentiousness I have just committed in using a word like
"cosmic."

Although, as I have indicated, it is not in principle
possible to enumerate all the kinds of interconnections that
engender the world of the literary text, I would point here to
four salient aspects of the poem which, together with the
expressive vagueness of something/someone, combine to
produce the distinctive mood and tone of this version of
apocalypse. These are: the chiasm and synesthesia of the first

line (more of which in a moment), the pervasive personification of natural forces, the prominence of looking, and the
allusions to the first chapter of Genesis. A formal element of
a literary text may contribute significantly to the building of a
world through its placement, through repetition, through the
rhetorical emphasis it gets, or through any combination of the
three. Thus, zeugma and catalogs help define the world of
The Rape of the Lock because they are repeated so frequently,
with such inventive variations; and on the smaller scale of
"Once by the Pacific," that is true of personification and the
reiterated verb "looked." On the other hand, the first line
features two spectacular rhetorical devices that do not occur
again in the poem, but because they form the archway
through which we enter into the world of the poem, they play
an important part in determining our vision of that world. The
line is symmetrical (two nouns, two modifiers, joined by the
verb "made" at the midpoint of the line) in the form we call
chiastic: ABBA (shattered/water/misty/din). The formal crossover of the chiasm reinforces a crossover between different
sensory realms in the imagery (that is, synesthesia): the din is
"misty," though mist logically belongs to sight and touch, not
sound; and the water is "shattered," as though it were hard
and solid, not quite a synesthetic image but coming close in
its transgression of the borders between different physical
states. This coupling of chiasm and synesthesia begins the
poem with a terrific sense of the violent interfusion of
opposing spheres, solid and liquid, sight and sound, land and
sea, and that interfusion is the precondition for the poem's
apprehension of apocalypse. The violent mixing of realms is a
reversal of one of the organizing thematic features of Genesis
1: there, creation begins with the spirit of the Lord hovering
over the face of the formless waters, and it proceeds through
an ordered sequence of acts of separation, between the upper
and the lower waters, between sea and dry land, between
night and day. The allusion becomes explicit only at the end
of the poem, but it is prepared for at the beginning.

As befits a reversal of the work of the anthropomorphic God of the Bible, the force of destruction pulsing through the breakers is personified and felt throughout as a malevolent will: "Great waves looked over others coming in, / And thought of doing something to the shore. . . ." Perhaps the pronounced personification somehow justifies the rather strange image of the clouds as locks of hair, though I am not so sure of that. In any case, the active "looked" of the personified waves is disturbingly reflected by the impersonal "it looked as if," twice stated, which betokens the looking of the observer at the appearance of those looking waves, that cliff, that descending night. What I called the mnemonic power of the literary work, citing Pope's Lap-dogs as an illustration, here operates more visibly within the limits of fourteen lines. The mind shuttles back and forth among the three occurrences of "looked," finds itself in a world of menacing appearances behind which there lurks some kind of baleful presence endowed with will.

The kind of cohesion we see here is so dense and various that it is qualitatively different from the cohesion of nonliterary texts.[9] One of its defining features, moreover, is its dimension of literary allusion. To be sure, ordinary language can scarcely work without recourse to allusion. Roland Barthes observes somewhere—rather bleakly, I should think—that no one can say "I love you" to someone else without implicitly quoting an antecedent speaker who has recited those same words. Such a notion may push allusion beyond the borders of conceptual usefulness. In any case, in the language of literature, allusion of a much more specific sort is a primary coordinate, not an occasional resource. (Allusion is so central to almost all literary expression that it will need to be considered at length in a separate chapter.) Making a world in a literary text, a writer joins it to a known class of literary objects, and his world will in one way or another, at varying levels of explicitness, incorporate bits of previous texts, changing them to suit its own immanent laws. God's *Put out the Light* in the last line of "Once by the Pacific" is, of course, a canceling of the divine *Let there be light* in Genesis 1, and, as we noted, makes explicit the intimations of an undoing of biblical creation earlier in the poem.

Because literary tradition repeatedly recapitulates itself, allusions may be layered, and I suspect that is true here. A reversal of Genesis, running the reel back, as it were, from seventh day to chaos and void, presides over the conclusion of Pope's *Dunciad:*

> Lo! thy dread Empire, CHAOS! is restor'd;
> Light dies before thy uncreating word;
> Thy hand, great Anarch! lets the curtain fall;
> And Universal Darkness buries All.
>
> (IV:653–656)

Put out the Light is also exactly the sentence Othello says, twice, in the brief soliloquy just before he murders Desdemona. Are we intended at the end of Frost's poem to recall Shakespeare's image of a dark man enraged with jealousy about to destroy the beautiful woman he passionately loves? There is no way of knowing whether Frost meant that echo to be heard, but the very possibility of its presence suggests how the accumulated images, themes, and actual verbal formulations of literary tradition become charged particles in the mind of the writer (and "mind" is surely more than what is conscious and intentional) and of the reader.

The presence of these layered associations and meanings, of this fine network of internal connections, does not imply that the literary work is inherently a model of perfection. Poems and plays and stories are, after all, created by human beings like you and me, and even some of the greatest exhibit moments when the imagination flags, when the weaving of meaningful patterns slackens, when contradictions slide in that may not contribute to any ultimate richness of paradoxical statement. There could in fact be just such an unproductive dissonance in the hairy clouds blown across eyes of Frost's poem, however much one might try to accommodate those two lines to the structure of the poem by linking them both with the personification and the theme of looking. The possible presence of flaws in any literary achievement—and in my view "Once by the Pacific" remains a very remarkable poem—ought to steer us away from a mystification of the literary text, which is by no means a necessary consequence of recognizing its distinctiveness. The performance of the language of literature can be as uneven as the performance of any other kind of language. There are, of course, more and less accomplished speakers, but even the most eloquent may from time to time lisp or slur. This means that as readers we will sometimes run the risk of inventing a connection in the text where there is only a gap. For the most part, however, the dangers of overreading are far outweighed by the dangers of underreading, a habit to which modern culture, with its popular journalism and its rapid electronic messages, predisposes us.

It can be reasonably objected that I have made things too easy for myself by illustrating the language of literature with two such tightly woven poems composed in rhyming couplets. In fact, I have chosen my prooftexts because they are beautiful realizations of an intrinsic potential of literary language that elsewhere may work more diffusely. The multifarious aspects of cohesion, the mnemonic power, that we have observed in *The Rape of the Lock* and in "Once by the Pacific" have their counterparts even in sprawling or ragged literary texts—say, a poem by Allen Ginsburg or a novel by Zola—though they may not always operate with the same high degree of concentration and formal elegance. It is another question how or whether these features are present in downright bad literature, like pulp fiction and greeting-card verse, but I think it will be most useful to take up that question in a later chapter as part of our consideration of style. In any case, it should be evident that the distinctive resources of literary language do not work like a simple on-off switch, marking this as literary and that as not. A piece of philosophic or historical writing, a legal opinion, the exposition of a psychological theory, could exhibit some or even many of the characteristics of literary language we have noted, and that is why, as emphases change in the academic study of literature, many such texts can become the subject of literary scrutiny. But it is only the literary text that as a matter of intrinsic purpose marshals all these resources for the construction of a "world"—a reordering through language, and language made prominent, of the elements of experience in order to express a certain vision or understanding or visceral apprehension of them.

The language of literature abundantly draws on ordinary language and achieves its coherences through operations that are sometimes instructively analogous to those of ordinary language, but it carries them to a higher exponential power, transmits through them messages of a different order. To read this language adequately requires a prehensile activity of the mind on the details of the text as it unfolds, a willingness to entertain multiple and unresolved meanings, an openness to the pleasures in the sound and look and combination of the words. All three of these capacities are bound to grow the more one reads, and that is probably why at the moment they are in a general state of decay. But there is a necessary, if subordinate, place for literary studies alongside reading. Analytic attention to the distinctive formal resources of literature is never a substitute for the immediate experience of reading, but it can give us a sharper focus on the dynamic play of elements in what we read. And precisely because so many of our reading habits these days are acquired through exposure to thinner, more univocal, less complexly pleasurable uses of language, we need to understand more clearly the inflections and the underlying patterns of the special language of literature.

CHAPTER TWO

Character and the
Connection with Reality

Literature is quintessentially a representational art, but the relation between the literary text and the world it represents has always been something of a puzzle, and recent trends in literary theory have compounded the puzzlement. The objects of literary representation belong to a wide range of heterogeneous categories, material, conceptual, emotional, relational, personal, and collective. They include states of feeling, moments of perception, memories (all characteristically treated in lyric poetry); buildings, neighborhoods, industrial processes, social institutions (as, for example, in the novels of Balzac); world-historical forces and theological ideas (as, respectively, in *War and Peace* and *The Brothers Karamazov*); imaginary personages and historical personages imaginatively reconstructed, which amounts to the same thing.

Fictional character is probably the crucial test case for the link between literature and reality. Very few people will take the trouble to read a novel or story unless they can somehow "identify" with the characters, live with them inwardly as though they were real at least for the duration of the reading. Modern avant-garde experiments in fiction that seek to block all possibility of such identification give signs of being not the wave of the future but no more than the exception that proves the rule. Literary theorists, among them critical promoters of such experiments, have frequently inveighed against the naïveté, or, indeed, the delusional habit, of reading fictional characters as though they were real people.

One objection that can be dismissed at the outset is that ordinary habits of reading betray a "metaphysics of presence," ignoring the ineluctable absence of all purported objects of representation in those columns of conventional signs of linguistic elements that constitute the printed page. The critic Denis Donoghue has pointed out with eminent good sense that such a reader is a straw man.[1] That is, unless a reader is delusional in a clinical sense, he or she never actually imagines that Emma Bovary or Isabel Archer or Huckleberry Finn is a real person. It is Don Quixote, in a fit of madness, who leaps onto the stage of Master Pedro's puppet theater, slashing at the evil Moors with his sword, but Cervantes' novel from the beginning is contrived to elicit from its readers a much saner and more complicated attitude toward the status of fictional personages.[2]

But if on some level we always know that characters in fiction are mere constructs, congeries of words, compounds of convention and invention, what is it about them that leads us to take them so seriously? Although there has been a great flowering of speculation on, and systematic description of, narrative in the past two decades, it offers little guidance, and in fact a good deal of misguidance, on this essential question. Let me describe briefly how this situation has come about before proposing an alternative way of thinking about character. As with the contemporary objections to the distinctiveness of literature, a move toward the marginalization of character has been undertaken on two fronts, one formal (and in part, linguistic), the other, in a much more intentional way, ideological.

The first great wave of contemporary narrative theory surfaced in France in the 1960s and, taking its models from Structuralist anthropology, sought to create a new discipline with a new name, narratology—that is, the systematic analysis of narrative as a set of formal relations and functions. Implicit in much of this discussion was a central metaphor of Structuralist thought, elsewhere applied to cultural systems and here to the literary text: the self-regulating machine. The systemic operations of narrative had largely been neglected by Anglo-American criticism, and by French criticism before the sixties, so there was definitely something to be learned from the new movement, but one may wonder whether the mechanizing conception of narrative as a system of functions offers an exhaustive account of it, as narratologists have tended to assume. What precisely is left out is the possibility of talking coherently about the nexus between text and what by consensus we are willing to call reality. It is symptomatic that narratology should be most conspicuously inadequate in its treatment of character because with its conception of narrative as a system of structural mechanisms, character can be little more than a function of plot. The narratologists have scarcely any critical vocabulary for encompassing the mimetic dimension of character.[3]

This inadequacy of Structuralist thinking about narrative is compounded by a fondness for seeing literary works in reductively linguistic terms. Because literary narrative is made up of words, it is imagined to be a language, or at the very least, a language-like system in which the purely internal differences among the components (tip from top or tap, villain from hero or helper) generate meanings. The elements of narrative, then, are conceived as analogous to or isomorphic with the elements of language, a notion that has led to some of the most embarrassing moments of the new narratology in which attempts have been made to identify in configurations of plot and character narrative adverbs, narrative adjectives, and so forth. In all this, there are scarcely grounds for helping us understand why the great fictional characters engage us so powerfully and even provide illumination for our lives.

Although the cluster of related intellectual trends called post-Structuralism withdraws from the Structuralist interest in system and rejects the project of a science of culture, it tacitly assumes as its point of departure in thinking about mimesis the supposed Structuralist demonstration that character is a mere function of narrative mechanisms. From the more ideological perspective of post-Structuralism, all the fuss and bother about a lowly function becomes suspect, if not actually ominous. Purportedly realistic character is now deemed a camouflage device or a mask (a notion already adumbrated in some of the Structuralists), or worse, a pernicious illusion working to sustain an oppressive ideology. Thus, the idealist, theological, and "logocentric" biases of Western culture are all encouraged by the illusion of character (an idea popular among the followers of Derrida and of Foucault); the notion of a coherent, unitary self embodied in realistic character is an evasion of all that is fissured and repressed in the self (an argument heard from Lacanians); the appealing consistency and meretricious intelligibility of character are merely instruments for enhancing the market value of literature (the objection of the neo-Marxists). All these lines of attack on character have been conveniently drawn together in a single article by the French critic Hélène Cixous, which is at once Derridean, Freudian, and Marxist.[4] She is so skeptical about the reality of character that she uses the word in inverted commas only. Imparting an ideological impetus to the Structuralist metaphor of the machine, she describes the literary work in which character occurs as a "machine of repression," and does not hesitate to conclude that "The marketable form of literature . . . is closely related to that familiar, decipherable human sign that 'character' claims to be."

What I would like to propose about all these attempts to undercut the mimetic validity of character is that they reflect the kind of sophistication that becomes its own egregious naïveté. Thus, Tzvetan Todorov, in an essay on verisimilitude that reflects French Structuralism in its heyday, proposes four different meanings for the term "verisimilitude" (correspondence to received opinion, correspondence to generic expectation, and so forth) after having announced flatly, "We shall discard only the first naive meaning, according to which a relation to reality is expressed."[5] This way of talking, which in various inflections has been in vogue since the sixties, is a means of exhibiting cleverness at the cost, as I have intimated, of a new sort of naïveté. To begin at the most rudimentary level, verisimilar fiction seeks to adhere to the laws of physical reality. If somebody throws an apple into the air in a story and it keeps going straight up, you know you are not reading verisimilar fiction, and this has nothing to do with received opinion. If someone in a novel runs a fever of 104° Fahrenheit, verisimilitude has been observed; if the fever is 114° Fahrenheit, verisimilitude has been violated. (Science fiction is an instructive mixed case because it tries to make fantasy seem verisimilar by extrapolating the physical laws of our own world to other worlds where somewhat different quantitative limits and relations may obtain.) Though there are not such easily measurable laws of human behavior, we nevertheless are able to make judgments when we read—and judgments not chiefly dependent on ideology, received opinion, genre, and so forth—about whether a bereaved father, a rejected mistress, a rebellious son is acting in a way that seems persuasively like reality. How such judgments are made will become clearer presently through illustration.

The very notion that literature is severed from reality because it is composed of conventions, both linguistic and literary, is an unexamined dogma of both Structuralist and post-Structuralist thought. The essential point of refutation,

which ought to be self-evident but has been neglected in the
general rage for sophistication, has been made with beautiful
concision by A. D. Nuttall in his admirable book, A New
Mimesis:

> Why should the presence of convention preclude refer-
> ence to reality? The truth is almost exactly converse. All
> reference to reality (including pointing with the finger) is
> conventionally ordered. Language is an immensely rich
> system of conventions and is the best means we have of
> referring to the real.[6]

What this observation suggests is that discussion of the
internal relations among elements of a literary work, however
instructive, is never sufficient: ways have to be found to talk
about how literature through its manifold conventions manages to address reality. To be sure, "reality" is a notoriously
slippery term. I will use it here as an umbrella for the
underlying aspects of our being in the world—the psychology
of the individual; its matrices in biology and family; the
complications of relating to others; social institutions; historical forces and events. About all of these we can talk with one
another because to a large extent we share them as the
common stuff of our human existence.

The simplifications of the ideological assault on mimetic
character are as pronounced as those of the linguistic formal-
ists, and attention to them will bring us closer to what occurs
in literary mimesis. The whole idea of the realist work as a
"machine of repression" is a piece of ideologically radical
naïveté, for in the interests of displaying an impeccably
liberated consciousness it entirely collapses the distinction
between literature and propaganda. What is ignored is the
polysemous, open-ended nature of literary texts; the evidence
they abundantly offer for imaginative freedom variously exercised in the act of literary creation, often working against the

grain of ruling ideologies; and hence the fundamental fact that ideology, like convention, is a context of literature but not its determinant, except when the writer slides into the propagandist. As for the idea of unitary character, comfortingly familiar and decipherable, and as such both a market mechanism and an instrument of idealist deception, there may be some grounds for such a notion in modern popular literature from Western to romance, but in view of what serious writers have been doing with character since Homer and the Bible, it is as much of a straw man as the delusional reader naively addicted to a metaphysics of presence. In fact, many of the great fictional characters—King David, Othello, Captain Ahab, Anna Karenina, Leopold Bloom—are compelling precisely because there proves to be something ultimately indecipherable about them as they move through unforeseen twists and turns of self-revelation and self-concealment that put us in touch with what is uncanny, imponderable about our existence as human beings—and I begin my examples with one from the tenth or ninth century B.C.E. to stress that such purposefully troubling representation of character is hardly the invention of modernism.

The unity of character so often denounced as a sham by new wave critics is neither monolithic nor static, as they claim, but, on the contrary, is mobile, unstable, elusive even as it seems palpable in our reading experience—precisely like the complex unity of the literary artwork itself. Baruch Hochman astutely observes that the unity of character inheres in dynamic contradictions, which is also a basic fact of our psychological lives and as such helps explain the realistic persuasiveness of successfully achieved fictional character.[7] This is a perception shared in different terms by a good many writers but too often missed by contemporary theorists. The British novelist Elizabeth Bowen once proposed that character should seem unpredictable before any given act, inevitable after it. Vladimir Nabokov spoke in a chess metaphor of a "knight's move," in which the character hops over other pieces and then to one side, in ways that are unanticipated but prove after the fact to conform brilliantly to the rules (the rules in this case being the verisimilar dynamic unity of the character). And as long ago as 1927, E. M. Forster proposed that the test for what he called "round character" was that it was "capable of surprising in a convincing way" and in doing this possessed "the incalculability of life."[8]

How do we make such recognitions as we read, and what is the source in the writer's art for the mimetic power of such representations? The second question is probably unanswerable, though something may be gained by pondering it; the first question, at any rate, should come into clearer focus through some examples. Let us proceed from the unsurprising to the surprising, from pawn's march to knight's move.

A common mode of presenting character in the nineteenth-century novel, still occasionally used by novelists today, is a formal introductory portrait that defines the character's essential traits. As literary historians have noted, this practice derives from a minor nonnarrative genre popular in the seventeenth and eighteenth centuries, the Theophrastan character, which consists of a thumbnail sketch of a recognized social or vocational type (the country bumpkin, the pastor, the fop, and so forth). This is a convention that displays the familiar and the decipherable with a vengeance. Here, on the second page of Stendhal's *The Red and the Black* (1830), is the initial portrait of M. de Rênal, the pompous mayor of Verrières who will become Julien Sorel's employer and who will be cuckolded by Julien:

> At the sight of him all hats are quickly raised. His hair is graying and he is dressed in gray. He is a knight of several orders, he has a high forehead, an aquiline nose, and on the whole his face does not lack a certain regularity: one even finds, at first view, that it combines the dignity of a

village mayor with that sort of appeal which can still be encountered in a man of forty-eight or fifty. But soon the visitor from Paris is shocked by a certain air of self-satisfaction and complacency mingled with a hint of limitation and unoriginality. One feels finally that this man's talent is limited to seeing that he is paid exactly what is owed him, and to paying on his part as late as possible when it is he that owes.

Such is the mayor of Verrières, M. de Rênal.

(I:1; my translation)

Everything about the mayor is related to social and characterological stereotypes. He has "that sort of appeal" we are all expected by experience to associate with certain men pushing fifty (and the indicative "that," reflecting an assumption of shared familiar knowledge, occurs frequently in these nineteenth-century thumbnail portraits). He has the smugness and provinciality of a small-town mayor, the narrowly calculating monetary habits of a perfect bourgeois, even a concert of gray hair and gray wardrobe to match the drab propriety of his life. Only the aquiline nose and the high forehead are a perfunctory effort to give him some individual physical traits. It is no wonder that the urbane narrator, who has assumed the stance of conducting a Parisian visitor on a tour of Verrières, can tightly tie up the whole package in an ostentatious ribbon: "Such is the mayor of Verrières, M. de Rênal."

The mayor is, I suppose, one variety of what E. M. Forster would call "flat character," a kind of character necessary to the artistic economy of the narrative; Stendhal can afford to box him for public presentation in this fashion because no surprises will be required of him. Is such a procedure, with all its reliance on stereotype, antimimetic? At first thought, stereotypes may seem intrinsically unrealistic, but a little reflection will suggest that they are often approximations rather than misrepresentations of reality and that no one can get along without them. Baruch Hochman reminds us that relating individual character to general types is one of the principal mental operations we use in order to know people in real experience, and so the recourse to general types in fiction actually simulates a cognitive process repeatedly employed outside of reading.[9] Let us say we meet a bearded young man in a tie-dyed T-shirt, faded jeans, and sandals, with a little ponytail. A sixties type, we say to ourselves, a belated flower child. The stereotype calls to mind a whole cluster of associated traits, and we use it as an instrument of knowledge that enables us to "decipher" the individual by relating him to general categories. If all we see of the young man with the ponytail is what is caught by the passing eye in the street, there is an end to the matter; he remains a stereotype, like a flat character in a novel. Should we engage him in conversation, or actually enter into a continuing relationship with him, the stereotype might conceivably be confirmed (hence its initial function as an approximation); might require minor or major modifications; might need to be rejected altogether (if, for example, we discovered that the young man, despite appearances, was an investor in the stock market or a genetic engineer). A fiction with no dependable stereotypes would be radically disorienting, and that is indeed one way of describing the uncompromising iconoclasm of certain modernist writers like Kafka and Beckett. In the realist tradition, the approximation that is the stereotype serves as a foil of clear decipherability against which are played the more dynamic and more elusive major characters, for whom mere approximation will not do. What also sometimes happens is that the stereotypical character in the end manages to step outside the cage of stereotype. *The Red and the Black* offers the most instructive examples of the rendering of elusive unity in contrast to the stereotypical secondary character; for an instance of the self-transcendence of stereotype, we will have to look beyond the novels of Stendhal.

A few pages after the initial portrait of M. de Rênal, his
wife is introduced—it should be noted, without the benefit of
any thumbnail sketch. Instead, we see her in action, strolling
with her husband and her three small sons, suddenly alarmed
when her eleven-year-old threatens to climb up on a parapet.
The narrator's sole initial comment is that she "appeared to be
a woman of thirty, but still quite pretty." The age and the
prettiness are needed narrative data because both will figure
in her subsequent affair with Julien. Why doesn't the narrator
simply tell us that she was thirty instead of saying that she
looked thirty? If he knows that M. de Rênal is a knight of
several orders, surely he could know Mme. de Rênal's exact
age. It is a momentary renunciation of omniscience that goes
hand in hand with his refusal to package Mme. de Rênal for us
as he has just packaged her husband: we are kept on the
outside, reminded that what we can know of this woman is a
matter of inference from appearances, gestures, and speech.
Her initial gestures show her as a solicitous mother calling her
boy away from the parapet, and a loyal, indeed subservient,
wife, patiently listening to her husband's tirade and praising
him. He is incensed because a liberal Parisian journalist has
arrived in town to investigate the local poorhouse and hospital
for which he is overseer. The mayor expresses indignation to
his wife over the scandalous articles such a fellow might place
in the liberal newspapers. To which Mme. de Rênal, in what
is only her second piece of dialogue in the novel, responds:
"You don't read them, my dear" (I:2). The wonderful thing
about these words is that we can't be sure how to take them.
They may betray nothing more than naïveté, and that is
surely how the husband construes them. They may conceal an
ironic superiority of the demure wife to the fuming husband,
her supposed naïveté perhaps exploited as a self-protective
mask. Or they may reflect something we could call the
incipience of ironic consciousness, in which the naïveté about
politics and public opinion bears the seed of a cool shrewdness
of perception that sets off the resourceful wife from her

limited husband. In immediate context, the first of these three readings seems the most plausible—Mme. de Rênal has already been described as speaking "timidly" to her husband. But we read character developmentally, so that later discoveries compel a reconsideration of earlier views; and Mme. de Rênal's later behavior as Julien's passionate mistress exhibits a subtlety and a capacity for fine manipulation that make us suspect the presence of the ironist within the guise of the naive provincial wife.

These half-dozen words of dialogue, then, are a moment of formidably rich mimesis; the character's statement offers a revealing glimpse of those teasing ambiguities of motive and identity working in the frame of social institution about which we are obliged endlessly to infer in our lives outside of reading. Our recognition of the authority of the representation has to depend finally not on any internal mechanisms of the narrative but on a matching of experience and reading. Whatever we have gleaned from experience about men and women, marriage and politics, veiled irony as a weapon of the powerless, is instantaneously scanned as we imaginatively reconstruct the exchange between the spouses, and, if everything fits, this background of experiential knowledge confirms the rightness of the moment.

How did Stendhal manage to *know* this about Mme. de Rênal when he invented (writing, as a matter of fact, at breakneck speed) this line for her? Any explanation will remain highly conjectural, but it is important to note where no explanation is to be found. There is surely nothing in the structural necessities or formal requirements of the novel that could bring the writer to this moment of subtle comic illumination. And though as a novelist he must work with linguistic and literary convention, it is hard to imagine how convention, or even the swerving from convention, could in itself lead to such an insight. If we look beyond the formal configurations of the text to the man that produced them, we will find scant support for a mystique of the writer as a special repository of wisdom. Stendhal was in fact a shrewdly intelligent observer (something that could not be asserted of a good many great writers), but, particularly in his relations with women, he exhibited an astonishing capacity for repeated self-delusion that led to a long string of painful pratfalls and protracted frustrations. The case of Stendhal is exemplary. Between the unpredictable pattern of illumination in the work and the touching human foibles of the life, one is compelled to conclude that when fictional invention is going well, it is an activity that "privileges" the writer in some uncanny way: in the incandescence of the imagination that produces good fiction, elements of knowledge and bits of perception variously collected, many of them no doubt stored subliminally in the mind of the writer, coalesce, take on revelatory form in the speech and acts of imaginary personages. It is as if the very process of writing allowed the writer to tap unguessed levels of his own self, to achieve a kind of nonvolitional heightening of ordinary insight, as, analogously, the process of free association in psychoanalysis is supposed to do.

Fiction, then, involves above all an imaginative intercourse between the experience of the writer, beautifully focused as it would not be elsewhere, and the experience of the reader, which is both necessary to recognize adequately what the writer has produced and capable of being deepened by what the work of fiction offers. A. D. Nuttall nicely characterizes what has coalesced in the achieved fiction as a set of persuasive possibilities, probing hypotheses about human lives: "The fiction evokes from us, as we entertain the hypothesis, all the human energies and powers, the incipient commitments and defenses which occur in experiential knowing, but are absent from cool, conceptual knowing."[10] Such knowing, he goes on to say, is acquired through a gradual process of deepening and intensification, both in life and in the sequence of episodes that constitutes the work of fiction.

Mme. de Rênal, even though she is kept offstage for long stretches in *The Red and the Black*, provides an apt illustration of such a process of progressive revelation. Once she has fallen in love, the narrator observes that "her soul was entering unknown territory" (*des pays inconnus*), and Stendhal's characterization of her might be described as a continual, plausible destabilizing of any fixity of character we might at first have been tempted to attach to her. First she is compliant wife and devoted mother, then passionate mistress, then also cool actress in the interests of her love, then contrite penitent, and at the very end, passionate mistress again. But this instability is plausible because we sense certain common denominators, not easily specified, through all her changes. These would include: a spontaneity of feeling, a capacity for selfless devotion, a loyalty to her own emotions and to what she perceives as her values, a responsiveness or even malleability which sometimes has the look of passivity but is never quite that. There are, to be sure, other, less sympathetic ways of describing her character. Some critics, for example, have seen in her a morbid dependency exhibited first in her relationship with her husband and then with Julien. Different readings of this sort are possible both because we bring different predispositions and different backlogs of experience to the text and because the manifestations of character in fiction as in life leave a large margin of ambiguity. What is important for our concern with the dynamic unity of character is that most readers intuit some set of common denominators, though they may debate over their precise nature.

It should be stressed that this dynamic complexity of character is relational and not just a matter of the individual self. A final example from *The Red and the Black*, one of the small, subtle knight's moves in the novel, will illustrate this relational dimension. After M. de Rênal has received an anonymous letter denouncing his wife and Julien, he confronts her, and in a conversation that goes on for two hours, she manages through the most ingenious histrionic contrivances to allay his suspicions, to make him feel guilty for having entertained them, and altogether to exhaust the poor man. In summarizing this interview, the narrator observes: "Once or twice, during this grand scene, Mme. de Rênal was on the verge of experiencing a certain sympathy for the emphatically real distress of this man, who for twelve years had been her friend [ami]. But true passion is selfish" (I:21). A momentary door is opened here on an unsuspected horizon: the possibility that such a man, now rendered helpless, might tempt such a woman to sympathy. This perception has that revelatory rightness of which I spoke earlier. M. de Rênal, mayor and man, is no doubt pompous, overbearing, conceited, obtuse, but all that does not preclude the possibility of a thread of companionship in the fabric of their marriage: he has been, after all, her *ami*. It seems equally right that the impulse of compassion is no more than a fleeting temptation: "But true passion is selfish." Note that the reversal is effected through the introduction of a moral maxim— of the sort, in fact, that Stendhal previously had put together in *De l'Amour*.

Although fictional character does not offer an abstract, conceptual kind of knowledge, the writer may draw on such knowledge to support his perception of character. Mme. de Rênal is splendidly individual, as her momentary turn of sympathy toward her obnoxious husband demonstrates, but the behavior of the individual can also be expected to conform in some ways to the laws of what Stendhal, with his roots in the eighteenth-century French philosophic tradition, conceived as a generally valid moral psychology. Most ages have their equivalents of such a body of knowledge. (Some version of Freudianism would probably serve for our own era.) To make character entirely contingent on general precepts would be to reduce fiction to didactic illustration, but as an ancillary device, the general principles enable writers to link the "incalculability of life" manifested in individual character with the elements of recurrence and typicality that allow us to decipher experience.

So far, I have stressed dynamic contradiction, subtlety, the capacity to surprise convincingly as measures of the mimetic force of character. We are all complicated creatures, but both introspection and observation of others suggest that we are not always or only complicated, and this is an understanding that is also registered in fictional mimesis. There are, that is to say, fictional characters that seem lifelike not in being complex but rather in being intensely, quite simply, themselves. The comic grotesque figures in Dickens and Smollett, those walking synecdoches, embodiments of a recurrent tic or metaphor, are not an abandonment of verisimilitude but bold stylizations that catch the terrible, absurd simplicity to which some people can reduce their lives—and so it may be a little misleading to call them "flat" characters. The realistic representation of simplicity of character is not, moreover, restricted to comic figures. There is a kind of serious character in which the sheer intensity of being consistently oneself becomes as compelling a hypothesis of human possibility as complexity in another kind of character. Let me offer an example which also illustrates the transcendence of stereotypes that is often produced by the momentum of fictional imagination in the realist novel.

Balzac is one of the most shameless traders in stereotype among the great nineteenth-century novelists. As a result, there are passages in his books that many of us today have to read in a spirit of camp as resounding expressions of the kitsch of his era. Nevertheless, he remains a major realist not only in his representation of places and processes and social institutions but also of character. His *Splendeurs et misères des courtisanes* (1847), a novel which in its most widely available English translation is called, with a certain music-hall jingle, *A Harlot High and Low*, provides a particularly instructive instance of a movement through stereotype to verisimilar characterization. The harlot in question is Esther Gobseck, the dazzling young woman who is Balzac's most memorable version of a nineteenth-century French stereotype of which he was particularly fond—*la belle Juive,* the beautiful Jewess. In one great set piece which is a kind of hymn to the pseudoscientific racism of his age, he stresses the potency of genetically transmitted traits, even when the stock has been transported from one climate to another, and then associates Esther's beauty and her glowing sensuality with the brilliant azure of the Mediterranean skies, the smoldering sands of the desert, the rattle of Oriental tambourines, the sultriness of the seraglio (in all this rather extravagantly confusing the Hebrew Bible with *The Thousand and One Nights*). This cultural stereotype is crossbred with another one: the Whore with the Golden Heart, subspecies, True-Loving Courtesan. In a society of relentless self-seeking, Esther is the one person capable of total selfless devotion to the man she loves. This trait is an absolute given of her personality from the first pages of the novel; nothing she can undergo will induce her to swerve from it in the least degree.

The double stereotyping of Esther is reinforced by a characteristic Balzacian propensity to represent the character through a series of mythological images, sometimes actually arranging her as he describes her in iconographic poses. Thus, this "sublimist type of Asiatic beauty" is variously Mary Magdalen, the Madonna, and, with a switch of cultural spheres, Venus herself. These sundry stereotypes are much less defensible as approximations than, say, the social stereo-types Stendhal invokes in representing M. de Rênal because, deriving from literary and cultural conventions, they are fantasy projections of the mysterious Other (*la belle Juive*), sentimental simplifications (the Whore with the Golden Heart), and in sum, they seek less to understand than to heighten or monumentalize contemporary figures by assimilating them to mythic archetypes. In historical retrospect, all this may have a certain amusement value, but it is obviously not why we still read Balzac.

It might seem that Esther Gobseck as a plausible hypothesis of a real woman could not possibly extricate herself from the weight of stereotypical bric-a-brac with which the novelist has loaded her. In fact, she does, quite remarkably. Let us see how before speculating why. At first, she appears to be merely a pretty pawn manipulated by the sinister Vautrin, masquerading as a Spanish priest. Her absolute devotion to her lover Lucien—Vautrin's protégé—fits her nicely for this role of perfect passivity. From the moment Vautrin determines that she must give herself to the odious Baron de Nucingen in order to get the money needed for Lucien's social ascent, she begins to exhibit qualities of spunkiness, of self-protective shrewdness, at least in relation to the baron, that make her more believable as a precociously seasoned prostitute fanatically in love and utterly trapped by social circumstances.

Esther's great self-revelation, however, is posthumous. In the third of the four parts of the novel, after she has committed suicide and Lucien has been thrown into prison accused of complicity in her death, a letter written by Esther to Lucien on the morning of her death, delivered to his address after his arrest, falls into the hands of the police. Some quotation will be necessary to suggest the flavor of the letter—and it is eminently a text with a flavor—but since it goes on for five pages, a few excerpts will have to suffice. Balzac's punctuation here abounds in suspension points, presumably to indicate the broken, zigzag rhythm of Esther's last communication, so I will indicate my elisions by suspension points with brackets around them. Esther sits with a miniature of Lucien done on ivory, promising to send it with the letter. Then she thinks of Clothilde de Grandlieu, the flat-chested, unprepossessing young woman of good family whom Lucien seeks to marry in order to further his social ambitions.

> This portrait, my darling, hide it, don't give it to anyone . . . unless as a present it can win you the heart of that walking lath wearing dresses, that Clothilde de Grandlieu, who will make you black and blue when you sleep, her bones are so sharp. . . . Yes, I agree to that, I would still be good for something as when I was alive. Ah! to give you pleasure, or if it had just made you laugh, I'd have held myself close to a fire with an apple in my mouth to roast it for you! [. . .]
>
> Don't you see, I mean to make a beautiful corpse, I shall lie down, I shall stretch out in bed, I shall *pose* myself, eh! Then I shall press the berry against the soft palate, and I won't be disfigured either by convulsion, or by a ridiculous posture [. . .]
>
> You offered me a whole life the day before yesterday when you told me that if Clothilde still refused you, you would marry me. It would have been a calamity for both of us. I would have been all the more dead, so to speak; for deaths may be more or less bitter. Society would never have accepted us [. . .]
>
> Who will part your hair the way I did? Bah! I don't want to think about anything to do with life any longer, I have only five minutes left, I give them to God; don't be jealous of Him, my sweet angel, I want to talk to Him about you, ask Him to make you happy in return for my death and my punishment in the next world. It's such a nuisance to have to go to hell, I would have liked to see the angels and find out whether they are like you . . .[11]

Even in excerpt, one scarcely needs the context of the novel as a whole to see the effectiveness of the letter. Esther, scant minutes away from self-destruction, cannot suppress a jealous swipe at her skinny rival (she herself, needless to say, has a voluptuous figure), whose bones are so sharp they will bruise

Lucien in bed. In one breath, her satiric language reveals the feisty young tart; in the next, the horrendous picture of roasting an apple in her mouth suggests her fanatic devotion, not without a strong tincture of masochism, to the feckless Lucien. (At this point, there is a strong resonance with what has preceded in the novel because in effect she *has* been roasting herself for Lucien's pleasure.) Then we encounter the exquisitely feminine narcissism of Esther's contemplation of suicide. (Her lover exhibits his own style of narcissism which is a good deal less engaging.) Through all her brief life, she has had only her beauty to trade on, and so it seems powerfully right that even in suicide she should be concerned to pose herself for a perfect death, with no disfigurement, anticipating the touch against the palate of the rare, painless poison as a sensual fulfillment.

Alternately spunky, self-sacrificing, and theatrical, Esther is also capable of shrewd perception, as in her comment that no happy ending was possible for them because society would never have accepted Lucien's marriage to a kept woman. It is Lucien, not she, who, as she understands, desperately needs society. The last paragraph about God and the angels, which occurs just before she signs the letter, is a wonderful climax of self-revelation. Before the moment of death, she recalls an intimate gesture of amorous solicitude: "Who will part your hair the way I did?" Then she must excuse herself for devoting her last minutes to prayer by begging her lover not to be jealous of God: even confronting eternity, she can, after all, imagine things only with the reflexes of someone whose life has been defined by passion, jealousy, the threat of sexual rivalry. Heaven and hell themselves are conceived in the image of her unflagging devotion to her "angelic" Lucien, though the reader is sharply aware that her lover is in fact a will-less instrument of the satanic Vautrin.

What is this posthumous letter doing in the penultimate

section of Balzac's novel? It plays no real role in the plot;
thematically, it does no more than reinforce an obvious irony:
the life of its intended recipient has been shattered, and he,
too, will commit suicide, not out of the pride of passion like
Esther but out of the weakness of despair. Any claim, then,
that this revelation of character primarily serves a function in
the internal mechanisms of the narrative is implausible. But
the functionally superfluous passage is really what fictional
character is all about. W. J. Harvey, in a happy phrase, has
observed that character tends to exhibit "a surplus margin of
gratuitous life,"[12] and this encore performance by a dead and
buried Esther illustrates the aptness of that formula in the
most literal way. From the viewpoint of the novelist, what is
involved is a kind of zest in the sheer "doing" of Esther that
has no strong relation to the structural necessities of the
novel. One easily imagines Balzac entering into the pleasure,
the powerful imaginative momentum, of embodying (it would
be nice to be able to say ensouling) this individual woman,
here made more splendidly individual in her last moments
than she was at any point earlier in the novel. The stereotypes
to which he had frequent recourse before are set aside like a
discarded scaffolding as he invents these last individual
gestures of an arresting human probability, Esther Gobseck.

The answering pleasure we experience as readers stems
from the perception of a distinctive presence, and subtlety or
complexity does not play much of a role in this perception.
Granted, the character of Esther is not monolithic, as the
rapid, psychologically plausible leaps in the letter from
attitude to attitude indicate. But what engages the imagination, I think, is not the element of surprise that one encounters in novelists like Stendhal, Tolstoy, James, Proust,
Nabokov, but rather the fact that Esther is so intensely
herself: the traits, the motives, might all have been predicted
from her previous representations in the novel; the pleasure
of discovery is in the verisimilar details of speech and gesture

which manifest those traits and motives so vividly. If one wants to use a spatial metaphor for Esther and the whole class of fictional characters who resemble her, one should say they are neither round nor flat, but deep. If the fascination of human types is an end in itself (and the novel generically reflects such an assumption), the deepened experiential knowing of the imagined individual is a process that justifies itself, and for which no formal limits or functions can be prescribed.

The sense of illuminating connection we feel as readers between fictional character and real human possibility does not depend on a particular narrative technique. Ultimately, I suppose, it flows from the kind of leap of intuition by the writer that I tried to describe earlier. Some writers realize such intuition through a purely external presentation of character. Balzac generally restricts himself to outside views of Esther (as he does with most of his characters), and then uses the final letter as a kind of soliloquy. Stendhal, on the other hand, renders Mme. de Rênal (and his other major characters) through mixed means of presentation: we are offered summaries of her thoughts and feelings, the third-person miming of inward speech that is called *style indirect libre,* the narrator's analysis of her motives and acts, and the report of her speech and actions. These shifting techniques of presentation may help suggest a quality of dynamic fluidity in the character, but that is by no means the only way to achieve such an effect.

As a matter of literary history, the novel devotes much more attention than do earlier narrative genres to the minute emotional and cognitive fluctuations of inner states, and in a later chapter we will consider in detail the technical operations of this attention. Beginning in the eighteenth century with the epistolary novels of Richardson, Sterne's fantastically associative narrative, the emotional perspectivism of novels like Prévost's *Manon Lescaut* and Diderot's *The Nun,* the novel perfects subtle new techniques for representing the movements of consciousness—new, though not without certain remarkable anticipations in biblical and classical literature. The most supple of these is the *style indirect libre,* though by the first decades of our own century some writers would step beyond it to interior monologue when immediacy, difficulty, and the sheer sense of process became central mimetic values. I would guess that many readers of the great realist novels carry around in their heads little anthologies of perfectly realized moments of experiential realism, novelistic equivalents of the hand-held camera: Kitty ascending the great stairs to the ball early in *Anna Karenina* with eyes open to the wondrous glitter of the scene; Emma Bovary at the end of all her resources, running through the woods with the trees spinning around her nightmarishly; the child Pip on the second page of *Great Expectations* confronted by the looming figure of a fierce man dressed in gray, his body lacerated, one leg in a great iron. It should be recognized, however, that these are only one set of possibilities for the realism of character; elsewhere—for example, in the novels of Fielding, Scott, Mark Twain, Trollope—such realism is achieved with little or no representation of the kinesis of consciousness.

It is important to keep this variety in mind because it will help us to see the continuities between the mimesis of character in the novel and in earlier and other genres. In fact, the supposedly pure conventionality of novelistic realism has been argued on historical grounds in the following terms: What we call the individual is a product of emergent capitalism, Protestantism, the breakdown of village society, the dissolution of the extended family, and so forth. It would have made no sense to a medieval person or to someone living in classical antiquity. The novel, then, does not represent men and women as they "really" are but rather gives us a historically conditioned, ideologically slanted conception of individual identity that may always have been partly illusory. In any event, its time is now passed and it will be replaced by some new notion of the serial self, the collective self, or whatever answers the requirements of a new era. The argument is by no means a foolish one. There were significant forces in intellectual and cultural history only recently in evidence around the year 1600 that put new value on the individual and that in the course of time would lead to a concept of the originality of the self which would have been unintelligible to earlier eras. Without such a concept, the novel would scarcely have been what it proved to be. And yet, it strains credibility to imagine that the individual is solely a product of transient historic conditioning. There are, perhaps, human societies in which a person feels himself to be no more than a component of some corporate identity, but the evidence of the Western literary tradition beginning with the Greeks and the Hebrews suggests that at least in this tradition there have been no close approximations of this sort of human beehive. The individual has certainly been modified through the ages but not rebuilt from the ground up.

What enables us to become imaginatively engaged with characters in works of fiction produced in the early nineteenth century, the turn of the seventeenth century, or even the eighth century B.C.E.? Obviously, even a moderately sophisticated reader has to be capable of a certain amount of historical reconstruction. Jane Austen's heroines live long before feminism, the sexual revolution, the electronic environment, the drug culture, and their quandaries will seem nonsense to a late twentieth-century reader unless he or she is able to imagine the different moral coordinates that defined the life of a young woman in rural England during the time of the Regency. Nevertheless, many people still read Jane Austen, quite avidly, not as an exercise of archaeological reconstruction because, for all the drastic historical changes, there remain strong and meaningful continuities between the human possibilities so finely represented in her novels and the human possibilities with which we still contend in our lives.

Let me illustrate the point with two episodes involving

fathers and sons that are historically removed from us by nearly three millennia. The first is from the sixth book of the *Iliad*. Hektor, in full battle gear, has been taking leave of his wife, Andromache, before going out to fight the Achaians.

So speaking glorious Hektor held out his arms to his baby,
who shrank to his fair-girdled nurse's bosom
screaming, and frightened at the aspect of his father,
terrified as he saw the bronze and the crest with its horse-hair,
nodding dreadfully, as he thought, from the peak of the helmet.
Then his beloved father laughed out, and his honoured mother,
and at once glorious Hektor lifted from his head the helmet
and laid it in all its shining upon the ground. Then taking
up his dear son he tossed him about in his arms, and kissed
him. . . .

(VI:466–474; Lattimore translation)

The heroes and heroines of the Homeric epics are not yet the highly particularized individuals of the realist novel. It is not only that individuating details of personal history are usually much sparser but, more crucially, that these figures belong to a much more stable world of fixed roles and values. The heroic epithet, however much it served the technical needs of oral-formulaic composition, is a key expression of this stability. Like an eternal force of nature, Hektor is repeatedly "glorious Hektor," and the family relations are preassigned and universalized, "beloved father," "honoured mother." These elements of distance from our own cultural situation need to be registered, even in a passage which, out of context, looks as though it could serve the disarmament movement of the 1980s. (Homer's poem, of course, actually celebrates martial virtues, though with a pained consciousness of the cost they exact.)

Yet with all that has changed, some things have not changed, and that is precisely what enables us to be moved by these lines 2,700 years after their composition in a world alien to ours. The terror of the startled, uncomprehending child;

the affection of the laughing father; the throat-catching contrast between human father revealing himself to his son and
terrible man of war, features hidden beneath horse-hair and
bronze—none of this needs explaining to us because we still
are conscious of many of the same things about fathers and
children, about the terrible tension between familial love and
the savagery of war. It need not be claimed that human nature
is fixed and unchanging, but after three millennia, sufficiently
powerful continuities persist in the literary representation of
human realities to make us feel when we read that writers
then and now are engaged with many of the same fundamental
objects of representation.

My other illustration is an equally memorable moment
from ancient literature, in a narrative written perhaps 150
years or more before the *Iliad* (the dating remains quite
uncertain), several hundred miles to the east. King David's
throne has been usurped by his son Absalom, and David has
fled to Transjordan with fighting men still loyal to him. When
the rebels and the loyalists are about to meet in battle, the
aging king, who will not himself now enter the fray, gives
explicit instructions that no harm be done to "the lad Absalom." However, David's hard-bitten commander-in-chief
Joab concludes that paternal sentiment should not be allowed
to interfere with the need to be rid of this dangerous
adversary, and when Absalom is caught in the oak tree, Joab
himself stabs him to death. In a spectacular scene, David sits
waiting between the two gates of the city while a watchman
overhead makes out first one runner, then another hurrying
toward them. When the second of these responds to David's
anxious question by at last conveying the news of Absalom's
death, the king mounts to the chamber over the gate,
weeping as he climbs and crying out these words: "O my son
Absalom! my son Absalom! Would that I had died in thy
place, O Absalom, my son, my son!" (2 Samuel 19:33).[13]

Although biblical narrative often uses distinctive techniques that involve subtleties of perception which may easily

be lost on later readers, David's words here readily move us
without any guide. Altogether, David is more of an individ-
ualized character, full of dynamic psychological contradictions, than any of the Homeric heroes. Elsewhere a master of
poised, politic speech, and of poetic eloquence, bereavement
here reduces him to a stammer of anguish. We may no longer
live in a society where lines of relation, as in the David story,
are defined by polygamy, vendetta, anointed monarchy,
exercise of cultic functions, and public sexual possession of a
rival's concubines; but the bond between father and son is a
biological given of our shared human condition that continues
to dictate essentially the same spectrum of emotional and
moral possibilities. In the first part of his story David is chiefly
a public—and hidden—person; we begin to see the private
David only after the catastrophe of his adultery with Bath-
sheba and his vicarious murder of Uriah in 2 Samuel 11.
Absalom's rebellion forces an absolute conflict between David's public and private roles. When he learns of his son's
death, the public man collapses, leaving only the helpless old
father with his unbearable loss. David's long gasp of pain
rendered in these few repeated words addressed to a dead son
seems as immediate as though it were written yesterday.

The claim I am making is a fairly modest one, which it
seems to me is variously and abundantly confirmed by the
evidence of five millennia or more of cultural artifacts: not
that there is an immutable human nature but that there are
certain lines of persistence that cross over from one era and
one culture to another. Much about the way we perceive
ourselves and the world manifestly changes as society, language, ideology, and technology change; but we also continue
to share much as creatures born of woman, begotten by man,
raised with siblings, endowed with certain appetites, conscious of our own mortality, confronting nature from our
various locations in culture. To say that humanity continues to
hold some things in common across the ages is not to imply
that what is held in common is confidently known. On the

contrary, the most arresting writers, even in the ancient period, often treat the human awareness of being in the world, in the family, in society, in history, as something to puzzle over endlessly. The characters and life situations of the narratives of different eras speak to us not because they reflect a knowledge which never changes but rather because they express a set of enigmas with which we continue to wrestle.

My examples from antiquity highlight the aspect of continuity in the mimetic enterprise of literary tradition. The complementary, and necessary, perspective of literary history concentrates on evolution and transformation. Formal analysis of literature in turn focuses on conventions and technical devices, in which quite often the shifting of aesthetic values and cultural codes is most perceptible. But what needs emphasis at this late point in the course of criticism is that literature cannot be adequately accounted for merely as a set of changing and arbitrary codes. What is left out in such a view is the powerful capacity of the literary work to refer its readers to a complex order of moral, emotional, and psychological realities. A criticism with no coherent vocabulary for discussing that power of reference will provide only a feeble guide to literature.

Literary fashions, generic constraints, cultural assumptions, manifestly change from era to era, but literary tradition constitutes itself as a trans-historical human community. In fact, a good many of the cultural codes invoked in literature may not be arbitrary but rather may be stylizations of certain perdurable aspects of human existence perpetuated from one era to another—perpetuated precisely because they answer so well to what we share as people. It is not only that later writers, by allusion and imitation, converse with the writers of earlier ages, but that through this polyphonous conversation all of them point toward shared objects of representation, turning and turning the sundry artifices of language to reveal the incalculability of life.

CHAPTER THREE

Style

> ". . . in general the symbol-using animal takes pleasure in using symbols: the passions may be terrible, but the syllables are a relief."
>
> Denis Donoghue, *Ferocious Alphabets*

Style is at once the most self-evident and the most elusive aspect of the literary text. Since language in a work of literature is never simply a transparent envelope of "content," most of us are conscious at some level as we read of style, and we quite naturally say of a novelist: his style is overwrought, she is a brilliant stylist, and so forth. It is nevertheless not altogether clear what literary style is, what its functions may be, and whether it can be firmly discriminated from the more general sense of style as "manner of writing or of speaking" which covers a vast multitude of verbal sins from the society pages of the local newspaper to the instruction pamphlets of the Internal Revenue Service. In the present age of sophisticated linguistics, one might expect that stylistics would be the great growth industry of literary studies, but so far that has not proved to be the case. Definitions of style tend to seize on two complementary conceptual handles: deviation from the norm of general usage (the norm, as has often been observed, being a somewhat problematic notion) and the internal emphasis in the writing on certain formal features that produce conspicuous cohesiveness (a particular kind of

recurring sentence structure, vocabulary, imagery, or whatever). Such generalizations seem valid on the whole but not
especially helpful in the particular case. At the other end of
the spectrum, much attentive stylistic analysis has been
devoted to individual authors and passages, analysis often
exhibiting the perceptive virtues of close reading but rarely
throwing light on the general phenomenon of style. And,
given the propensity of literary style to resist the obvious and
easy way of saying things, it is a phenomenon that becomes
increasingly perplexing to readers nurtured on a thin gruel of
journalistic formulas and textbook platitudes. Perfectly earnest, reasonably intelligent undergraduates, exposed for the
first time to the fantastic proliferation of metaphor in Melville,
the exquisite syntactic convolutions of the late Henry James,
the sonorously extravagant paradoxes and the arcane terms in
Faulkner, are often simply baffled as to why anyone should
want to do such strange things with words, and to make life so
difficult for a reader.

I shall not pretend in the pages that follow to articulate a
general theory of style that will hold cogently in all cases, but
I would like to offer an orientation toward what style does that
might serve as a modest guide to the perplexed. Style of
course equally embraces poetry and prose, but in order to
avoid the complicating considerations of prosody and poetic
diction, I shall concentrate on prose, moving quickly from
essayistic to fictional style.

Literary style, to begin with, is a manifestation of writing
that elaborately embodies the essential discontinuities between writing and speaking, even in the case of writers who
highlight certain colloquial elements in their prose. Indeed,
Denis Donoghue, a critic interested in establishing, in opposition to one trend of contemporary theory, the primacy of
voice over writing, makes the suggestive proposal that style
be regarded "as compensation for defects in the conditions of
writing, starting with the first defect, that it is writing and not

speech."[1] The literary stylist, in other words, precisely because he addresses himself to an absent and indeterminate audience, is impelled to knead and twist and stretch language in order to make it an instrument of subtle communication that will serve instead of the living voice guided from one moment of utterance to the next by the eyes and posture and gestures of a flesh-and-blood interlocutor. One should add that the very act of writing in one respect makes the writer more craftsman than communicator, for he is directed in the first instance not to his—necessarily, eventual—audience but to the medium of words, which has its own intricate allure, and which he works and reworks as a sculptor models his clay, to produce the pleasing curve, the intriguing texture, the satisfying symmetry. "The passions," as Donoghue says, "may be terrible, but the syllables are a relief."

A person may also take pleasure, of course, in manipulating the spoken word, and thus speech can have its own style, but it is a style that flows inevitably from an art of improvisation and of performance, quite different from the writer's patient practice with language in the privacy of his study. Most writers, I suspect, get so addicted to the activity that they are constantly warming up for it, trying out the striking image in conversation and still turning over the smart phrase as they prepare to drift off to sleep. This may mean that the style in conversation of certain writers is at times a kind of preliminary sketch for their prose, or an effort to appear consistent with the persona they have created in their prose. But the moments of contact between conversational and literary style merely underscore the essential difference between the two, illustrating how prose as the product of composition, whether rapid or slow, follows its own peculiar momentum, creates its own laws.

Samuel Johnson is an instructive case in point because he is justly famous both as one of the great English conversationalists and as one of the great English prose stylists. If we assume that Boswell's record of Johnson's speech is a fair approximation of his actual words, it is safe to conclude that there are two different Johnsonian styles, one oral and the other written. What connects them is the special emphasis of his personal presence, the ring of peremptory authority he imparts to words, and the incisive wit. But in the formal deployment of the language, in its diction, cadence, and syntax, Johnson's conversation cannot be said to exhibit the style of his essays. Authority, for example, is conveyed not through the architecturally grand periodic sentences that are the hallmark of his prose but, on the contrary, through brisk, often clipped utterances that replace architectonics with colloquial attack. Although he sometimes gives an ostentatiously Latinate turn to his speech, the diction of his conversation is more homespun than anything one encounters in his writing. Thus, observing in 1777 the contradiction between the clamor for independence of the American colonists and their exploitation of slave labor, he tartly remarks: "How is it that we hear the loudest *yelps* for liberty among the drivers of negroes?"[2]

There is often a monosyllabic muscularity in Johnson's spoken diction that marks it off from the more orotund rhetoric of his prose. When Boswell tries to argue that a powerless schoolboy's sufferings exceed those of a grown man, Johnson replies, "Ah! Sir, a boy's being flogged is not so severe as a man's having the hiss of the world against him." The very next sentence in Boswell's transcription, however, a weighty aphorism turning on a pointedly Latinate word choice for its central term, is an instance of the master critic tuning up for his prose in his conversation: "Men have a solicitude about fame; and the greater share they have of it, the more afraid they are of losing it."[3] Such an utterance might easily launch or cap a paragraph in the larger sweep of Johnson's written style, but a passage like the following is built around a typically elaborate periodic sentence that by no stretch of the imagination could have been spoken. It is from his "Preface to Shakespeare," an essay which in intellectual subtlety and rhetorical power remains one of the glories of English criticism. Johnson is contrasting Shakespeare's ability to encompass ordinary life with the convention-bound propensity for the preposterous that, as he sees it, characterizes the theater elsewhere:

> Upon every other stage the universal agent is love, by whose power all good and evil is distributed, and every action quickened or retarded. To bring a lover, a lady, and a rival into the fable; to entangle them in contradictory obligations, perplex them with oppositions of interest, and harass them with violence of desires inconsistent with each other; to make them meet in rapture and part in agony; to fill their mouths with hyperbolical joy and outrageous sorrow; to distress them as nothing human ever was distressed; to deliver them as nothing human ever was delivered is the business of a modern dramatist. For this probability is violated, life is misrepresented, and language is depraved.[4]

This is, preeminently, writing that exhibits style, which I will define provisionally as a summoning of the resources of language to convey the precise nuance of attitude and concept the writer desires and also as an orchestration of those very resources that is repeatedly felt to be in fine excess of the occasion of communication. Both these components of style, but especially the second one, need some explaining; both should become clearer through an analysis of details in the passage. The paragraph begins with a relatively brief sentence that inverts normal English syntactic order. If style is, among other things, the deviation from a norm, or at least from statistically preponderant usage, the "normal" way to make this statement would be: Love is the universal agent upon every other stage. Johnson gains at least three advantages by the syntactic inversion. By placing "upon every other stage" in the initial position, he makes it a kind of topic phrase for the whole paragraph, which is devoted to the absurdities of non-Shakespearian modern theater, and he also flaunts the absolute lack of qualification of the assertion (certainly an exaggeration), thus insisting on his uncompromising authority of judgment through a rearrangement of language when, because this is writing, not speech, he has no Boswell to stare in the eye and address with a peremptory "Sir!" In addition, the inversion produces a small-scale periodic pattern: we don't know what the subject is, what is this universal agent—with Latinate precision, "that which causes the action"—until we reach the end of the clause and discover "love."

That syntactic pattern is then deployed flamboyantly in the next, long sentence, which withholds the revelation of its subject until the climactic flourish of its last seven words, "is the business of a modern dramatist." Such grand periods are a celebrated feature of Johnsonian prose. What they communicate above all is not idea but attitude, serving as a syntactic correlative for magisterial authorial control. For sentences like this one are triumphal marches, not run-ons; we palpably feel that the artificer who solidly balances the clauses and buttresses the segments with the steel braces of his semicolons will complete the structure with a last resounding stroke. More than with other kinds of writers, we are in his hands; the syntax is the vehicle of his authority.

In regard to the communicative function of style, Johnson's word choices exhibit a formidable precision that manifests the continuously *composed* character of his language. Here I would like to introduce a concept that seems to me essential to the understanding not only of style but of literary form in general, and that is overdetermination. Just as in Freudian psychology a given neurotic symptom or dream image is often presumed to have been produced by more than one unconscious motive, in literary

texts a word choice dictated by some formal consideration—rhythm, rhyme, alliteration, parallelism—may simultaneously be determined by the desire to discriminate
meanings, to discover connections, to release the expressive
force of etymological backgrounds. Or, to put this in slightly
different terms, the attention to formal necessity leads to a
series of small serendipities in the discovery of meanings,   )
unanticipated relays of memory and association having been
activated in the mind of the writer as he writes. Johnson
wants the authoritative abstraction of "universal agent" at the
beginning, and then, in a nice progression we already
touched on, "agent" leads to "action" at the end of the
sentence. The action is said to be "quickened or retarded" by
this universal agent. Why "quickened" rather than "accelerated" or "sped up"? The five syllables of "accelerated"
would have been a rhythmic abomination, the spondee
and the down-shift of "sped up" a blatant awkwardness.
"Quickened," then, helps preserve a cadence at the end
of the sentence, but it also introduces a teasing possibility of a secondary meaning, "to bring to life," an operation
that is perhaps only ironically applicable to a kind of
dramaturgy that depends on the convention of amorous
intrigue.

   Reinforcing secondary meanings are also played into the
passage as etymological ghosts. Near the beginning of our
long middle sentence, the triadic series of infinitives "to
entangle . . . perplex . . . harass" revolves around a hidden
pun in the Latinate middle term (Latin being very much part
of Johnson's mental relays of association). In context,
"perplex" obviously means to confuse, but etymologically it
also means to twist together and so overlaps, or in a way is
generated by, "to entangle" before it. Near the end of the
periodic sentence, etymology confirms lexical precision: the
two parallel clauses, "to distress . . . ," "to deliver . . .", are
aligned by alliteration and by anaphora ("as nothing human

ever was . . .") and bracketed by antithesis, since "distress" means to constrict, strain, put in straits, and "deliver" means to set free. The pair distress/deliver is then picked up by a third term with a *de-* prefix, the climactic final element in the brilliant triadic series that drives home the argument: "For this probability is violated, life is misrepresented, and language is depraved." This last sentence, of course, also illustrates a wonderful sense of counterpoint: after the architectonic period, the conclusion is hammered out in a sentence of a dozen words, through three compact parallel clauses.

Since language, after all, is concerned with meaning, it is hardly surprising that literary style should be, as we have been observing, the instrument of an attitudinally defined act of communication. But to imagine that all aspects of style are determined by the need to get across a message is to commit what I would call the expressive fallacy. Although it is often difficult to distinguish the two functions, style also comes into being because the writer is drawn to words as a plastic medium in which he can create formal configurations that please him, that have an intrinsic beauty. I have mentioned triadic series in the passage, to which one must add the flourishing of paired terms ("to make them meet in rapture and part in agony; to fill their mouths with hyperbolical joy and outrageous sorrow," and so forth). Architectonic prose of various sorts often tends to a fondness for groupings of two and three because through them we most readily perceive order, sequence, balance. The pairs and the triads, then, could be taken as another correlative for authorial control in Johnson's style, but beyond any suggestion of attitude, I think one must grant that they also constitute an aesthetic object. Almost no one who deserves to be called a stylist would be that without a delight, which Johnson surely evinces, in making harmonious, interesting, surprising patterns with words as the words convey their meanings.

The little triadic series, "a lover, a lady, and a rival" offers a nice microscopic illustration of this aesthetic impulse in the creation of style. All three terms are perfectly right for Johnson's meaning, but they also yield a small musical theme in the prose. The "lady" could not be designated a "beloved" because that would destroy the rhythmic pattern of three trochaic nouns. She would not be called a "mistress" because that would derail the alliteration of "a lover, a lady." Alliteration makes a delicate pirouette as we move on to "rival," where the repeated *l* sound is at the end of the word, with the consonants of "rival" symmetrically mirroring those of "lover" in reverse order. This sound pattern, as far as I can tell, does not "mean" anything; it is there because it pleases. I am obviously not suggesting that Johnson paused to calculate this whole phonetic effect, but it no doubt sounded just right to him as he struck off the phrase and he would not have surrendered it for another. It reflects the aesthetic shaping of language in accordance with the individual sensibility of the writer that is much of the pleasure of style both for the stylist and for the reader.

The relation between the aesthetic and the expressive in style is never a regular or predictable one. In many instances, specific details will be overdetermined by aesthetic and expressive considerations. At some points, we may feel that the writing is driven by one of the two motives, independent of or even at the expense of the other. But in any event, the stylist is impelled by a desire to convey thought and stance with optimal precision through a verbal vehicle that has formal integrity and textural consistency. These generalizations are, of course, by no means limited to the resounding formality of a style like Johnson's; they hold equally true, despite all the differences in the aims of communication and aesthetic sensibility, for writers of expository prose as disparate from one another as Thomas Carlyle, Matthew Arnold, H. L. Mencken, Edmund Wilson, Tom Wolfe.

The operations of style that we have been observing also obtain when prose is the vehicle for fiction, but here there are further complications in the uses to which language is put. Instead of the writer's pitching the artifice of his prose to the (absent) reader, we have a triangular situation: the writer— through the agency of a narrator—addresses the reader, reporting the actions and motives and feelings of imaginary personages who are assumed, for the purposes of this verbal intercourse, to be virtually real, so that the reader relates to them as the writer relates to them, or even as the writer relates to the reader, with the salient difference that the writer's knowledge of the personages is infinitely superior. A novelist is perfectly free to short-circuit the illusion of reality in his fiction and remind us that the characters are mere constructs of invention and convention, but, except in the most extreme antirealist fantasy, even practitioners of self-conscious artifice repeatedly, and paradoxically, revert to the as-if-real status of their personages. In general, then, a triangular relationship remains intact in which a constructed persona, the narrator who stands in for the real person of the writer behind him, addresses an indeterminate person, the reader, about hypothetical people, the fictional personages. The triangle is not equilateral because the characters, as creatures or prisoners of the narrative, cannot talk back to the narrator or to the reader, though in a few experimental fictions (like Unamuno's *Mist*, Nabokov's *Pnin*) they end up doing just that, in a sense actualizing the personhood of the hypothetical persons they represent.

We will have occasion in a later chapter to look at this triangle from another perspective when we consider narrative point of view. For the moment, what concerns us is the role style plays in this complicated situation of communication. I would like to begin with an example from Fielding because his narrator, unblushingly flaunting the first-person singular and constantly indulging in disquisitions on a broad variety of general topics beyond the immediate concerns of the narrative, ostentatiously exhibits the overlap between essayistic and novelistic writing. Some of the splendid excurses in *Joseph Andrews* and *Tom Jones* employ grand balanced periods that might almost be Johnsonian, were it not for the elements of exuberant playfulness and flamboyant irony they reveal. (Johnson, as a matter of fact, dismissed Fielding, telling Boswell that life was too short to waste time reading such a writer.) For our purposes, it will be more instructive to observe Fielding's language when he is being more characteristically novelistic, when he is reporting the multifaceted transactions between characters with an eye to their motives, their individual temperament, their moral nature.

In the initial section of *Tom Jones*, we may recall, Squire Allworthy's sister Bridget commits the indiscretion of marrying the egregious Captain Blifil, a bond from which she is happy to be released by early widowhood—she was, the narrator informs us, "not over and above pleased with the Behaviour of her Husband; nay, to be honest, she absolutely hated him, till his Death at last a little reconciled him to her Affections" (III:6). The two hypocritical tutors Allworthy has engaged for Tom and young Blifil, Thwackum and Square, whom the narrator respectively designates the Pedagogue and the Philosopher, both begin to pursue the widow, impelled more by the allure of lucre than by lust, since they imagine she will inherit her brother. Bridget, however, remains impervious to courtship, as the narrator, in his characteristic fashion, explains:

> Whether Mrs. *Blifil* had been surfeited with the Sweets of Marriage, or disgusted by its Bitters, or from what other Cause it proceeded, I will not determine; but she could never be brought to listen to any second Proposals. However, she at last conversed with *Square*, with such a Degree of Intimacy, that malicious Tongues began to

whisper things of her, to which, as well for the Sake of the
Lady, as that they were highly disagreeable to the Rule of
Right, and the Fitness of Things, we shall give no Credit;
and therefore shall not blot our Paper with them. The
Pedagogue, 'tis certain, whipt on without getting a Step
nearer to his Journey's End.

(III:6)

Fielding's prose can be a good deal more elaborate than this,
especially in its mock-epic flights, but the middle range of his
style represented by this passage is particularly instructive in
regard to how style creates the "world" of a novel. We should
note at the outset that the paragraph does not render any
discriminated scene—there is no dialogue, no description of
the characters or the setting, no evocation of furtive embraces
or rumpled bedclothes—but it does manage to convey a
morally interesting narrative datum: Bridget's sexual liaison
with the philosopher Square. As is invariably the case in
literary narrative, the datum is not raw because it is communicated from a certain perspective, inviting us to think about
it in a certain tonality, within a fixed range of moral judgment.
The role of style here is essentially to provide a rhetorical
equivalent for the network of rumor and supposition in which
wayward sexual activity is caught in the real social world—a
rather elaborate instance of style compensating for the defect
of writing's being something other than speech.

The chief trick is fashioning a kind of prose that will
suggest something of the easy familiarity of polite conversation, in keeping with the figure of the narrator as genial
companion to the reader introduced at the beginning of *Tom
Jones*, and yet preserve its own formal decorum. The diction
is eminently cultivated but eschews the high-falutin language
of Fielding's spectacular set pieces, and is noticeably different
from the weighty Latinate authority of Johnson's prose. There
is elaborate syntactic inversion that has a composed quality

("Whether Mrs. *Blifil* . . . , I will not determine"; "to which . . . , we will give no Credit"), but in sentences that do not produce the effect of a formal period. That is, the revelation of subject and predicate is postponed to the end of a chain of clauses, not so much to impose a grand rhetorical impression as to create a moment of suspense, almost a kind of toying with the reader, reenacting on the microscopic level of the sentence what happens globally with the celebrated comic plot of *Tom Jones*. The postponement of syntactic revelation is, like Johnson's, also an implicit correlative of authorial control, but control to a different purpose, coyly playing with attitudes and moral possibilities rather than enunciating a ringing conclusion.

The quasi-vernacular effect that Fielding seeks to achieve makes him avoid the symmetries of rhythm and wording we observed in Johnson, and which he himself pursues elsewhere. Thus, the two long initial sentences of the three that constitute the paragraph are a series of repeated stops and starts, of deliberately irregular length and syntactic shape, typographically indicated by Fielding's abundant commas. He yields to one explicit formal symmetry here because it is too good to pass up—in other words, because it exerts an aesthetic allure in keeping with the general formal disposition of his style, and perhaps in excess of its expressive function. I refer, of course, to "surfeited with the Sweets of Marriage, or disgusted by its Bitters." This is a nice instance of the elevation of a cliché into a witty antithesis. "Surfeited with sweets" is a worn formula, usually followed by "of love" rather than "of marriage." The association of the phrase is with sensuality, so the implication is that Bridget may have had altogether too much of the marital bed with the irascible captain. Then "Bitters," perfect lexical antithesis to "Sweets," comes as a surprise. Bitters are unappetizing medicinal substances like quinine, their metaphorical application to the married state requiring a certain interpretive agility on the part of the reader. Surfeit and disgust aptly round out the image of ingestion, the former term directly referring to gluttonous indulgence, the latter, at least etymologically, implying the idea of revulsion because of a bad taste. Locally, this symmetrical antithesis both pleases and teases, but Fielding is quick to break it up by adding, "or from what other Cause it proceeded," an addition which at once helps to preserve tonal consistency (the conversational asymmetry of ambling movement) and to complicate the information communicated (what other motive, indeed, might account for Bridget's resistance to remarriage?).

Fielding's main strategy in creating a rhetorical equivalent of a rumor network is innuendo, reinforced by his characteristically ironic disclaimers of what he is in fact asserting. In the eighteenth century an illicit sexual union was called "criminal conversation," so the reader would be expected to realize at once what the narrator implies when he decorously says that Bridget "at last conversed with *Square*, with such a Degree of Intimacy . . ." The "malicious Tongues" the narrator then introduces are really also his, and ours, and we can hardly take at face value either his stated solicitude for the lady or his concern for "the Rule of Right, and the Fitness of Things," the latter terms having been already exposed in the novel as Square's empty, self-serving philosophic slogans. This is hardly an irony that tries to cover its own tracks, and the added flourish that the writer would not deign to blot his paper with such accusations serves mainly to underscore his exposure of Bridget and Square. That exposure is doubly confirmed by the last, brief sentence because an obvious antithesis is implied: " 'tis certain" that the Pedagogue never enjoyed Bridget's favors, inviting the inference that the Philosopher did.

The final sentence illustrates in another way the pleasures of style in the experience of reading: quite beyond the "information" conveyed about the character, we delight in the elegant wit and ingenuity (in other styles, it might be musicality, metaphoric brilliance, compactness, or half a dozen other qualities) of the formulation, which is in fine excess of the communicative occasion. Thwackum is said to have "whipt on without getting a Step nearer to his Journey's End" for three related reasons that fit inside each other like a nest of Chinese boxes. First, he whips on quite literally, in keeping with his comic villain's name, thrashing Tom while favoring Blifil because he assumes this discriminatory treatment of his pupils will ingratiate him with Blifil's mother. Then he whips on metaphorically in a standard figure of speech, driving his metaphorical horse but never reaching his destination. Finally, behind this familiar metaphor stands a veiled metaphoric innuendo of sexual activity, either the male sexual motions that Bridget frustrates or (Fielding is by no means above such suggestions) a possible onanistic substitution for what she refuses to grant.

The style, in sum, establishes a mental set in which we as readers imaginatively reconstruct the personages, their actions, their motives, the moral and psychological meanings of the narrative. I do not mean that the style absolutely determines our response. Different readers will pick up different emphases and draw different inferences; some no doubt will reject one or two of those I have just drawn. But style elicits a certain range of thoughts and feelings about the narrative data, a certain way of thinking and feeling about them, and a certain predisposition toward the distinctive pleasures of the verbal medium provided by the writer in question. We can encounter smug hypocrites in Jane Austen, Dickens, George Eliot, Edith Wharton, Faulkner, as in Fielding, but in each instance the narrator's style (among other things) encourages us to imagine and judge such figures in a different way. Fielding's urbane prose, happily wedding the formal and the vernacular, combining a knowing worldliness with a polite verbal decorum, playing wittily with innuendo and double

meaning, draws us into a community of cultivated intelligence, and it is from that standpoint that we condone or
condemn, or simply *understand,* what is happening morally,
socially, emotionally, psychologically, in the narrative. Every
original style will create its own distinctive standpoint, and
this is the sense in which the world of a novel ultimately
depends on its style. Conrad's London in *The Secret Agent*
and James' London in *The Princess Casamassima* refer, quite
persuasively, to the same city (twenty years apart), but the
metropolis of each belongs to its own world not only because
of the details included or ignored but also because of the
stylistic medium through which the city is evoked.

One particularly telling expression of the determinative
force of style in fiction is metaphor. This does not mean that
metaphor need be a dominant stylistic feature, and in fact our
examples from Johnson and Fielding manage nicely without
figurative language, though both writers elsewhere sometimes make spectacular use of it. But it is a fact of linguistic
life that metaphor is intrinsic to the use of language, from
small children learning to speak, who quite naturally extend
the applicability of their limited vocabulary by using terms
metaphorically, to speculative thinkers, who rarely can dis-
pense with metaphor in articulating thought. If, then, a writer
rigorously excludes metaphor from his prose, as Hemingway
does sometimes and as Alain Robbe-Grillet does programmat-
ically, we sense this absence itself as a strong stylization—as
if, say, a painter represented a landscape suppressing all
parallels and correspondences of contour and line.

Given the interest in metaphor evinced by most stylists,
and the positive addiction to it shown by some, it is remarkable how many different kinds of style, how many different
novelistic worlds, can be shaped through the central agency of
metaphor. Many variables are involved in these differences:
the objects to which the metaphors refer; the semantic fields
from which they are drawn; the level of diction and the

syntactic form in which they are presented; whether a single metaphor is developed at length or a rapid sequence of different, perhaps conflicting metaphors is offered; the degree of explicitness or hiddenness of the metaphor; and the fit between the operation of the metaphor and the novel's characteristic procedures for making meaning. Like other features of style, literary metaphor is a radical extension of a function of ordinary language, often used with an exuberance of invention that bespeaks the writer's delight in his medium and repeatedly evoking the atmosphere, with its specific gravity and coloration, through which we see the represented objects of the fiction.

Let us consider a sampling of three conspicuously metaphorical texts from novels written from the mid-nineteenth century to the beginning of our own century. The writers in question, Dickens, Melville, and James, could scarcely be more different from one another as stylists, yet metaphor is an indispensable tool for each.

Here is Dickens' first full-scale presentation—the narrator himself calls it a "description" but that hardly seems accurate— of the Six Jolly Fellowship-Porters, the ramshackle riverfront tavern frequented by the lowerclass characters in *Our Mutual Friend* (1863–65). It is the opening paragraph of Chapter 6 in Book the First:

> The Six Jolly Fellowship-Porters, already mentioned as a tavern of a dropsical appearance, had long settled down into a state of hale infirmity. In its whole constitution it had not a straight floor, and hardly a straight line; but it had outlasted, and clearly would yet outlast, many a better-trimmed building, many a sprucer public-house. Externally, it was a narrow lopsided wooden jumble of corpulent windows heaped one upon another as you might heap as many toppling oranges, with a crazy wooden verandah impending over the water; indeed the whole house, inclusive of the complaining flag-staff on the roof,

impended over the water, but seemed to have got into the
condition of a faint-hearted diver who has paused so long
on the brink that he will never go in at all.

The propensity for personification exhibited here, together
with a complementary fondness for representing people as
things, is one of the most often remarked features of the
Dickensian world. Nobody has described this peculiar operation of metaphor in Dickens more aptly than Dorothy Van
Ghent, who in her essay on *Great Expectations* speaks of a
"general principle of reciprocal changes, by which things have
become as it were daemonically animated and people have
been reduced to thing-like characteristics—as if, by a law of
conservation of energy, the humanity of which people have
become incapable had leaked out into the external
environment."[5] The passage scarcely gives us a coherent
visual image of the Six Jolly Fellowship-Porters, only the
general sense that it is tumbledown, crooked, precarious,
warped. What is most strongly conveyed through the figurative language is a perception of the public-house as a bent-
over, swollen, ailing, yet oddly durable old man, with its
"dropsical appearance," its "hale infirmity," and, less explicitly, "its whole constitution."

As with other features of style, the use of metaphor
generates its own momentum that begins to exceed any
representational purpose. What, for example, are "corpulent
windows"? Presumably, the reference is to a bulging look,
whether because the windows are architectural excrescences
or waterlogged and swollen. But the metaphor is hard to
visualize, and visualization is perhaps beside the point, which
is to be sought rather in the sheer fun of the surprising verbal
collocation (like Falstaff's "alacrity for sinking") that carries
forward the dominant metaphor of dropsy. It is Dickens'
general practice to drive on headlong with a single controlling
metaphor until a kind of displacement is effected of the

referent by the metaphor. He does this here with the image of the dropsical old man, which is then compounded by a more local metaphor drawn from a different semantic field and introduced in more colloquial language: "heaped one upon another as you might heap as many toppling oranges." The "complaining flag-staff" punningly picks up the initial association with disease—it complains (that is, cries out) because it creaks in the wind, and also because, like the building to which it is connected, it suffers from a complaint. The concluding image of the reluctant diver is perhaps linked to the illness metaphor by the term "condition"; in any case, it is a variant personification of the tavern, perhaps even comically complementary to the first personification: to begin with, the place is a man bloated by water retention, suffering dropsy, then a man afraid of the contact with water.

What may be most interesting, as well as most difficult to determine, about the play of metaphor here and in novelistic prose in general, is its tonality. For if style, as I have proposed, is a way of thinking and feeling about the fictional world, metaphor is likely to impose a certain affect on us as we read. There is surely a note of jocularity in the way the metaphorization of the public-house calls attention to itself, a jocularity particularly evident at the moment we already observed when the windows are said to be "corpulent." The fantastic evocation of the rickety structure, in other words, displays a kind of lunatic zest, which is the writer's in his verbal inventiveness and in which we as readers are invited to join (if we don't, there's little point to reading such prose). The joking stance is reflected in some of the formal turns of diction—most notably, in that odd "impending over the water," a phrase sufficiently appealing to Dickens that he contrived to repeat it. "Impending" here means "hanging," a sense listed as rare in the *Oxford English Dictionary*; more commonly, of course, "impending" is used with abstractions, as in impending decision, impending doom. Dickens' latinizing use of the term is an anomalously Johnsonian touch that reinforces through diction the feeling already conveyed through metaphor that the characterization of the Six Jolly Fellowship-Porters involves an element of exuberant fooling around with words and images. Flaunted playfulness is also felt in the obtruded paradox of "hale infirmity." Let me observe that though paradox is not necessarily an essential property of literary expression, as the American New Critics once claimed, it is a kind of statement encouraged by the purposeful dislocation of ordinary language that is literary style. Paradox is not readily expressed in music or in the visual arts; but because the language of literature opens up so many possibilities of superimposing significant images, establishing unlooked-for connections, stretching lexical and syntactic constraints, it often lends itself to paradoxical perceptions.

In the present case, I would propose that it is not only the notion of a vigorous sickness that is paradoxical but the tonality of the whole passage—and, by implication, of much of the late Dickens. There is an undertone of uneasiness in what I have called the jocularity of the prose. The subject of the fantastic metaphor is, after all, an ugly, distended slum building miraculously teetering on the safe side of the verge of collapse, and the materials of the metaphor are disease and physical distortion. The image of the diver is a local joke—the tavern is too cowardly to take the plunge—but it catches up a larger, more ominous resonance of the novel. The Thames is the great clotted artery of filth that runs through the London of *Our Mutual Friend.* Desperate scavengers drag it for dead bodies and wealth; death by drowning is a shadow that hangs over several of the main characters. The figurative diver frozen forever on the brink is not proffered as a symbol, but in keeping with the integrative function of style, it surely reinforces a sense already established at this early point in the novel that we are being led through a world in which the Thames is more than a geographical indication and in which the slippery brink between river and bank is a tense junction of meanings.

In the highly wrought metaphorical style of *Moby-Dick* (1851), meanings are palpably made to exert a terrific pressure. From another viewpoint the construction of meaning has become radically problematic—one recalls the famous chapters on the whiteness of the whale and the gold doubloon—a predicament that repeatedly produces a violent scramble of figurative language. Sometimes the violence is felt simply in the juxtaposing of shockingly antithetical images, as when, after a costly encounter between the crew of the Pequod and the White Whale, the narrator invites us to envisage "the chips of chewed boats" underneath "the serene, exasperating sunlight, that smiled on, as if at a birth or a bridal" (Chapter 41). Sometimes this violence takes the form of a stroboscopic sequence of alternative images for the same object, as when Ahab (Chapter 28) is likened to a man cut away from the stake, a bronze statue of Perseus, a lofty tree branded by lightning. Sometimes a metaphor generates one fantastic elaboration after another in a dizzying rapid series, as when Ahab (Chapter 34) is compared to a grizzly bear, the bear to a defiant Indian chief, his old age to a fierce winter ("inclement, howling") in which "Ahab's soul, shut up in the caved trunk of his body, there fed upon the sullen paws of his gloom."

There is more to be said about the reasons for this riot of metaphor, but first it should be observed that the operation of metaphor here, as elsewhere, cannot be considered apart from the other aspects of style with which it is associated, such as diction, rhythm, and the orchestration of phonetic effects. To follow this interaction of stylistic elements, we will need to look at a continuous passage. Here is one of the Pequod's boats caught in a squall:

The wind increased to a howl; the waves dashed their bucklers together; the whole squall roared, forked, and

crackled around us like a white fire upon a prairie, in
which, unconsumed, we were burning; immortal in the
jaws of death! In vain we hailed the other boats; as well
roar to the live coals down the chimney as hail those boats
in that storm. Meanwhile the driving scud, rack, and mist,
grew darker with the shadows of night; no sign of the ship
could be seen. The rising sea forbade all attempts to bale
out the boat. The oars were useless as propellers, performing now the service of life-preservers. So, cutting the
lashing of the waterproof match keg, after many failures
Starbuck contrived to ignite the lamp in the lantern; then
stretching it on a waif pole, handed it to Queequeg as the
standard-bearer of this forlorn hope. There, then, he sat,
holding up that imbecile candle in the heart of that
almighty forlornness. There, then, he sat, the sign and
symbol of a man without faith, hopelessly holding up hope
in the midst of despair.

(Chapter 48)

Unlike our specimens from Fielding and Dickens, a first-
person narrator—Ishmael—is speaking here, recalling the
experience as one of its participants. But stylistically, as many
critics have noted, the difference between Ishmael and
Melville is scarcely distinguishable, and though *Moby-Dick*
may be an extreme case in this regard, few novelists are able
to renounce altogether the resources of authorial style for the
sake of preserving a plausibly mimetic language for their
first-person narrators. "Authorial style" may be a little misleading because it implies that style for a novelist as for an
essayist is a kind of personal signature. That is entirely true
for some writers and partly true for most, but style is also
guided, as I have been arguing, by the need to shape a
distinctive world for a particular novel. *Moby-Dick* is in
certain ways unlike any other novel by Melville, and though
there are manifest stylistic connections with his other books,
nowhere else does he push his language to such lengths.

What lengths, and to what purposes? Because Melville wants to cast the story of this mad pursuit of the fabulous whale as a vast, sonorous prose poem, alternately epic and dramatic, he very frequently suppresses the kinds of vernacular elements most novelists weave into their style and instead flaunts the formal poetic properties of his language. The prominence of metaphor is of course one central reflection of this flaunting of poetic artifice. Another is the diction, which is often Shakespearian, with especially abundant reminiscences of *King Lear*, as here in "howl," "roared, forked, and crack[l]ed" (compare, for example, Lear in the storm, III:2: "Blow, winds, and crack your cheeks! Rage! Blow! . . . / You sulph'rous and thought-executing fires. . . ."). The question of allusion is complicated and deserves consideration in its own right, but we should note that style never operates in a vacuum; it inevitably plays against a background of previous styles and even specific previous literary texts with their various associations of meaning, aim, attitude. There is no work of literature in English that gives us more powerfully than does *King Lear* the image of man over against the sky, an impotent creature raging at the fierce fates and the elements. *Moby-Dick* ultimately has a different vision of reality, but the tonality of the style is often Learian.

The Shakespearian resonances are amplified, moreover, by the language of another early seventeenth-century text, the King James Version of the Bible, and, more particularly, of the Hebrew Bible. I refer here not to the many specific allusions to Job, Jonah, and Genesis but again to the diction, as in the first metaphor of our passage, "the waves dashed their bucklers together," with its reminiscence of the martial imagery of Psalms. No specific biblical text is brought to bear, but the poetic muscularity, the solemnity, of Old Testament language is invoked.

We noted the role of paradox in Dickens' metaphoric imagination: in the chatty, jovial vehicle of his prose, it tends to be playful, perhaps a bit coy, though with a serious underside. In Melville's poetic world, paradox is the great source of illumination, and he brandishes it like a torch. It is felt, to begin with, in the joining of opposed semantic fields through the metaphors: the storm on the ocean is "like a white fire upon a prairie"; the boats bobbing in the dark on the unstable water are like live coals down the chimney of a furnace. In between these two original images is an explicit paradox that turns on a specific biblical allusion: "unconsumed, we were burning," like Moses' bush that burns and is not consumed. (The same language is attached to Ahab when he is described as a man cut loose from the stake.) This paradox is then picked up in what amounts to poetic parallelism (the central formal mechanism of ancient Hebrew verse), in a clause that scans nicely as iambic tetrameter: "immortal in these jaws of death!" The paragraph goes on to conclude with a flourish of contradictions. The waif pole (a pole used to mark dead whales left adrift) with the lantern hanging from it becomes a standard of "forlorn hope," and Queequeg holding it is, in a final burst of alliterative emphasis, "the sign and symbol of a man without faith hopelessly holding up hope in the midst of despair." The poetic formality of this conclusion is appropriately reinforced by the use of anaphora in the last two sentences: "There, then, he sat. . . ."

Unlike the passage from *Our Mutual Friend*, where the building afraid to dive into the water is at the most a subliminally symbolic image, Melville takes pains, here and elsewhere, to remind us that reality as it is figured in his language is the womb of allegory, that every image engenders large meanings, however contradictory or disturbing, that every scene is potentially a representative image of man's fate on earth. These are not, moreover, static allegorical tableaux; rather, the process of symbol-making is self-consciously caught at the moment of fiercely intense experience. Later, Ishmael observes that when you are dragged out into the depths by a plunging whale, "you bid adieu to circumspect life and only exist in a delirious throb" (Chapter 87). There are changes of pace, moments of circumspection, in *Moby-Dick*, but a large part of the narration is undertaken at the pace and pitch of delirious throb, and the maelstrom of metaphor is one of the chief resources of style for conveying us from the no doubt easier rhythms of our own sundry worlds to the relentless pulsations of the world of this haunting novel.

I would add that even for a writer so intent, so devoid of playfulness for its own sake, style is not merely instrumental. In all the gloom of Melville's cosmic despair, the syllables are a relief, the pleasure of fashioning a resonant style is manifest in every cadence, every play of sound. "Scud, rack, and mist" are a fine trio of nautical terms (the first two mean "wind-blown ocean spray" and "storm"), aptly descriptive in context; but in their monosyllabic, Anglo-Saxon compactness they also have a wonderful *sound*, their appeal being as much musical as mimetic. The phonetic effect, moreover, jibes nicely with the flurry of monosyllabic words at the beginning of the passage: "wind," "howl," "waves," "squall," "roared," "forked." Whether Melville intended a real distinction of terms in calling Queequeg both "sign and symbol" is far from certain, but the appeal to the ear of the alliterative flourish is clear.

The "imbecile candle" at the end of the passage is a more complicated illustration of the double function of style as communicative vehicle and aesthetic medium. It is a strikingly compressed metaphor, the lantern personified or rather seen as a metonymic extension of the human hand that holds it up. Behind it, I would guess, stands the "brief candle" of Macbeth's last soliloquy ("all our yesterdays have lighted fools/ The way to dusty death"). The image surely focuses the whole sense of painful paradox with which Melville wants to end this moment, but it also calls attention to itself as a splendid verbal invention, reveling in the surprise of this adjective attached to this noun—quite like Dickens' corpulent windows, though with the most somber tonality instead of a bizarrely jocular one. In each instance, style at once illuminates dimensions of existence we recognize as part of the world of our experience and transports us into a realm that we can enjoy only through the artifice of language.

I noted before that there is a whole set of variables which influence the stylistic effect of metaphor. Two such variables we have so far scanted are the nature of the referent of the metaphor and the point of view of the narrator. In Dickens we observed an omniscient narrator using figurative language to represent a static object, the building that is the setting for the action at hand. In Melville, a first-person participant-narrator uses figurative language to represent an event in terrific kinesis, the squall that threatens to overwhelm the whaling boats. In the example we will now consider from *The Wings of the Dove* (1902), the perspective of the third-person narrator is finely interwoven with that of the protagonist, and, equally typical for the late Henry James, the object of figuration is the presence and nature of one of the other characters. In the second chapter of the novel, Kate Croy, who since her mother's death has been living with her formidable Aunt Maud, has a panicked perception of herself as a "trembling kid" awaiting the imminent moment when she will be introduced into the cage of the lioness.

> The cage was Aunt Maud's own room, her office, her counting-house, her battlefield, her especial scene, in fine, of action, situated on the ground-floor, opening from the main hall and figuring rather to our young woman on exit and entrance as a guard-house or a toll-gate. The lioness waited—the kid had at least that consciousness; was aware of the neighbourhood of a morsel she had reason to suppose tender. She would have been meanwhile a wonderful lioness for a show, an extraordinary figure in a cage or anywhere; majestic, magnificent,

high-coloured, all brilliant gloss, perpetual satin, twinkling
bugles and flashing gems, with a lustre of agate eyes, a
sheen of raven hair, a polish of complexion that was like
that of well-kept china and that—as if the skin were too
tight—told especially at curves and corners.

The efflorescence of metaphor and the hesitations of syntax in
the late Henry James have been the subjects of abundant
commentary, but it may be helpful to say something about the
correlation between those two stylistic traits. The narrator,
voicing a comparison that has silently occurred to Kate, calls
the room a cage, but then neither the literal designation nor
the figurative one can contain the multiplicity of functions and
feelings which that space presents to the mind of the protagonist, so it is also an office, a counting-house, a battlefield, a
scene of action, a guard-house, a toll-gate. The multiplication
of metaphors goes hand in hand with a restless accretion of
syntactic particles, as though an endless patience of accumulation were necessary to approach an object of thought that
was intrinsically elusive. The Jamesian fingerprint in the
prose of the first sentence is the expression "in fine," inserted,
with characteristic oddness, between "scene" and "of action."
Syntactically, it introduces a peculiar little hesitation before
completing the first series of six figurative alternatives offered
for the room; it throws one a bit off stride, as the style in
general, I think, is meant to do, interrupting the flow of words
at the wrong moment, conveying what is almost an uneasiness
about this process of accretion.

The phrase that introduces the seventh and eighth
figurative alternatives for the room, "figuring rather to our
young woman," is another preeminently Jamesian locution,
one of the many he uses in his later novels to remind us that
what is being reported is from the character's post of observation. Another characteristic indicator of the location of
narration in the mind of the protagonist is the comment "the

kid had at least that consciousness" which is made as we return to the metaphor of the lioness and her appointed victim; and the syntactic interpolation of the comment, once again a retarding movement in the prose, is equally characteristic. It should be noted that "figuring" points explicitly to the process of figuration going on in Kate's consciousness, a notion picked up punningly in the third of our three sentences when Aunt Maud is said to be "an extraordinary figure"—that is, a presence, but also a potent source of metaphor, "in a cage or anywhere."

The long final clause of the last sentence illustrates even more elaborately the general movement through accretion of James' prose. Because the series begins with "brilliant gloss," we are momentarily inclined to read all the terms as metaphors of a metaphor, figures for the lioness's pelt, until, as in the resolution of a *faux raccord* between scenes in a film, we recognize that these are all literal details of the lady's dress and appearance ("bugles" being not the musical instrument but the tube-shaped glass beads used to ornament women's garments around the turn of the century). But because this prose is conspicuously in pursuit of an ensemble of impressions, it rarely rests for long on the literal level, and here the nonfigurative details generate a new metaphor: from the sheen of satin and lustrous ornaments we move to the "polish" of complexion, which is then figured as "well-kept china," an image for the possessor drawn from one of her possessions. The unsparing scrutiny of Aunt Maud's taut skin is still Kate's, and there is a strategic compactness in the judgmental force of the concluding verb: "[a polish] . . . that . . . told especially at curves and corners."

In Dickens and Melville, figurative language is deployed chiefly to produce a complex set of rhetorical effects, persuading the reader to imagine the status and nature of the objects of representation more or less as the informing authorial intelligence wants to imagine them. In the later nineteenth century and on into the twentieth century, as novelistic narration comes to be more subtly situated in the fluctuations of consciousness of the characters, figurative language is increasingly used in exploratory ways, as the instrument of a process of cognitive discovery. James' affinity for metaphor is motivated by an assumption that we inevitably think in metaphors, that we constantly try on different metaphors for size in an effort to find more precise approximations for our understanding of things. And when the metaphors refer not to a house or a storm or, let us add, a person confidently known because he is presumed to have a fixed nature, but rather to a personality that, like most which affect us intimately, looms too large to be taken in all at once, then figuration becomes a restless, implicitly endless process instead of a rhetorical product. The sequence of different images Melville offers for Ahab mirrors in finished form the violently paradoxical nature which Melville perceives as the sum total of the character. Aunt Maud (and by extension her room), like most other Jamesian characters, has a "foglike" presence, in which "there were parts doubtless magnified and parts certainly vague," but no sum total, and so something further can always be added in the imaging of the character and in the hinging together of language. As far as the latter is concerned, James for the most part abandons the pleasing formal orchestrations of syntax and sound that all of our previous examples have exhibited in order to represent the movements of the mind— at times, in a language so finespun or tortuous as to be almost exasperating.

Yet even such a style fashioned to meet the requirements of experiential realism is never entirely explicable in terms of mimesis. The novelist who composed our passage from *The Wings of the Dove* has done an admirable job of representing the protagonist's efforts to imagine her overwhelming aunt, but the language, in its own unrhetorical way, is, like the work of most stylists, preeminently composed. We may learn a good deal about Kate's relationship with her aunt from the metaphor of the lioness and the kid, but we are also invited to delight, as James has clearly done, in the very articulation of the metaphor, as we are meant to delight in the triplet of spanking epithets, "majestic, magnificent, high-coloured" and in the vivid catalog of gleaming objects that follows.

As I have said, metaphor is by no means an indispensable instrument of novelistic style, but it occurs often enough as a primary resource to have provided us a convenient focus for seeing the range of possibilities for creating distinctive fictional worlds through style. In each instance, in different ways and with varying degrees of extremeness, ordinary language is purposefully distorted into some new configuration that gives coherence, attitudinal and emotional definition, to the world of the novel. But not everything we call literature is written at the pitch of genius. If what we have observed about style is a particular application of that power to generate multiple connections which I proposed as a hallmark of the language of literature, can such a concept of style apply to the derivative, popular, or downright bad writer?

Clearly, I have been using both "literature" and "style" as honorific terms. This usage seems to me a needed corrective to the vehement "deprivileging" of literature that has enjoyed such currency in criticism over the past two decades. The masterworks of literary tradition, as I have tried to illustrate in regard to style as well as in regard to other issues, effect a reorganization of linguistic resources that amounts to a transcendence of the capacities of ordinary language. The full perception of this transcendence requires special modes of attention and provides a distinctive order of imaginative pleasure. A run-of-the-mill work of fiction or an egregiously bad one usually reflects not an abandonment of the language of literature but an extreme, inadvertently parodistic, simplification of it.

Popular fiction may evince a certain openness to contamination from other kinds of discourse—journalism, instruction manuals, sermons, political speeches, and, especially, advertising—but on the whole it actually emphasizes its own literariness. (Some original stylists have consciously quoted, imitated, parodied extraliterary discourse, but that is quite a different matter from being contaminated by it.) The aim of such writing is not merely to purvey vicarious experiences but also to convey a sense that the vehicle of the experiences has the prestige of literature. Sometimes this is done quite cynically, sometimes perfectly earnest writers strain all their artistic abilities to produce what reads like the consequence of mechanical manipulation.

If intensity, complexity, subtlety, and, above all, significance are generally assumed to be the hallmarks of literature, the derivative writer, well-intended or otherwise, tends to execute a series of gestures that point to these values without realizing them. On the level of style, the result is a high degree of interchangeability from one book to the next. Instead of a style that is both a personal signature and the defining medium for a distinctive fictional world, any given novel sounds more or less like hundreds of others. For this reason, it is easier for the average reader to "get into" such a book—there will be no "imbecile candles" and "hale infirmities," no strange coils of syntax, no zigzagging between figurative and literal, to disorient him. A good deal of bestselling American prose, for example, is written in a mode one might call Standard Contemporary Novelistic, representing, I would guess, a homogenization and formulaic reduction of certain features of robust and muscular style introduced in the twenties and thirties by Hemingway, Dos Passos, Farrell, and others. This writing often reflects a certain workmanlike competence, but the suspicion of a cliché lurks around the corner of all too many sentences. Thus, figurative language can be almost as abundant as in Melville and James, but instead of linking vitally with the hidden center of the work, it seems to be dragged in from elsewhere, recycled from a vast heap of other middling texts: if something is hard, it is hard as steel; eyes pierce or burn; a ravine gashes the side of a hill; a clubbed man falls as though pole-axed. In all this, the derivative writer is not doing something different from literary style; he is only doing it deficiently.

To move down the slippery slope from middling to bad: uninspired style strives so self-consciously to be literary that it parodies the mechanisms of literary style. The "tempestuously heaving breasts" (in the worst case, they will also be "alabaster") that tend to obtrude in the pages of genteel erotic fiction are in one sense meant to do the same kind of thing as the figurative language of Shakespeare and Melville, but through a grotesquely hackneyed metaphor that instead of bridging a gap of perception is inert, and laughable. Nothing could be more painfully literary than the style of this climactic moment in *Royal Punishment*, a romance by Barbara Cartland, author, according to the publisher's note, of over 390 books that have sold more than 370 million copies throughout the world. She follows the peculiar typographic convention of beginning a new paragraph for each brief sentence, apparently for the purpose of distending a long story into a short novel:

> It was then the Marquis's lips came down on hers, and pulling her close against him until it was almost impossible for her to breathe, he kissed her.
>
> To Clotilda, it was as if the heavens opened and the sunshine outside suddenly enveloped the whole room with a dazzling light.
>
> Then the light was within herself and the Marquis, and she felt as if everything she had longed for and believed in was there on his lips.
>
> He gave her not only the sun, but the moon, the stars, and the flowers that filled the garden.
>
> It was so beautiful, so perfect, and at the same time so

wildly exciting that she knew this was what she had always
thought love would be like.[6]

The language here is nothing if not composed, manifestly
deviating from nonliterary language. But the reshaping of
vernacular syntax (as in the dramatic flourish of "It was then
. . . he kissed her") is heavy-handed and predictable, just as
the obtruded metaphors of heavens opening and light flooding
in, with their vaguely religious associations ultimately going
back to Revelation and John respectively, are effusive clichés.
Though style involves more than surprise, successful style
always makes repeated discoveries of the unlooked-for. This
kind of popular prose, on the other hand, goes through the
motions of figuration and significant cadence of literary style
while constantly succumbing to the obvious, the undifferen-
tiating image or term or phrase. Clotilda's discovery of love is
conveyed in an emphatic triplet, "so beautiful, so perfect, . . .
so wildly exciting," but the terms chosen are so hopelessly
vapid that they merely point to an automatic idea of rapture,
written by romantic recipe (two parts idealism, one part erotic
arousal). The style, aspiring or pretending to convey, like the
best literary prose, more than ordinary language, really
conveys less. As to making a fictional world through style, it
is safe to assume that the world of this novel is essentially
interchangeable with those of the other 390 or so the author
has written, and almost equally with the 39,000 or more
novels with which she may be competing.

If bad writing works—and sells—through the effortless
ease of access it affords readers by adhering to familiar
formulas, good writing revels in difficulties—technical, emotional, and conceptual difficulties overcome by the writer in
innovative configurations of language which then become
both the challenge to the reader and the reader's delight.
Style is the clearest single measure of the language of
literature, which also involves abundant nonstylistic elements

such as structure, narrative point of view, the ordering of narrative units, and prosody. But style remains, after all, the medium in which we swim as we read. In writers of the first rank, across a broad spectrum from the convolute grandiloquence of Faulkner to the chaste precision of Isaac Babel, style is the writer's means of realizing the cogency, the integrity, of a certain vision of reality, but it is also the distinctive pleasure of one person's way with language, which in the best of circumstances will elicit an answering pleasure in that other incurable language addict, the reader.

CHAPTER FOUR

Allusion

Allusion is not merely a device, like irony, understatement, ellipsis, or repetition, but an essential modality of the language of literature. It is important to understand why this should be so, but first some clarification is necessary about the term itself. In common usage, an allusion is any "indirect reference," and even the best of literary handbooks tend to mingle this general sense of the term with "literary allusion," though in fact the two kinds of allusion are different in formal structure and semantic thrust. When, for example, the Southern writer Katherine Anne Porter, in a magazine article written in the mid-1960s, invoked the distorted prominence of a group of writers in New York, raised on an immigrant jargon, with no roots in the authentic language of America, this thinly veiled reference was an allusion in the first sense. The point of alluding to rather than actually naming "New York Jewish intellectuals" would be to express a decorous disdain, a haughty distance, from the object of reference, together with a knowing wink of shared superiority with the readers who would immediately decode the oblique reference. There is little more to be said about the meaning and function of such allusions, and though this one occurred in a published text, we also use allusions in this sense all the time, whether motivated by hostility, humor, modesty, prurience, nervousness, fear, or whatever, in our daily speech.

Literary allusion, on the other hand, which will be our concern in all that follows, involves the evocation—through a wide spectrum of formal means—in one text of an antecedent literary text. The consequence, as Ziva Ben-Porat has observed, is a "simultaneous activation of two texts" in patterns of interrelation that are usually quite unpredictable.[1] Since the early 1970s, under the influence of French usage, there has been a pronounced tendency to substitute "intertextuality" (a term coined by Julia Kristeva in 1967) for "allusion" as a critical term. I would like to resist that tendency here. "Intertextuality" is a much more general concept, which occasionally may be warranted for that very reason, and the adjective "intertextual" in certain contexts may be particularly useful. But this more abstract term finesses the crucial question of authorial intention: you can allude to a poem or a play but you can't "intertextual" it.[2] Whereas allusion implies a writer's active, purposeful use of antecedent texts, intertextuality is something that can be talked about when two or more texts are set side by side, and in recent critical practice such juxtaposition has often been the willful or whimsical act of the critic, without regard to authorial intention. A critic is, of course, free to join any texts he wants—*Oedipus Rex* and *Hiawatha*, Nietzsche and Kurt Vonnegut—and the results may be perfectly intriguing, but one cannot claim, as would be the case with allusion, that the analysis follows a process which is intrinsic and central to literary expression.

Why intrinsic and central? Every act of literary expression necessarily implies the context of a literary tradition, just as every individual speech act implies the context of a shared general language. Logically, there ought to have been a moment when someone composed the first poem or told the first story, but as an empirical fact of cultural history such origins are absolutely unrecoverable, and in a sense are unimaginable. All that we have of literature builds on literature that precedes it. The Homer of the eighth century B.C.E. who is, more or less, the source of our canonical *Iliad*, is a crystallization or culmination of centuries of bardic tradition. (Since he, like the bards before him, is an oral-formulaic composer, we should note that the act of writing is not strictly necessary for the process of literature.) The Hebrew Bible, though it represents a radical revolution in consciousness, draws on a Syro-Palestinian tradition of poetry antedating it by half a millennium for its poetic forms and imagery; makes abundant use of a much older narrative literature from Mesopotamia; and in all likelihood exploits prebiblical strata, whether written or oral, of an indigenous Hebrew literature. Such promiscuous borrowing occurs again and again in literary history not because of any poverty of imagination but rather because the language in which the literary imagination speaks is constituted by all the antecedent literary works available to the writer.

It is, let me stress, an unnatural act to compose a poem or write a story. No one would think of perpetrating such an act without having been exposed to poems or stories that present themselves as objects of emulation or rivalry. If, say, you decide to put your love, exultation, or misery into a sonnet, the immediacy of your experience may be quite terrific, but since English speech does not normally bubble out in fourteen intricately rhymed pentameter lines, your choice of the sonnet reflects the awareness of a tradition that winds its way from Sidney, Spenser, Shakespeare, Milton, and Wordsworth down to modernists like Yeats and Frost. I drop these resounding names in order to emphasize that the form is never entirely separable for the writer who adopts it from the particular achievements previously realized in that form. A writer embraces a given form, whether it is as precisely defined as a sonnet or as baggy as a novel, because he or she admires what has been done with the form. Every act of literary creation springs from the conviction— often, perhaps, the illusion—that the writer has something new and interesting to say, but it is no use pretending that your illustrious literary forebears, whose formal achievements you are exploiting, never existed.

In one way or another, then, all writers are forced to enter into a dialogue or debate with their predecessors, recycling bits and pieces of earlier texts, giving them a fresh application, a nuance of redefinition, a radically new meaning, a different function, an unanticipated elaboration. Since antecedent texts can neither be ignored nor repeated verbatim (except in the teasing fantasy of Borges' Pierre Menard), this process of infinite combination and permutation of texts, of "simultaneous activation" of texts, is ineluctable in the making of literature. The bristling allusions of T. S. Eliot's *The Waste Land* may have been meant as a kind of implicit manifesto of poetic modernism in 1922, but, whatever aggressiveness and self-consciousness they reflect, they are no more than an extrusion of a process intrinsic to literature. In this respect, one could say of *The Waste Land* what Viktor Shklovsky said of *Tristram Shandy* as a novel—that it is the most typical poem of world literature.

John Hollander, bringing to bear a fine combination of erudition and perceptiveness, repeatedly demonstrates the variety and pervasiveness of this internal dialogue of literature with itself in *Melodious Guile: Fictive Pattern in Poetic Language*. He aptly defines this essential dynamic of literary tradition in his account of one mode of what he calls "poetic answering." "A poem treats an earlier one as if it posed a question, and answers it, interprets it, glosses it, revises it in poetry's own way of saying, 'In other words. . . .' In these terms, the whole history of poetry may be said to constitute a chain of answers to the first texts—Homer and Genesis—

which themselves become questions for successive generations of answerers."[3]

It is true, of course, that the density of allusion increases
noticeably in certain schools and eras, for reasons that variously have to do with ideology, with assumptions about
literary convention, with cultural engagement in the past. To
touch on just a few moments of high density, I would mention
medieval Hebrew poetry in Spain; Dante; Spenser, Ben
Jonson, and Milton; English Augustan verse; Eliot, Pound,
and Joyce. The abundant recourse to allusion is by no means
limited to moderns who are troubled by their belatedness,
struggling under the burden of the past. We find it, as I have
said, in the earliest texts that have come down to us, which
give frequent evidence of engaging in subtle colloquys with
their own literary antecedents.

The aspect of intentionality of allusion in contradistinction to intertextuality is worth emphasizing. I have already
mentioned the species of intertextuality that is solely the
product of the critic's decision to bring together two texts, and
where, presumably, the chief interest lies in the ingenuity of
the critical argument itself, for which the juxtaposed texts
serve as springboards. There is a second kind of intertextuality that derives from certain generally shared properties of the
language of literature. Consider, for example the opening
sentences of *Pride and Prejudice* and *Anna Karenina*. From
Jane Austen: "It is a truth universally acknowledged, that a
single man in possession of a good fortune, must be in want of
a wife." From Tolstoy: "Happy families are all alike; every
unhappy family is unhappy in its own way." There is an
identifiable literary-historical relation between these two
texts as instances of the nineteenth-century realist novel,
early and late (1813 and 1878, respectively). Much could be
said about the convention of beginning a novel with an
aphoristic generalization in order to establish the authority of
the narrator's overview; about the explicit irony of Jane

Austen's satiric realism and the muting or exclusion of irony in Tolstoy's more somber psychological and social realism. The very nature, moreover, of these two opening sentences raises the question of the play between general knowledge and individual experience that is central to the representation of reality in so many nineteenth-century novels. The two texts, then, may be said to share a dialect of the language of literature. Nevertheless, it is highly unlikely that Tolstoy was in any way *invoking* Jane Austen when he devised his own initial sentence, so what we see here is a potentially instructive instance of intertextuality without allusion. Allusion occurs when a writer, recognizing the general necessity of making a literary work by building on the foundations of antecedent literature, deliberately exploits this predicament in explicitly activating an earlier text as part of the new system of meaning and aesthetic value of his own text.

Since this is in fact a process as old as the earliest literature that we possess, let me offer as an initial illustration a bit of dialogue from a story that goes back to the early Iron Age. In the second chapter of the Book of Joshua, two spies are sent out by Joshua to Jericho, the first Canaanite city west of the Jordan in the path of Israelite conquest. They are given refuge, we may recall, by the harlot Rahab, who responds to the King of Jericho's command to produce the men by hiding them in the thatched roof of her house and pretending they have already fled. Her very first words of explanation to the spies about why she is helping them are as follows: "I know that the Lord hath given you the land, and that your terror is fallen upon us, and that all the inhabitants of the land faint because of you" (Joshua 2:9). It is a speech that makes perfect sense in context, but the second and third clauses are also a close prose paraphrase—virtually the same words but without the rhythmic regularity— of the end of one line of poetry and the beginning of the next in the Song of the Sea, with the order reversed: "All the inhabitants of Canaan faint. / Terror and dread fall upon them" (Exodus 15:15–16; the translation is mine because the King James Version here does not make clear the verbatim conformity of the Hebrew in Exodus and in Joshua). It would scarcely have been any trouble for the author to make Rahab convey this message in different words, so we are entitled to ask what a Canaanite harlot is doing quoting from the song chanted by Moses, according to the traditional account, after the drowning of the Egyptian host, forty years earlier in narrated time. A realistic motivation for the citation—i.e., that the Song of the Sea had somehow become a kind of hit tune among the inhabitants of eastern Canaan—must be excluded on grounds of improbability. For the audience of the story, however, the recurrence of Moses' words in Rahab's mouth is a great moment of recognition. The Song of the Sea (by scholarly consensus, a composition that considerably antedates Joshua) had sketched out a grand historical plan of fulfillment prophetic of further fulfillment: the triumph over the Egyptians in the first two stanzas followed by the imminent triumph over the Canaanites depicted in the third stanza. Rahab's unwitting citation of the language of the Song becomes a splendid confirmation of the prophecy: it was no empty poetic boast on the shore of the Sea of Reeds, for a Canaanite woman now attests that the terror of the Israelites has indeed fallen on her people, that the inhabitants of the land faint because of them.

The conquest that Joshua is about to initiate is in fact carefully defined through allusion as a reenactment of the Exodus victory, in conformance with a general biblical pre-disposition to see history as a chain of duplicating patterns. In the next chapter (Joshua 3), the crossing of the Jordan by the tribes, with the waters miraculously parting, is turned into an explicit repetition of the miraculous crossing of the Sea of Reeds. Rahab herself, in the verse immediately after the one I have quoted, pointedly mentions the drying up of the Sea of Reeds. Under the force of this central allusion, other echoes of the Exodus story begin to suggest themselves. Is the hiding of the spies in the thatch a reminiscence of the hiding of the infant Moses, who is afterward placed in an ark among the bulrushes? A lexical similarity and a grammatical peculiarity may provide clues here. Of four or more biblical terms for "hide," the same verb, *ts-p-n*, is used in both texts (Exodus 2:2; Joshua 2:4), and oddly, even though she is hiding "them," as all the translations plausibly say, the received Hebrew text actually has a singular object of the verb, "him," which could be either an authorial choice to make us think of Moses or a scribal error caused by the recollection of Exodus 2:2 that the language of the verse has triggered. Finally, when Rahab gives the spies instructions for safe flight, she tells them, "get you to the mountain" (v. 16). Though in context "mountain," *har,* may mean hill country, it is lexically identical with the often stated goal of the flight from Egypt, and the two men wait there three days—admittedly, a formulaic number in biblical narrative, but also the number of days that the Israelites are enjoined to wait at the foot of the mountain before the giving of the law.

As this ancient example illustrates, allusions often radiate out to contiguous allusions, and it is also fairly characteristic that one allusion should be superimposed on another. Thus, the two successful spies in Joshua recall the two courageous spies in Numbers, Joshua and Caleb, whose view is out-weighed by the other ten spies fearful of the Canaanites—a lack of resolve that leads to forty years of tarrying in the wilderness. Through the double set of allusions, we get a sense of restitution made in Joshua for the espionage fiasco of Numbers. Now there are only the two loyal spies, without ten pusillanimous ones, and in taking the first step of the con-quest, they recapitulate from the beginning the interrupted process of the Exodus—hidden like Moses, eliciting a recol-lection of Moses' exemplary triumph at the Sea of Reeds, heading off to the mountain as Moses led the people of Israel.

Our initial example also suggests something of the multiple possibilities of form and function inherent in allusion. There are three categories of variables involved in allusion: the form given to the signal for the allusion (what Ziva Ben-Porat calls the "marker" in the alluding text); the function of the allusion in the alluding text; the relation of the alluding text to the evoked text. It will not be feasible to illustrate all the possibilities generated by this conjunction of variables, but a general overview of the terrain may be helpful.

How does an audience identify an allusion? The whole system of signaling depends, quite obviously, on a high degree of cultural literacy—an easy assumption in traditional societies with fixed literary canons and a high capacity for verbatim retention of texts, but something of a problem for contemporaries, who often come to literary texts from a background of loose canons, little reading, and languid memory. The question of cultural literacy, which of late has begun to exercise the American public for good reason, lies beyond our concerns here, but I would observe that because of the intrinsically allusive nature of literary expression, there is simply no substitute for careful, retentive reading as a guide to good reading: literature is always its own best teacher. Most writers, working on the assumption that the lessons of literature have been thoroughly absorbed, feel free to use a variety of different kinds of allusive markers, direct and oblique.

The most explicit marker is actual citation. Even citation, however, is susceptible to degrees of variation. At one end of the spectrum, we encounter the prominent embedding of one text in another—as, for example, in *Crime and Punishment*, when the entire story of the raising of Lazarus from John is read out loud by Sonia to Raskolnikov. Here, allusion is no longer a technique of indirection: the character opens the book and reads, so the reader is unambiguously confronted with the antecedent text, and the embedding text provides direct exegesis on it, or rather, the two texts produce mutually illuminating commentary on each other. A more common allusive procedure is Rahab's citation of the Song of the Sea, where the embedded text is relatively brief and not reproduced verbatim. Because, moreover, this close paraphrase of an antecedent text occurs in dialogue, the effect resembles the collusion between author and audience produced in dramatic irony. Rahab presumably does not know she is quoting the great Israelite song of triumph; we do, and in all likelihood the two spies do as well, so we, the Israelite audience of the story, recognize the confirmation of a large historical design that the Canaanite woman can grasp only partially, from her perspective as a member of the invaded population. In any case, the minor modification of the lines from Exodus 15—the switching of their order and the relaxing of the verse rhythm into prose dialogue—is hardly intended to camouflage the source.

Elsewhere, a cited text may be deliberately recast or distorted in order to produce a particular effect. One of the most beautifully economical examples of such allusive alteration is provided by a brief sequence from "Churchmonuments," a poetic meditation on mortality by George Herbert: "Flesh is but the glass, which holds the dust / That measures all our time; which also shall / Be crumbled into dust." The initial clause here is a citation of the King James Version of Isaiah 40:6: "All flesh is grass," with the crucial substitution of a single liquid letter, l for r. The line wonderfully illustrates the serious playfulness which allusion, like other aspects of the language of literature, often exhibits. Through what amounts to an intertextual rhyme ("grass" and "glass"), Herbert conveys a sharp dissonance of images together with a complete consonance of theme. Both his poem and the biblical one are concerned with the frailty of flesh (elsewhere in the Bible associated with "dust" as in Herbert), the ephemerality of human life, but the prophet couches this idea in an agricultural imagery of flourishing and withering while Herbert restates it in a technological image of the body as an hourglass holding within it the inexorable flow of the sands of time. The result of this joining through allusion of consonance and dissonance is a spark of revelation that leaps from one text to the other. Since Herbert surely presumed in his readers a verbatim familiarity with the text from Isaiah, he could count on a recognition of the wit of his discovery (the element of play) and a perception of the small shock as the fragile blade of grass is transformed into the otherwise fragile transparency of the hourglass.

As signals in the allusive marker become more microscopic, the dimension of teasing game may become more prominent. Thus, a single word can serve as a marker—in the Rahab story, *watitspeno,* "and-she-hid-him"—but perhaps only some of the audience will pick it up. For others, it may operate as a subliminal clue, affecting their perception of the story in ways of which they are not conscious; and in general it is likely that a good deal of allusion is either meant to have or ends up having a subliminal effect. Some readers— or in the case of the ancient story, listeners—may get no signal at all from such microscopic markers, which nevertheless make sense in their own right in context without the background of allusion, and one can hardly expect that all readers will take away all encoded messages and implications from all texts.

What I have said of the effect produced by single-word markers is also often true when a name or a motif is borrowed, without actual citation, from one work by another. Thus, some readers of Kafka's *Amerika* may pay no attention to the odd fact that the town where Karl Rossmann serves as a menial hotel employee, somewhere within a day's travel of New York City, is called Rameses. Others may pick up the Egyptian·association without much further reflection, though that very recognition will in some degree subtly affect their perception of what happens in the novel. For readers who ponder the background of the peculiar name choice, a whole pattern of allusion begins to emerge. Rameses in Exodus was one of the storage cities built for Pharaoh by Hebrew slave labor. In Kafka's novel, it is the site of incessant frantic labor, another kind of slavery. The allusion points toward a radical ambiguity in the America of the novel, which is at once the Promised Land and the house of bondage. The children of Israel went down to Egypt because Joseph was first sold there as a slave; this may lead us to contemplate a partial parallel with Karl Rossmann's fate, peremptorily banished from his father's house for no real fault of his own and packed off to America. His surrogate father upon his arrival in New York is an uncle named Jacob, like the father of the biblical Joseph, and from Jacob's at first welcoming home Karl suffers a second banishment. With all these ramified connections, we may even begin to wonder retrospectively whether Karl's being virtually raped by a servant woman back in Europe, the incident that precipitates his disgrace, might not be a parallel with reversed denouement to the story of Joseph and Potiphar's wife. The almost teasing procedure here is to camouflage the allusive possibilities, to set up partial but suggestive analogies between the two texts, with the single obtrusive name clue of the Egyptian city leading us, or some of us, to look for links that are elsewhere submerged.

Finally, as our example from Kafka suggests, it should be observed that the marker may be situational, without any verbal borrowing, direct or veiled, from the evoked text. The account in Joshua 3 of the parting of the waters of the Jordan uses none of the language that reports the parting of the Sea of Reeds in Exodus, with the solitary exception of the word "heap" (*ned*), which also occurs as a simile for the piling up of the waters in the Song of the Sea. But we would easily identify the allusion even without this small verbal clue because the similarity of situation is so striking—the tribes of Israel marching dryshod through a watery body that marks

the border between one realm and another in their passage
from slavery to national independence.

Faulkner's *Absalom, Absalom!* is a much more complicated instance of the use of situational markers. The title of
the novel, of course, is an actual quotation of the bereaved
David's words (2 Samuel 19:1) and follows a twentieth-
century convention of using phrases from biblical, classical,
and older English texts as titles for novels (*The Way of All
Flesh; The Sun Also Rises; Look Homeward, Angel;* and so
forth). But in the body of the novel, there are no citations,
even oblique ones, from the David story. The closest approximation to verbal markers is a recurrent vocabulary that
underlies an affinity of concern, a connection of tone, with
ancient Hebrew narrative—terms like "blessing," "curse,"
"seed," "flesh," "birthright," "land," "inheritance." But
Faulkner's use of such biblical terms does not direct us to
particular texts; they are invocations of a whole corpus, and a
world, rather than allusions proper. With the solitary clue,
then, provided by the title, we follow out the intricate
patterns of Faulkner's plot, slowly constructing the partial but
meaningful parallels with the biblical tale: Sutpen as David
(with whom he shares red hair, a motivic clue), the man who
comes from nowhere to build himself a kingdom out of sheer
force of will; Bon, Judith, and Henry as a fraternal triangle
recalling the triangle of Amnon, Tamar, and Absalom that
moves from incest to fratricide. The motives, to be sure, of
the principal figures as well as significant elements of plot are
quite different in the two stories, allusion being here as
elsewhere a dynamic interplay between two texts rather than
the dressing-up of an old text in new form.

The situational parallels, moreover, between the story of
the house of Sutpen and the story of the house of David are
still further complicated by the superimposition of a second
set of allusions, here with explicit verbal markers in the text
of the novel, to Greek tragedy, and in particular to the

Oresteia. Faulkner's novel, in sum, represents the most global use of allusion. It is not the interplay of line against line—an image in Isaiah and an image in Herbert, a verse from Exodus and a snatch of dialogue in Joshua—but of plot against plot and world against world. The evoked text becomes a fundamental ground of reference for the alluding text (something already true, but with the more immediate link of historical contiguity and complete thematic consonance, for the connection between Joshua and the Exodus story). That is, *Absalom, Absalom!* is a story about primal sin, the tainting of an inheritance, the loss of a promised land, the violent twisting of the fraternal bond; as it is a story about inexorable fate, *hubris*, the destruction of a presumptuous king, the embodiment of the furies in filial hatred—and the respective grounds of reference that give resonance to these two cognate sets of concerns are the Hebrew Bible and the tragedies of Aeschylus.

The second set of variables in the dynamics of allusion consists of the different functions a given allusion may serve in the text in which it occurs. The fact that the phenomenon of allusion is central to literature does not mean that every allusion is central to the work in which it appears. The effect of an allusion may be purely local, discontinuous with the larger patterns of meaning of the work; sometimes an allusion is a mere throwaway, a wink to the wise that is a small expression of what I called earlier the high fun of literature. The general significance, moreover, of a given allusion in a text is not determined by the amount of space it occupies or by the explicitness of the marker. A brief and isolated allusion can be a key to a work while an elaborated allusion can be incidental to the larger structure.

In the fourteenth line of Wordsworth's *The Prelude*, the autobiographical poet-speaker says, "The earth is all before me," and then goes on to reflect that "should the chosen guide / Be nothing better than a wandering cloud, / I cannot miss my way." The marker here consists of a mere nine words, the first six I have quoted and, two lines down, "guide," then "wandering" and "way." These lead us back to the concluding lines of *Paradise Lost*, like *The Prelude* a long poem in blank verse, and arguably the greatest in English composed in that form:

> The World was all before them, where to choose
> Thir place of rest, and Providence thir guide:
> They hand in hand with wandring steps and slow,
> Through *Eden* took thir solitarie way.

Wordsworth's poem makes only occasional allusions later on to *Paradise Lost,* but the single emphatic allusion of the beginning of one poem to the end of the other has powerful reverberations. Wordsworth's tracing of the "Growth of a Poet's Mind" is in one aspect a return to Eden, or a Paradise Regained. In the vision of benign nature with which the poem opens, the elements of earth and sky are themselves providential, and so "a wandering cloud" can be a fit substitute for "Providence thir guide" in the evoked text from Milton. The affiliation with *Paradise Lost* as we enter into the world of *The Prelude* tells us not so much that Wordsworth claims to be heir or rival to Milton but rather that his poem is directed to the same large arena of significance as Milton's: if *Paradise Lost* tells the story of mankind's fall and the beginning of its arduous journey to redemption, *The Prelude,* by working instead with the poet's individual experience, seeks also to encompass the character of human nature, man's relation to the world around him, and the redemptive powers of the human imagination. Thus the marker of the allusion is local and limited, but the implications of the allusion are global for the poem.

On the other hand, an allusion may be articulated in flamboyant detail but with only local effect. Swift, for example, in his urban-pastoral mock-epic poem (the conflation of genres is quite pronounced on his part), "A Description of a City Shower," describes a fashionable London fop caught by the sudden downpour in his sedan-chair, trembling within as the rain pounds against the leather roof:

> So when *Troy* Chair-Men bore the wooden Steed,
> Pregnant with *Greeks*, impatient to be freed;
> (Those Bully *Greeks*, who as the Moderns do,
> Instead of paying Chair-Men, run them thro')
> *Laocoon* struck the Out-side with his Spear,
> And each imprison'd Hero quak'd for Fear.

The entirely explicit allusion is to the *Aeneid* II:40–56, in which the suspicious Trojan warrior Laocoön prods the wooden horse with his spear but is interrupted by the appearance of Sinon before he can carry his investigation further. There is nothing about the general significance of the *Aeneid* or about the Trojan Horse episode in particular that speaks to the meanings of "A Description of a City Shower." The only point of the juxtaposition of texts, beyond the sheer ingenious joke of it—the sedan-chair as Trojan Horse—is the mock-epic shuttle between disparate realms, ancient and modern. The ancient is irreverently modernized ("Those Bully *Greeks* . . ."), while the distinctly sub-epic character of the modern is stressed by its being rendered ironically in epic terms: the pusillanimous fop, a latter-day "imprison'd Hero," quakes within his sedan-chair at the threat of rain as the Greek warriors quaked when they heard a spear thrust against their hiding place. For the space of six lines, this particular allusion is a splendid resource, and one has only to imagine how senseless or insipid the lines would appear to a reader who had never heard of the Trojan Horse in order to see how the allusion gives satirical liveliness and cultural depth to Swift's description of the beau trembling in fear that the rain will ruin his finery. But nothing is meant to radiate out from these six lines to the other fifty-seven of the poem. In contrast, for example, to Pope's use of the *Aeneid* in *The Dunciad*, where the Virgilian plot of founding a second Troy recurs pervasively as a new founding of the empire of Chaos which spells the end of an era in British culture, Swift's witty exploitation of Virgil is strictly the occasion for a piece of local fun.

In any case, the richly associative possibilities of expression that allusion makes available have led many writers to reiterate a key allusion and multiply variations on it. In these instances, the allusion is a key to the work not merely through strategic placement, as in our example from Wordsworth, but through being a recurrent thread in the formal design of the work and thus part of the imaginative definition of character, theme, and world. When Joyce's *Ulysses* appeared in 1922, T. S. Eliot published what would become a famous manifesto, "*Ulysses*, Order, and Myth," in which he argued that casting a modern work on the pattern of an ancient story was an innovative means of imparting poetic coherence to the chaos that characterized modern life. In fact, the technique is an old one, virtually dictated by the allusive logic of literature. Pope's use of the *Aeneid* in *The Dunciad*, which we just noted, is scarcely different in kind from Joyce's use of the *Odyssey* as a kind of armature for his contemporary materials; and a decade after the last version of Pope's poem, Fielding utilizes the Virgilian epic, which he called his "noble model," with a more Joycean intricacy in *Amelia*, contriving episode-for-episode parallels between his novel and the Latin poem. Still earlier, the eleventh-century Hebrew poet, Samuel Hanagid, vizier and commander-in-chief of the armies of Granada, writes two triumphant battle poems each with the same number of lines as there are chapters in the Book of Psalms, identifying himself as speaker both with the thanksgiving mood of Psalms and with the victorious figure of divinely elected monarch represented by the biblical David.

A key allusion may provide the whole ground plan for a work, as in the examples I have just touched on, or the allusion may be a kind of imaginative center to which the work reverts as it amplifies its own distinctive resonances. Some novels, for example, use snatches of poetry in a refrain-like technique. In the first few pages of *Mrs. Dalloway*, Virginia Woolf has her protagonist open a book to two lines of verse, not identified, which will recur half a dozen times in the course of the novel: "Fear no more the heat o' the sun, / Nor the furious winter's rages." These are the opening lines of the dirge sung over the supposedly dead Imogen in Shakespeare's *Cymbeline* (IV:2). There is a tonal as well as a thematic affinity between the play and the novel, as one can see from the words immediately after the first citation of the poem, "this late age of the world's experience had bred in them all, all men and women, a well of tears."[4]

The affinity is evident in a related way in the first stanza of the song:

> Fear no more the heat o' the sun,
>   Nor the furious winter's rages;
> Thou thy worldly task hast done,
>   Home are gone, and ta'en thy wages.
> Golden lads and girls all must,
> As chimney-sweepers, come to dust.

Mrs. Dalloway is a book given to broodings over mortality, over the poignant transience of youth, beauty, and love (in the third stanza of the song, it is "lovers young" who come to dust). The fear of the sun's heat may lead by an association of antithesis to Septimus Smith's obsessional harping on shade as he prepares to commit suicide; and a movement along the Shakespearian axis carries us from the serenity of death in Clarissa's musing over the song from *Cymbeline* to Septimus' identification with Lear's revulsion from sexuality and with the maddened king's suicidal stance on the brink of the cliff. The dominant Shakespearian key, in any case, is the song's evocation of a world of brightness and beauty vanishing, as must all things ("The sceptre, learning, physic, must / All follow this, and come to dust"). That, I would suggest, is the imaginative point of reference of the whole novel, formally signaled through the recurrence of the lines as a refrain, but informing the vision of the novel even in passages where there is no citation, like this reflection on the imposing progress down Bond Street of a royal motor car with drawn blinds:

> . . . the enduring symbol of the state which will be known to curious antiquaries, sifting the ruins of time, when London is a grass-grown path and all those hurrying along the pavement this Wednesday morning are but bones with a few wedding rings mixed up in their dust and the gold stoppings of innumerable decayed teeth. The face in the motor car will then be known.[5]

The technique of allusive refrain brings us to the verge of the third set of variables involved in allusion, which is the relation of the alluding text to the evoked text. There is, to begin with, a quantitative issue: how much of the antecedent text is "activated" by the allusion? The formal indications of the marker in themselves provide no clue to what elements of the evoked text we are expected to align interpretively with the alluding text. As with most matters of reading, we need to depend not on some arcane "technique" of decoding but on common sense. Thus, the three stanzas of the song from *Cymbeline* are directly relevant to the world of *Mrs. Dalloway* along the lines I have tried to suggest, but it is highly implausible that the play as a whole, with its tale of false accusation of adultery, imagined death, and discovery of long-lost sons, should have much bearing on Virginia Woolf's novel. (It is possible, of course, to argue for a more encompassing relevance of *Cymbeline* to *Mrs. Dalloway*, as has one recent feminist critic who sees in Imogen's maltreatment by men a parallel to Clarissa Dalloway's condition. Such a reading, however, seems to me to strain credence.) The relation, then, of the alluding text to the evoked one is of whole to part. The global allusions to the *Aeneid* in Pope's *Dunciad* and Fielding's *Amelia* of course place the whole alluding text in relation to the whole evoked text, although as we read there will be all sorts of elements in the evoked text that we will ignore while we make sense of the work at hand. The relation of whole to whole need not be based on the later writer's taking over the episode-by-episode scaffolding of plot from an earlier one, as in *Amelia* or *Ulysses*. Refrain alone, in fact, can be used to signal a global relation between two texts.

In the opening paragraphs of Nabokov's *Lolita*, Humbert Humbert speaks of a poignant first love as a child "In a princedom by the sea," and then goes on to declare that the resurgence of this love in his passion for Lolita is something the "noble-winged seraphs envied." The minimally altered citation—in Poe's "Annabel Lee" it is "a kingdom by the sea," and the "wingèd seraphs of heaven" first covet, then envy, the speaker's love for the girl—is hardly intended to deflect identification of the source, which in any case is explicitly confirmed three pages later when we learn that the beloved girl's name is Annabel Leigh. Though one must be cautious in speaking of a key allusion in a book so luxuriant with allusions—to Dostoyevsky, Merimée, Byron, Baudelaire, and many other writers[6]—phrases from "Annabel Lee" do recur throughout the novel, the seraphs of the beginning making a last appearance in the "angels" of the penultimate sentence of the book. Rereading this familiar poem alongside the novel, one realizes that the plot and theme of the poem are preeminently the general plot and theme of *Lolita*, which construes Poe's text both literally and symbolically: "*She* was a child and *I* was a child / In this kingdom by the sea," like Humbert Humbert and Annabel Leigh on the Riviera; the beloved child in both instances perishes; Humbert, like the speaker in the poem, stubbornly asserts his undying love as he stands at a crossroad of angelic and satanic forces ("the angels in Heaven above . . . the demons down under the sea"); and in both texts the obsessive devotion to the one consuming love becomes in the end a wedding with death ("I lie down by the side / Of my darling, my darling, my life and my bride / In her sepulchre there by the sea— / In her tomb by the sounding sea"). The refrain from Poe, then, signals an allusive relation of whole to whole, the three-hundred-plus pages of the novel to the forty-one lines of the poem, with Nabokov clearly recognizing the melodramatic extravagance of the poem and incorporating it as a constitutive element of Humbert Humbert's character.

The other two logical possibilities of allusive relation between two texts are part to part and part to whole. This last option, in which a global invocation of the text alluded to has a merely local effect in the alluding text, is relatively rare because it is not easily feasible to bring a whole complex structure to bear on a relatively simple, limited structure. If, for example, you wanted to represent a protagonist who was momentarily indecisive, you might allude to *Hamlet,* but in all likelihood you would be isolating the element of indecision from *Hamlet*—an allusion of part to part—rather than evoking the whole world of the play in order to render, say, a character who was uncertain whether to go to a movie or stay at home. The relation of part to part is probably the most common occurrence of allusion. Swift's beau in the sedan-chair alluding to Virgil's Greeks in the Trojan Horse is a clear-cut example, but the allusive relation of local text to local text is not limited to episodes—the parts in question may be a motif, a theme, a character, even an isolated phrase or image.

These combinatory variables can be technically intriguing, but they are, I think, less interesting than the compelling question of the relation of value and outlook between the alluding text and the text it evokes. In this regard, allusion readily fosters every conceivable relation to the evoked text: complete consonance of purpose and viewpoint (the story of the spies at Jericho and the story of the Exodus); playful consonance (Dryden's "Absalom and Achitophel" and the David story); ironic dissonance ("A Description of a City Shower" and the *Aeneid*); antagonistic dissonance (D. H. Lawrence's *The Man Who Died* and the Gospels); dissonance in some respects and consonance in others (*Paradise Lost* and the *Aeneid, Ulysses* and the *Odyssey*). In every case, however, the writer's point of departure is that he cannot be indifferent to the text he decides to use allusively. Somehow, it has excited him, moved him, haunted or disturbed him, or presented itself to his writerly perception as a model of achievement in a particular genre or literary mode.

That extreme instance of whole-to-whole allusion which is a reconstruction or a rewriting of an antecedent text provides especially powerful testimony to the captivating effect of earlier works on later imaginations. Ziva Ben-Porat calls this kind of allusion "metonymic" because there is extensive contiguity between the worlds of the alluding text and the evoked one, in contradistinction to other kinds of allusion, where the two texts are linked by some perception of similarity between them, the connection thus being "metaphoric." The terms allude to the linguist Roman Jakobson's much-invoked distinction between what he sees as the two basic principles for making connections in language— metonymy, or the link of contiguity, and metaphor, or the link of resemblance. Because I am a little wary of the broad-gauge antitheses that this binary opposition of Jakobson's produces wherever it is applied, I would prefer to call this sort of global allusion "midrashic," remembering the tendency of the early rabbis in the Midrash to interpret

Scripture by fleshing it out, recreating it in contemporary narrative terms. Midrashic allusion is generated when one writer is under the spell of an earlier one, whether happily or not. *The Man Who Died* is composed as a polemic sequel to the Gospels because Lawrence feels the need to counter the compelling power of the New Testament vision, with all that it has led to in Western history, by imagining an antithetical spirituality, of the flesh and not beyond it. On a much more modest scale, Donne is impelled to rewrite Marlowe's celebrated "The Passionate Shepherd to His Love" in his witty poem, "The Bait," because against that Elizabethan model of mellifluous verbal magic which surely touched him he wants to proffer an ideal of poetry that is more ruggedly realistic in diction and imagery, more cannily intellectual in its relation to its subjects.

Although midrashic allusion, except when it is formal parody like "The Bait," tends to produce texts considerably longer than the texts it reconstructs, it is bound by no fixed quantitative rules. Thomas Mann, haunted by the characters, events, and meanings of Genesis, spun out of a mere thirteen biblical chapters the twelve hundred pages of his *Joseph and His Brothers*. Wallace Stevens was equally haunted by the story in the Apocrypha of Susanna and the Elders (a bare sixty-four verses), and out of it he fashioned the sixty-six lines of "Peter Quince at the Clavier," which is no less a vital recreation of the world of the ancient tale than Mann's tetralogy. The structure of Stevens' poem lays bare a characteristic impulse of midrashic allusion, which is an exegetical meditation through narration on a potent earlier text. The poem begins, one recalls, with the playing on the clavier, which carries the speaker back in a wave of associative musing to that distant "green evening" when Susanna bathed in the garden, her beauty making the thin blood of the peeping elders "Pulse pizzicati of Hosanna." The elliptic evocation of the story of Susanna has an exquisite suggestiveness occasioned by the ancient text but quite transcending it ("the winds were like her maids, / On timid feet, / Fetching her woven scarves, / Yet wavering"). Musical motifs are wound through the depiction of Susanna, continuously binding the evoked world of the ancient tale with the contemporary moment at the clavier that led into Susanna. The last section of the poem trumpets a grand conclusion: "Beauty is momentary in the mind— / The fitful tracing of a portal; / But in the flesh it is immortal. // The body dies; the body's beauty lives." It is always risky for poetry to state a moral, though I think the evocative power of Stevens' poem has earned him this generalization. But the very impulse to generalize in this fashion is instructive. The older text is not just something the poet reads but something that *possesses* him, and the recreation of the old work in the new is an effort to make sense of that experience of possession, to explain what cultural memory means, why a tale of lust and loveliness two millennia removed still lives in our imagination and speaks to our condition.

The most effective uses of global allusion, as "Peter Quince at the Clavier" suggests, occur when the introduction of the evoked text is dictated not by arbitrary choice but by a sense on the part of the writer that there is something in the nature of things that requires the allusion—in this case, the poet's perception of the mnemonic function of art playing against the paradox of beauty's transience and its eternal recurrence. The text of Exodus has to suffuse Joshua because the author of Joshua sees his story, quite literally, as a reenactment of the Exodus. Milton recreates classical epic in *Paradise Lost* in part because he is persuaded of a typological relation of the classical to the biblical, the pagan providing an elaborate set of memorable adumbrations of the Christian truths to come. Joyce can put his Homeric materials to such elaborate use at least in part because he gives some credence to Vico's notion of great cycles of historical recurrence, which as he construed it made the relevance of ancient to modern more directly compelling. Thus, behind many global allusions is a perceived structure of history, an assumed grammar of the imagination, that underwrite or even necessitate the wedding of the two texts.

Since all our examples have been excerpted from longer works or have been episodic comments on complete texts, it may be useful in conclusion to look at one integral text in order to see more coherently the strength of allusion as a dimension of literature. Gerard Manley Hopkins' sonnet "Thou Art Indeed Just, Lord" is an intensely personal confessional statement that is also a midrashic allusion, even though the evoked text, from Jeremiah, is not narrative. The directness of the allusion could scarcely be more explicit since the sonnet is headed by an epigraph from the Vulgate which gives us in Latin all but the last clause of Jeremiah 12:1. The first three lines of the poem then translate those words into English.

> Thou art indeed just, Lord, if I contend
> With thee, but, sir, so what I plead is just.
> Why do sinners' ways prosper? and why must
> Disappointment all I endeavour end?
>   Wert thou my enemy, O thou my friend,
> How wouldst thou worse, I wonder, than thou dost
> Defeat, thwart me? Oh, the sots and thralls of lust
> Do in spare hours more thrive than I that spend,
> Sir, life upon thy cause. See, banks and brakes
> Now, leavèd how thick! lacèd they are again
> With fretty chervil, look, and fresh wind shakes
> Them; birds build—but not I build: no but strain,
> Time's eunuch, and not breed one work that wakes.
> Mine, O thou lord of life, send my roots rain.

The poem presents what looks at first like an allusion of part to part—the first three lines of the sonnet to the first verse of

Jeremiah 12—but which turns out to be an allusion of whole to whole. I do not mean, of course, that the entire Book of Jeremiah, with its prophecies of doom and its historical narrative, is evoked by the sonnet, but that there is a global identification of tone, feeling, and predicament between the speaker and the biblical prophet tormented by his mission. The diction, to be sure, is distinctively Hopkins', with one deliberate modernization of Scripture in that reiterated "sir," striking a certain Victorian note in addressing a superior. For the most part, however, the English is more archaic, in keeping with Hopkins' fondness for the Anglo-Saxon elements of the language and in keeping with the biblical subject. We might note, for example, the extraordinary thickness of monosyllabic clusters: after the first quatrain, as segments of meaning are orchestrated through alliteration (first *w* and *d*, then *b* and *l*, then *w* again), there is only one trisyllabic word ("enemy"), and just half a dozen bisyllabic words, plus the two artificial bisyllabics, "leavèd" and "lacèd." The close sequencing of stresses makes us work our way laboriously through a density of sound: "How wouldst thou worse, I wonder, than thou dost / Defeat, thwart me? Oh the sots and thralls of lust . . ." The poet's language reaches back behind the Latin of the Vulgate he has quoted and the diction of the King James Version that has influenced him to the packed muscularity of Jeremiah's Hebrew, which as poet he intuits through the veil of translation.

Jeremiah, in any case, is an informing presence in the poem even after the speaker swerves away from the direct translation of Scripture beginning with the last three words of the third line. The verse in Jeremiah ends as follows: "wherefore are all they happy that deal very treacherously?" On the surface, the speaker, by switching to the topic of his personal disappointment, parts company with his biblical model. In fact, Hopkins' theme of galling frustration in assuming the vocation of priest is preeminently Jeremian, and the parallel with what Jeremiah felt about his unhappy vocation as prophet is reinforced by his lineage "from the priests of Anathoth." Jeremiah's great, harrowing poem about being "seduced" (KJV, "deceived") by God into being a prophet resonates powerfully with this sonnet, even though there is no direct reference to its language. Here are the opening lines:

> O Lord, thou has deceived me, and I was deceived:
>> thou art stronger than I, and hast prevailed.
> I am in derision daily,
>> everyone mocketh me.
> For since I spoke,
>> I cried out, I cried out violence and spoil;
> because the word of the Lord was made a reproach unto me,
>> and a derision, daily.
> Then I said, I will not make mention of him,
>> nor speak any more in his name.
> But he was in my heart as a burning fire shut up in my bones,
>> I could not hold it in, I was unable.[7]
>
>>> (20:7–9)

The sonnet manifests a profound psychological identification with Jeremiah together with a dialectical modification of the prophet's theme. Sterility is not a problem for Jeremiah; the word of the Lord bursts forth from him, against his will, like fire shut up in the bone. For the speaker in Hopkins' poem, no doubt troubled by priestly celibacy, the paradox of God's enmity toward his supposed friend is felt in the reduction of the friend to the role of "time's eunuch," unable to breed living work, whether in the realm of the spirit or of poetry. The imagery Hopkins uses to define this plight reflects further subterranean links with Jeremiah. At the beginning of the sestet, halfway through the line, there is a sudden sortie into the natural world, which is quickly construed as a painful countermetaphor (the first pronounced use of figurative language in the poem) for the speaker's curse of barrenness: "See, banks and brakes . . ." Although the image of well-watered roots is an archetypal one as well as a metaphor for which biblical poets evinced special fondness, it is immediately triggered here by the next verse in Jeremiah (12:2), which Hopkins does not quote. The prospering sinners, that is, of our opening lines are then the subject of the following outraged declaration in Jeremiah: "Thou hast planted them, yea they have taken root: they grow, yea, they bring forth fruit." Elsewhere, Jeremiah calls God himself the source of living waters ("they have forsaken me, the fountain of living waters, and hewed out cisterns, broken cisterns, that can hold no water" [2:13]). And two chapters after the verse Hopkins translates, divine wrath is figured in a grim prophecy of devastating drought: "And their nobles have sent their little ones to the waters: they came to the pits, and found no water; they returned with their vessels empty; they were ashamed and confounded, and covered their heads" (14:3). Rain for the roots thus evokes a whole complex of Jeremian images.

The daring—and, I think, brilliant—syntactic inversion of the sonnet's last line is a memorable illustration of how the curve of expression in the individual literary text follows not only its own force lines but those of a background of literary tradition which it can scarcely avoid addressing. "Mine" at the beginning of the line has a plaintive, desperate isolation, and we do not know what the word refers to until we reach "my roots" just before the end of the line. The emphasis of this odd positioning powerfully suggests the speaker's sense that in fact other roots have been getting rain. In immediate context, these would be the roots of the trees on banks and in brakes where birds nest, and, by metaphoric implication, the roots of those sots and thralls of lust who thrive. This connection in turn leads back to the rooted, fruit-bearing sinners of the contiguous but unquoted Jeremiah 12:2. Finally, one wonders whether the circle of identification with the biblical prophet is not completed here: he, too, suffered in his vocation, as his words that I made mine show, but in the end you gave him the gift of your quickening spirit, and now *mine*, send *my* roots rain.

Some may object that "Thou Art Indeed Just, Lord" is an atypical case because it can hardly be standard procedure for a literary text to build its own statement on a verbatim citation of an antecedent text. In fact, citation and close paraphrase are more common than is often assumed, from T. S. Eliot's lifting of lines from Laforgue and Mallarmé to the frequent "imitation" of passages of Latin and Greek poetry in the English Augustan poets, all the way back to the citation of the Song of the Sea in Joshua. In any case, the illustrative force of Hopkins' sonnet as an instance of allusion is by no means limited to its direct quotation of Jeremiah. We should of course not neglect the evident fact that the sonnet is not an exercise in exegesis or literary criticism but a strong expression of Gerard Manley Hopkins' personal anguish. It is exemplary, however, in showing what is always involved (if sometimes not so explicitly as here) when someone chooses a poem, or any other literary form, for the expression of personal experience. Literary form is always an elaborate *mediation* of experience—that is, an attempt to give it coherent definition by casting it in a certain style, structure, prosodic system, and against a background of earlier voices embodied in texts that have impelled the writer to the act of literary expression. Hopkins' speaker simultaneously becomes Jeremiah and measures his distance from Jeremiah, and the poet through the speaker discovers the depth and meaning of his feelings and longings by this double act of identification and differentiation. In one way or another, every writer is obliged to perform this same double act.

Looking at the process from the perspective of cultural history, we are entitled to say that literature, even as it fosters innovation, is an essentially conservative institution. In contrast to the evolution of technology, in which each subsequent stage makes previous stages obsolete, turns them into antiquarian stuff for the historians of science, each stage of literature *incorporates* the previous stages, the impulse of literary creation being constantly self-recapitulative. The self-recapitulation is also manifested in a recycling and reworking of formal structures, conventions, and genres, but it is most ubiquitous in the use of allusion.

As the corpus of literary works grows, writers are faced not with an exhaustion of possibilities, as some critics have claimed, but with more to say, orchestrating the voices of myriads of forerunners, in more and more complicated combinations. Obviously, such orchestration is by no means all that is involved in literary expression, which is more than a process of combination. But the example of Hopkins vividly demonstrates how the articulation of a strong individual voice, resonant with the writer's unique experience and temper, is achieved at least in part by the evocation and transformation of a voice, or voices, from the literary past.

CHAPTER FIVE

Structure

What is structure in a work of literature? A misleading but necessary metaphor for describing the formal organization of the work as a whole. It is misleading because structure suggests spatial extension and stasis, whereas literary texts, even very short ones, unfold sequentially, and our perception of the structure they manifest shifts as new elements are added from one word to the next, from one line to the next, and, in narrative, from one episode to the next. The metaphor, or some close equivalent of it, is nevertheless necessary because most literary works, in widely varying degrees of explicitness, do exhibit some formal design that plays a role in their aesthetic effect, or in their meaning, or often in both. The explicitness of the design and our individual predispositions as readers will determine the degree to which we consciously "see" structure, but even a subliminal awareness of it shapes our reading, affects the feel of the experience we conjure up for ourselves from the words of the text.

"Structure" as it is generally invoked by critics, and as I will be using it here, implies a constructor, and thus works on the analogy of structure in a building or even in a machine, rather than, say, molecular structure. In this regard, the metaphor is apt because every literary text is the handiwork of an artificer who seeks to give it purposeful shape. (Surrealist experiments in automatic writing are the rare exception to this fundamental rule.) Purposeful shape does not mean that structure is invariably dictated by conscious intention. In fact, intentionality is often more palpable in structure than in other features of a literary text—architectonics tends to imply architect and blueprints—and we will see the distinct thumb-prints of intentionality in several of the examples we will consider. However, as with sound, imagery, syntax, diction, and the invention of narrative episodes, a good deal goes on in the mind of the writer below or beyond the level of conscious awareness, and so structure, too, may be the product of intuitive elaboration, may be an unplanned emerging into formal coherence propelled by the momentum of the verbal and ideational materials with which the writer works.

"Structure" is a more restrictive term than "form," for the latter designates the deployment of words that constitutes the text and thus covers everything from the intricate con-vention of the villanelle to automatic writing, which may be said to have a free associative form but not a structure. In some literary works—say, the novels of William Burroughs, the longer poems of Alan Ginsberg—the elements of structure are so loose that the implications of coherent pattern and tensile interconnection of the metaphor are inapplicable, and it may be preferable to speak of form. Some critics, for example, talk about the "digressive structure" of *Tristram Shandy*, but Sterne himself appears to have conceived it more as antistructure. If one considers the elegantly architectonic novels of Fielding, one of the writers who both inspired Sterne and stirred him to parodic reaction, *Tristram Shandy's* penchant for fantastication, wild association, and zany impro-visation looks more like a raising of the roof and a knocking down of the walls than the erection of an alternate structure, and it may make better sense to speak rather of Sterne's digressive form.

Let me also stress that the notion of structure I am proposing runs counter to the application of the term that gained a certain currency in literary studies from the 1960s onward through the agency of French Structuralism. Under the twin influences of the anthropologist Claude Lévi-Strauss and the Russian folklorist Vladimir Propp, it was generally assumed that there were certain universal structural models which constituted a kind of grammar of the human imagination, and that any given text could then be studied as a transformational elaboration of one or more of these models. As Tzvetan Todorov put it quite frankly in a manifesto written at the height of the Structuralist vogue, "It is not the literary work itself that is the object of structural analysis. Structuralism instead investigates the properties of that special discourse which is literary discourse. Every work then is considered only as the manifestation of an abstract, much more general, structure of which it is only one possible realization."[1] By now, one hardly needs to debate the Structuralist program, which has repeatedly demonstrated its own severe limitations as a method of literary analysis. The abstract, general structures of which Todorov speaks may be in some ways instructive to the cultural anthropologist, but when one of them is proposed as the armature for an individual literary work, it usually proves to be among the least interesting aspects of the text. Even in the most conventionalized modes of literature, every writer seeks to make something new, and in regard to structure, the newness is felt by the reader not in the manifestation of a fixed, general model but, on the contrary, in the articulation of a distinctive pattern for the purposes of the text at hand. It seems to me that the concept of structure most useful for a critical account of the fullness of the reading experience is structure as something immanent in the particular text.

This does not imply a lapse into the mystifications of "organic form." A literary text does not wondrously grow like a tree or a flower, all its parts drawn together in a seamless perfection of vital unity. There are, to be sure, certain works that may tempt us to invoke such analogies, but the idea of human construction implied by structure is on the whole a good deal more accurate. Structure, as I have said, will often involve intention, sometimes even cold calculation, and a structure may also be incomplete, lopsided, ramshackle, or simply too obvious. In any case, attention to structure as an immanence in the particular text can help us see how the cluster of ideas and feelings, represented figures, situations, and relations, that are the "subject" of the text, is given coherent definition through formal design.

Our first examples will be short poems because they are the sort of text in which structure is most readily visible. The perceptibility of structure in longer narrative and dramatic texts is a question we will touch on later. I have said that structure is often related to meaning but not invariably. The closest relation to meaning would be imitative structure: a formal deployment of words meant to mime the experience, action, object, or event that is the subject. This imitative design would also be the clearest instance of the immanence of structure because it is fashioned ad hoc to embody formally the subject of the text. A case in point is a 1944 poem by William Carlos Williams entitled "The Dance."

> In Breughel's great picture, The Kermess,
> the dancers go round, they go round and
> around, the squeal and the blare and the
> tweedle of bagpipes, a bugle and fiddles
> tipping their bellies (round as the thick-
> sided glasses whose wash they impound)
> their hips and their bellies off balance
> to turn them. Kicking and rolling about
> the Fair Grounds, swinging their butts, those

shanks must be sound to bear up under such
rollicking measures, prance as they dance
in Breughel's great picture, The Kermess.[2]

Williams' intention here is quite obvious, and some readers
might object that the poem is no more than a stunt, though it
seems to me that the stunt is accomplished with such
virtuosity, with such a nice integration of poetic means, that
it becomes a highly engaging poem. Breughel's painting of
around 1568, *The Kermess,* or *The Peasant Dance,* depicts an
outdoor circle dance, and compositionally it is a series of
circles of different sizes looping into each other in spiral
fashion: the large circle of dancers in the middle of the canvas;
the high-stepping couple in the right foreground on their way
to loop into the circle; the drinkers at the table in the left
foreground whose outstretched arms suggest a circular design,
which is repeated by the circular outline of shoulders and
arms of the bagpipe player and the man with the extended jug
who are seated to the right with their backs to the table; and,
finally, in the nearest section of the left foreground, the two
wizened-looking little girls who hold both hands facing each
other, apparently moving together in their own small round
to the rhythm of the dance. Williams picks up the composition
as well as the subject of Breughel's painting by constructing
his poem as a series of circular patterns. "The Dance" aptly
illustrates the general character of literary structure because
it shows so vividly how all the formal features of the text, and
not just one or two of them, may participate in the creation of
structure. In this case, the circular structure inheres in the
meanings of the words, their sounds, the rhythm, the prosody, the syntax, the images. The "go round, they go round
and / around" of the opening lines announces the theme that
is at once formal and representational which will be worked
out through a whole set of complementary means.
    Most obviously, the poem ends where it begins, the last

line repeating the first. It is worth stressing in regard to this device that the same formal feature will have very different meanings in different texts, depending on the nature of the immanent structure in which it takes part. Ending a poem by repeating the opening line is a common procedure of closure but does not necessarily imply circularity. The great poem on the splendors of creation which is Psalm 8 begins and ends with the same line, "O Lord our Lord, how excellent is thy name in all the earth!" But the repetition at the end of this vertically ordered poetic review of cosmic hierarchy is felt as a climactic completion, a symmetric framing-in by praise of the panorama of creation. In "The Dance," on the other hand, because of all the semantic and formal signals of going round, the repetition of the first line in the last rolls us back to the beginning of the poem, inviting us to reread, round and round, as Joyce, in breaking off the last sentence of *Finnegans Wake*, expected readers to run it back into the first sentence which would complete it in endless circularity.

As a loose dactylic rhythm suggests the cadence of dancing feet, the repeated use of enjambement—most extremely, on the words "and," "the," "about," and on a hyphen—loops one line into the next. The only real end-stopped line beside the first/last is the sixth, "they impound," and that is an exception that confirms the rule because it is an end-stop at the conclusion of a parenthesis which interrupts a unit of syntax resumed at the beginning of the next line. The syntax itself sets up a spiral movement, with phrases and clauses braided together. The participial "tipping their bellies," for example, logically has to modify the first grammatical subject, "the dancers," but the intervening "blare and the / tweedle of bagpipes, a bugle and fiddles" produces a blur between instruments and dancers, whose bellies then blur into the roundness of the glasses in the parenthesis. Williams pointedly reinforces this fluidity by suppressing the comma that grammar would require at the end of the fourth line. "Whose wash they impound" refers to the former liquid contents of the glasses, now contained in the bellies, but it is a phrase that introduces another kind of ambiguity through a pun on the painterly term "wash" (a broad thin layer of color laid on by a continuous movement of the brush, strictly applicable to water colors and not to oil paintings like *The Peasant Dance*). Thus, for a hovering moment, we are not quite sure whether our attention is being directed to a detail of the represented scene or to the original painterly medium of representation. The slightly disorienting sense of fluidity is extended by the laconic syntax of the next string of phrases: "their hips and their bellies off balance / to turn them." This means something like, they dance with their hips and bellies off balance in order to turn (whether "them" refers to the dancers or to their hips and bellies is unclear). The effect of the suppression of syntactic specification is to make the off-balance hips and bellies stick out as almost autonomous objects, and to isolate and emphasize "to turn them," conveying an image of sheer pivotal motion, barely subordinated to syntactic function.

The quality of fusion of the poem's circular structure is further extended by overlapping and repeated sounds: to name the most prominent—the internal rhyming of "round," "sound," "impound" in an unrhymed poem; the alliteration of "blare," "bagpipes," "bugle," "bellies," "butts." (Breughel's painting is a soundless representation of a musical moment; Williams exploits the capacity of sound-mimickry of language to evoke the peasant music, introducing, by the way, two instruments not visible in the painting, which shows only the bagpipe.) Finally, since every literary text is an interaction between the formal disposition of words and their semantic function, we should note that an important element of the circular structure is the sheer accumulation of closely related terms that refer to the movement of the dance and to the music: tipping, kicking, rolling, swinging, rollicking; squeal, blare, and tweedle.

Consistently imitative form such as one finds in "The

Dance" is the most extreme instance of the immanence of literary structure. By no means typical, it is more likely to occur when a writer is consciously focusing on the formal challenge of mimesis, as Williams is in transposing the subject of a painting to a poem. Imitative structure on occasion will be attractive to writers drawn to formal experiment, like that great technical master among English poets, George Herbert, who in two remarkable poems, "The Altar" and "Easter Wings," contrived the typographical shape of the poem to represent the subject announced in the title. One encounters such image-poems from time to time in the Renaissance because of the various interests manifested during this period in extreme technical virtuosity, in emblems and symbolic correspondences, perhaps even in the "incarnation" of meaning in form. In later periods, experiments of this sort are rarer (in modern French poetry one could cite Apollinaire's *Calligrammes*). A more typical way of structuring the text is not to fashion a wholly new structure in every respect determined by the effort of mimesis but rather to hammer out a distinctive structure on the scaffolding of an inherited form. Most writers, in other words, do not feel impelled to reinvent the wheel, or to conceive a radical new alternative to the wheel, but almost all will want to do some imaginative redesigning of the wheels they use.

Structure as a fresh exploitation of the possibilities of traditional form is perhaps most strikingly illustrated by the sonnet, a form which poets have continually refashioned for over six centuries. Here is a 1925 sonnet by John Crowe Ransom called "Piazza Piece." The piazza of the title is not the Italian public square but, in the usage of the American South, a verandah.

> —I am a gentleman in a dustcoat trying
> To make you hear. Your ears are soft and small
> And listen to an old man not at all,

They want the young men's whispering and sighing.
But see the roses on your trellis dying
And hear the spectral singing of the moon;
For I must have my lovely lady soon,
I am a gentleman in a dustcoat trying.

—I am a lady young in beauty waiting
Until my truelove comes, and then we kiss.
But what grey man among the vines is this
Whose words are dry and faint as in a dream?
Back from my trellis, Sir, before I scream!
I am a lady young in beauty waiting.[3]

Ransom slightly modifies the fixed form of the Petrarchan sonnet by adding an eleventh unaccented syllable at the end of the two sets of repeated lines and of the lines that rhyme with them and by a small divergence from the conventional rhyme scheme (his is ABBAACCA DEEFFD). But the Petrarchan division between octet and sestet points toward the possibility of an opposition in statement between the two parts of the poem and Ransom's chief purpose in adopting the form is to effect an extreme realization of its antiphonal logic. "Piazza Piece" neatly illustrates the possibility of convergence of formal traditionalism and formal innovation in literary expression. Since the fourteenth century, countless hundreds of variously antiphonal sonnets have been written in the Petrarchan form. The text in question flaunts its affiliation with that tradition while drawing from the conventional division a distinctive dramatic structure that formally defines the relationship between these two particular speakers. The break between octet and sestet—typographically, the white space between the eighth line and the ninth—marks a chasm between age and youth, male and female, desire and the beautiful object of desire, and between the two different languages in which all these oppositions manifest themselves.
Though I hesitate to intrude with too much analysis on

the self-evident witty poignancy of the poem, let me explain briefly how this dialogue of the deaf is embodied in the formal structure of the sonnet. The gentleman is presumably wearing a dustcoat in 1920s fashion because he has motored to the young lady's house. One of the small, nice symmetries of the poem is that when she makes him out peering at her through the trellis and uttering inaudible words, she sees him as a "grey man," the color of his hair and perhaps his complexion blurring into and literalizing the "dust" of his dustcoat, even evoking the association of the term with death (in the traditional imagery exploited here, gray dust over against red rose). In the enjambement of the opening line, he is "trying / to make [her] hear." At the end-stopped conclusion of the octet, he is absolutely, definitionally, a gentleman trying. The words he speaks which she cannot hear are direct, simple, an apt expression of the elemental urgency and desperation of his desire. In the haunting fifth and sixth lines, he shows a certain knowing familiarity with poetic tradition as he has already shown an understanding of the cruelty of the laws of desire and response: "But see the roses on your trellis dying / And hear the spectral singing of the moon." The dying roses are of course poetic shorthand for the transience of beauty ("Gather ye rosebuds while ye may") and so constitute the essence of his argument to a coy mistress. The rhyme of "trying" and "dying" has the effect of implicating the gentle-man in death, suggesting he may be projecting on the rose his own feared condition of imminent demise. The moon is a standard prop for romance and serenades (our poem being a kind of grotesquely failed serenade), but as the subject of "spectral singing," it is also caught up here in the old man's morbid premonitions of death. The faint spookiness of his speech then reverberates in the young woman's perception that his unintelligible "words are dry and faint as in a dream." It is almost as though he were talking encapsulated in a bubble, and the two-part structure of the poem conveys a sense of two speakers effectively sealed off from each other.

The differences in how they speak are small but instructive. His speech is urgently directed to her, with the exception of the seventh line (and possibly the next line as well), which seems rather to be an exclamation of the speaker to himself: "For I must have my lovely lady soon." In her speech, the proportions of monologue and direct address are exactly reversed: everything she says is to herself, with the exception of the penultimate line (and possibly the last line as well) when, having realized that a man is standing among the vines, she cries out to him to go away. The gentleman's address is composed of brief declarative and imperative statements, with just one poetic inversion of syntax, in the third line, in which the knife twist of "not at all" is withheld till the end of the line so that the speaker can use it to stress the painfulness of his plight. The woman's speech, on the other hand, begins by flaunting the oddness of a double poetic inversion: "I am a lady young in beauty waiting." The mannered literary effect of this syntax goes hand in glove with her invocation of a balladic cliché in the next line, "Until my truelove comes," with the romantic fantasy completed in naive simplicity, "and then we kiss." In the antiphonal structure, age and youth are seen to have two different modes of romantic hunger. His is fixed on a specific but unattainable object, impelled by a pathetic sense of time's swift chariot at his back. Hers is dreamily spun out of the narcissism of newly blossomed beauty. The lovely haziness of that fantasy makes the intrusion of an old man in a dustcoat all the more shocking to her, and after commanding him to be gone, she immediately slips back into the filmy envelope of virginal self-regard: "I am a lady young in beauty waiting."

There has been a good deal of debate among literary theorists during the past couple of decades about whether a literary text can be said to represent anything outside itself. At first blush, the aspect of structure would seem to argue in favor of the antirepresentationalists, for it is verbal artifice, not life, that exhibits this kind of structure. Thus, the fact that the words of a poem or play or novel are deployed in a formal design could be construed as evidence of the literary text's correspondence to code, convention, or the rules of an internal game, and not to extraliterary reality. But what we have been seeing in the antiphonal structure of Ransom's Petrarchan sonnet suggests that the either-or alternative between artifice and representation violates primary readerly intuition. The elegant inventiveness of the poem of course depends on the play with generic codes, and the reader is surely not encouraged to construe the sonnet in any literal sense as a transcription of real speech. Real people, after all, do not address each other in rhyming iambic pentameter, with repeated refrains, eight lines counterposed to six. What most readers, however, would immediately recognize without any need for explanation is that the dramatic structure of the poem, built on the frame of the Petrarchan sonnet, is a means of defining and sharpening experience, giving insight into it. I realize that in certain critical circles the very concept of experience has been questioned, but what I mean by it here is simply this: almost all of us, of both sexes, in the slow course of living in the world come to know something about desire and its frustrations, about the self-absorption of youth and the self-conscious anxiety of age, and about the various comic or painful failures of communication between male and female. Ransom has not invented any of this experiential material, nor is it the product of generic conventions or of the play of literary artifice in the poem. The gentleman in the dustcoat and the lady young are persuasive projections of human possibility, endowed with the force of revelation through the formal coherence of the structural pattern in which their poignantly disparate destinies are set. One does not have to be over sixty or wear a dustcoat to feel that the gentleman's predicament is part of nature, not just art, as to grow old and to desire and to fear death are part of nature; but in Pope's sturdy eighteenth-century formula, it is "nature methodized," its elements made perspicuous by the artifice of structure.

Very often, however, the methodizing does not exhibit the clarity of formal design we have seen in our two initial examples. Literary structure is not only dynamic— one might say architecture in motion, assembled as it goes—but also is constituted of heterogeneous elements (sound, imagery, diction, motifs, syntax, and so forth). This means that many poems, many narrative and dramatic works, have complex structures produced by the interaction of different patterns which are severally made up of these different heterogeneous elements. Because no two readers will see the interplay of patterns in precisely the same way, such complex structures cannot be plainly charted as one can chart the mimetic circularity of "The Dance" or the neat antiphony of "Piazza Piece." But the absence of a formal schema that can be confidently diagrammed does not imply the absence of structure. And an element of indeterminacy in the character of a particular structure does not mean that all readings are equally admissible, that the interacting patterns of the text do not in some way determine the range of experience readers will enter into through the text. The complex issue of multiple and admissible readings deserves to be considered in its own right, and we will return to it in the concluding chapter of this study.

For many literary works it may be useful to think of structure as something open-ended that orients reading in a certain direction, at both the conscious and the subliminal levels, but with a large margin of uncertainties, a play of ambiguities flowing in part from the unstable borderlines of the structure itself. Such complex, open-ended structure in fact is extremely common in literature because as a rule structure is not planned all the way through, as in Williams' mimesis of the painted circle dance or Ransom's exploitation of the two-voiced sonnet, but intuitively discovered, often quite unconsciously, by the writer. If the successful literary work, as I have contended, is a junction of multifarious connections of a sort not encountered in extraliterary language, structure is the complex internal coherence these connections assume through the power of the creative imagination unlocking resources of language and possibilities of meaning which the writer may feel but not exactly know.

Let me try to alleviate the abstractness of these generalizations with a compact example of complex structure. Emily Dickinson's celebrated "After great pain, a formal feeling comes" (number 341 in the standard edition of her poetry, and composed around 1862) is not just a piece of arresting virtuosity, like our examples from Williams and Ransom, but a great American poem. Both technically and emotionally, it is a difficult poem, and what I have to say about its structural features will only underscore the intended difficulty.

> After great pain, a formal feeling comes—
> The Nerves sit ceremonious, like Tombs—
> The stiff Heart questions was it He, that bore,
> And Yesterday, or Centuries before?
>
> The Feet, mechanical, go round—
> Of Ground, or Air, or Ought—
> A Wooden way
> Regardless grown,
> A Quartz contentment, like a stone—
>
> This is the Hour of Lead—
> Remembered, if outlived,
> As Freezing persons, recollect the Snow—
> First—Chill—then Stupor—then the letting go—[4]

The poetic imagination here offers a profound glimpse into the nature of suffering, virtually every technical move contributing to the depth of insight. I will restrict my comments to the ways in which the represented experience of the aftermath of pain is given a structure. To begin with, the experience is segmented, broken down into what look like three temporal stages, by the division into stanzas. The middle stanza has five lines instead of four, but this added length is in a way counterbalanced by the two truncated lines it contains, "A Wooden way / Regardless grown," which make us slow down our reading and attend to these five words as the pivotal point in the poem turning from movement to stasis.

In fact, the relation of feeling to the metaphor of movement is a good deal more complicated than the initial statement of it I have just sketched out. The three stanzas embody three different sets of verbs referring to motion, three sets of metaphors, and three stances toward time and memory. Especially because "come and go" is an idiomatic collocation as well as a logical antithesis, it would be convenient for analysis if the poem exhibited a simple progress from "comes" at the beginning to "go round" in the middle stanza to "letting go" at the very end. But the complexity with which the subject of pain is grasped rules out such linearity, and the interplay of the three patterns I have named leads to a kind of focused emotional bewilderment. The New Critics might have spoken of a paradox at the heart of the poem, but I would prefer to see here an ambivalence, an inward vacillation, which is a psychological rather than a logical notion like paradox. Great pain both is and is not tolerable; it is and it is not possible to go on with life after such suffering. Something like that doubleness of feeling is registered in the complex structure of the poem.

Let us first follow the pattern of movement. At the beginning, in the immediate aftermath of great pain, feeling "comes" to the human subject as a kind of alienated reflex. "The Nerves sit ceremonious"—a minimal movement already on the brink of stasis, especially since the sitting is tomblike.

The middle stanza is marked by abundant movement in the feet going round a wooden way (evidently, the implied image is a circular wooden walkway), though the adjective "mechanical" marks a weird dissociation of feet from mind and so ties in the going round of the second stanza with the numbed sitting of the first. "Go" as the last word of the poem indicates movement only in the metaphorical sense of transition from one state of consciousness to another, or rather from consciousness through intolerable pain to a lapsing out of consciousness, a surrender of volition and inner coherence. (It is too simple, I think, to call that death, despite the comparison with freezing persons, for the poem is rather concerned with the deathlike in life.) The last line actually recapitulates the tripartite structure of the poem: chill in the first stanza, stupor in the second, letting go in the last.

Superimposed on this progression from minimal movement to circular movement to stasis and surrender is a sequence of related but differentiated images. Each of the three stanzas contains one image formally linked to the other two by its prominent position at the end of a line: "like tombs," "like a stone," "lead." (Did Emily Dickinson half-remember that the Song of the Sea in Exodus 15 which recounts the death of the Egyptian host marks the ends of its three stanzas by similes that alternate between "like a stone" and "like lead"?) The last two stanzas also each include a second, elaborated figurative comparison, the wooden way and the freezing persons. The effect of the three linked images in end-line position is in each case to set up a terrific tension with, or thematic transformation of, what immediately precedes it. To sit like tombs is to be stone or marble or any unfeeling thing, to be the emblem of death in the statuary mimicry of what was once alive. Thus the sitting of the first stanza is assimilated by deathlike numbness, while the seeming motion of the second stanza passes into absolute inanimateness in the extraordinary acerbic notation of "Quartz contentment" which is at once brutally defined—"like a stone." Quartz is semiprecious, stone ambiguous, lead merely heavy and dark (so much for the contentment). In the second stanza, the elaborated comparison of going round a wooden way precedes the compact comparison and is in a sense canceled out by it. In the last stanza, the compact comparison comes first, and then its meaning is unpacked by the elaborated simile of being trapped in snow. This concluding stanza plays richly with the polarity of stasis and motion by offering a little plot in which the persons caught in a snowstorm lose their grip by stages, and it is ambiguous whether the recollection is simply an immediate one of the snow in the moments before death or whether some possibility of their having "outlived" the experience to remember it later is implied.

Memory points to a third pattern that plays through the tripartite structure of the poem. The question of the first stanza refers of course to Christ bearing the cross and reflects a long vista of theological memory. In the chronometry of suffering, however, time spans are collapsed, and it is hard to know whether that agony happened two millennia ago, to the man from Nazareth, or just yesterday, to any one of us. The middle stanza excludes memory by representing the sufferer entrapped in the circularity of a repeated present constituted by automatic motion, consciousness hardened to quartz contentment. The strategy for moving out of this prisonhouse of the present in the last stanza is to project the highly tentative possibility of what it would be like to remember this present moment of pain's aftermath ("Remembered, if outlived") should it prove possible to survive it. The quality of such memory is spelled out in the simile of the freezing persons, and we have already noted the lethal ambiguity of that comparison.

Now, there are surely other ways to describe the three-stage movement of the poem, and it would be very surprising if all readers were to draw precisely the same interpretive conclusions from the details I have isolated. But the impossibility of unanimity among readers itself confirms the notion of complex structure that I have proposed. "After great pain" clearly exhibits certain aspects of orderly sequence, something which is marked by the very division into three stanzas. There is, however, more than one sequential pattern (arguably, more than the three I have traced), and these spiral around each other, intersect, qualify each other in ways that make the poem a semantic medium of terrific density. Structure powerfully contributes to the constitution of meaning in the poem, but because the structure is dynamic, what it generates is a set of permutations and combinations of meanings within a certain range.

The example of complex structure in Emily Dickinson brings us close to the characteristic manifestations of structure in narrative. Narrative structure will obviously inhere much more in elements of plot than is likely to be the case in a short poem. When one speaks, for example, about the climax of a story, the implication is that the sequence of events in the story possesses, at least implicitly, a formal design, rising to a peak near the end in a way that almost might be represented on a graph. As with poems, however, structure is made up of heterogeneous elements, and these could include images, motifs, allusions, shifts in style, as well as events. The most compelling function of narrative structure is as a process of meaning progressively enacted through the experience of the characters, but this description by no means covers all cases of narrative.

At one end of the spectrum, in fairy tales and folk tales a highly symmetrical structure is often dictated by generic conventions, the "immanence" for which I have been arguing being quite minimal. Goldilocks experiments with three different sets of the three bears' possessions, and in each instance a reversal occurs in the third member of the set, because the folk tale form conventionally structures climax and surprise as a sequence of two plus one (or in some cases, three plus one). At the other end of the spectrum, some sophisticated writers choose to elaborate formal design in their narratives because the elegance of symmetries and contrasts appeals to them, quite apart from any consideration of meaning. I am not sure, for example, whether any depth of thematic definition is gained in *Tom Jones* by the fact that Fielding neatly distributes the eighteen books of his novel geographically—the first six at the Allworthy estate, the middle six on the road, the last six in London. Town and country are an important thematic opposition in the novel, and are two important zones of moral experience for the protagonist, but the necessity of the structural symmetry is far from clear. One is tempted to conclude that Fielding found a purely aesthetic satisfaction in setting up his novel as a formal triptych, and the only inferable connection with meaning would be a general association with balanced control that one perceives on the level of sentence and paragraph and in the poised intelligence of the narrator. Joyce's *Ulysses* is a much more extreme case of the elaboration of structure for the aesthetic sake of structure because it appeals to the literary artificer. The Homeric scaffolding has come to make a good deal of sense to many readers, but if one follows the various schemata Joyce first explained to Stuart Gilbert, his plan for making the eighteen episodes correspond to different bodily organs, colors, arts, symbols, and "technics" seems in many ways capricious. The plot of *Ulysses* also has a perceptible structure, but it should be observed that the structural patterns derived from elements other than plot (allusion, motif, style) do not invariably interact with plot to produce the kind of complex total structure we observed on a small scale in Emily Dickinson.

Even when narrative structure is fully in the service of meaning, it may exhibit a formal explicitness scarcely less pronounced than that of a sonnet. This is far more likely to occur in prenovelistic narrative than in the novel. The story, for example, of Joseph and Potiphar's wife in Genesis 39 is symmetrically framed by the verses at the beginning of the chapter that report his rise to preeminence in the household of his Egyptian master and the verses at the end of the chapter that report his rise to preeminence in the prison into which he has been cast after the false accusation of sexual assault. It is not merely that the beginning and the end of the narrative unit mirror each other as sequences of events but also that they mirror each other *phrasally:* Joseph in Potiphar's house repeatedly "prospers," "finds favor in the sight of" his master, is privileged to have "all" entrusted "in his hand" because "the Lord was with him"; and these very phrases recur at the end when we hear of his fate in prison. The effect of the structural symmetry is not just aesthetic, as in *Tom Jones,* but pointedly thematic: Providence follows the hero; he is a man made to prosper and to cause everything around him to prosper; and even disgrace and imprisonment will prove no more than a temporary setback in his grand destiny of royal stewardship.[5]

The novel, because of its length and because of its relative freedom from the prescriptions of formal convention, provides the most intriguing test case for the uses of structure in literature. Many novelists evince little of the fondness for formal design we noted in Fielding and Joyce, and structure in the novel is often half-submerged, intermittent, dependent on glacial movements of plot over hundreds of pages. It was thus that Henry James, more elegant a fashioner of narrative shapes than most novelists, was led to denigrate (and misrepresent) the great Russian novels of the mid-nineteenth century as "baggy monsters." There are, however, meaningful continuities between the operations of structure we have seen on the scale of the short poem and structure in the novel. In the novel, as in the poem, structure channels the experience of the reader; and in the novel, that is often, though not inevitably, entangled with the experience of the principal characters.

In the traditional realist novel, which typically employs a uniform mode of presentation from beginning to end (the same narrator, the same tone and style, the same degree of narrative clarity), structure is more likely to be felt in the unfolding pattern of events than in any other single aspect of the narrative. The modernist novel, which has often evinced a fondness for switching perspectives, styles, and narrative techniques, sometimes displaces structure to the deployment of different means of presentation.[6] Thus, in Faulkner's *The Sound and the Fury* (1929), structure as a vehicle for meaning is manifested far less in the story than in the ways it is told. The narration flips back and forth among several pieces of anecdotal material ranging chronologically from 1902 to 1928: Caddy as a young girl muddying her underpants, the day of Quentin's suicide, Caddy's elopement and her brother Jason's futile pursuit of her, Benjy's thirty-third birthday. The characters are not cut out to learn from experience, but rather are doomed to be ground down and in some cases destroyed by it. The reader's perception of the vision of life implicit in the novel is not produced by following the recirculation of incident but by experiencing the graded progression of narrative clarity from one section of the book to the next.

The novel begins with the disorienting suppression of causal connections and syntactic coherence that constitutes the retarded Benjy's perspective ("a tale told by an idiot"). It moves on to the overripe lyricism and obsessive repetitions of Quentin's interior monologue, which is followed by the hard-edged surface clarity of Jason's first-person narration. In a pointed inversion, as narrative intelligibility increases from one brother to the next, moral character declines. Then the concluding section, linked with the black woman Dilsey who is the novel's great model of persistence in adversity, gives us the lucid overview of omniscient narration. After stumbling through the labyrinth from Benjy to Quentin to Jason, we stand in the dawn light of an Easter Sunday beholding the human scene through the generalizing amplitude of Faulkner's own authoritative baroque style: "now her skeleton rose, . . . as though muscle and tissue had been courage or fortitude which the days or the years had consumed until only the indomitable skeleton was left rising like a ruin or a landmark above the somnolent and impervious guts. . . ."[7] If the pattern of incident in the novel registers a course of progressive entrapment, the pattern of narration that is the most visible structure of the book makes us experience progressive discovery, leading to the sense of liberation of this culminating vision.

More typically, however, novelists deploy the sequence of events that constitute plot to provide structural definition for the experience of the main characters. There is little point in trying to classify, graphically or otherwise, the varieties of novelistic structure because, as I argued with examples from lyric poetry, the chief interest of structure is its immanence, the way it is elaborated ad hoc for the distinctive purposes of the particular literary work. Let me illustrate the range of possibilities with two novels that stand at opposite ends of the spectrum— one in which there is a chronologically continuous report of events that form a clear pattern of linear progression, the other in which narrative exposition is discontinuous and partly retrogressive, with the effect of arranging the events in a spiraling pattern. In both instances, the plot culminates in a suicide (in the second novel, actually two suicides separated by time, place, and motive). The spectacular differences in structure between the two books thus demonstrate how any human event may have infinitely variable meanings and literary definitions.

Edith Wharton's *The House of Mirth* (1905) begins with a splendid illusion of unfolding possibilities for the heroine,

Lily Bart. Though she is without financial resources and has been circulating unmarried in New York society a little too long (she is twenty-nine), Lily is still radiantly beautiful, full of vivacity and charm, and exhibits a subtle sense of how to manipulate men. In the first chapters, one man, whom we guess she might well come to love, offers his friendship, and another, a nincompoop with the palpable advantage of a vast fortune, is captivated by her and seems a likely if not altogether appetizing matrimonial prospect. Lily first mildly compromises herself in the opening chapter when she is seen coming out of the building in which Lawrence Selden has his bachelor apartment, though in fact her daytime visit to him has been perfectly innocent. The events that follow, covering three or four years of narrated time, form a steady progression of ever graver compromising incidents, flowing from Lily's imprudence, her naïveté, her self-absorption, and the fact that she has been trained to be nothing but a beautiful flower in a social world actuated by brutally cynical considerations of money, power, and class standing. Each imprudence has dire social consequences for her that prove to be irreversible. Step by step, she is cut off from the socialites she thought were her friends, from the prospects of marriage, from the inheritance she had expected her aunt to bequeath her. At first a welcome if dependent frequenter of the fashionable salons of old New York, she eventually slips into a kind of *demimonde*, becoming the companion of a sexual adventuress scheming to make a profitable marriage, and then she slides into the working class, struggling and failing as a milliner's assistant. She refuses to use the one resort that is offered her to escape this fate and firmly establish herself in the glittering world where she began because it would violate what is a fundamental point of conscience for her.

If one chooses to imagine narrative structure of *The House of Mirth* spatially, one could say that it has a kind of funnel shape: from one episode to the next, the walls of circumstance of Lily Bart's life become narrower, her social, economic, and romantic possibilities more and more restricted. At the end, she is trapped in her wretched little room in a shabby residential hotel, without resource or human solace, her only way out the overdose of sleeping powders with which she ends her suffering. The steadily progressive structure of events in the novel formally embodies the experience of inexorable destiny which is what Lily's life proves to be. Outside the frame of literary representation, a life may be, as we often rather casually say, "tragic." The difference that narrative structure makes is to translate the painful inevitability of tragedy into an intensifying sequence of events that leads us each time to hope desperately that the gifted protagonist will find a way to escape disaster, and each time to see more clearly how truly hopeless her predicament is.

The various disasters, on the other hand, that attend four of the five central characters in Ford Madox Ford's *The Good Soldier* (1915) are not the consequence of the entrapment of the individual by society. Instead, moral or psychological character sedulously constructs its own catastrophes, beginning with the mutual selection of partners of intimacy who will inadvertently but ineluctably turn life into hell for each other. Ford, then, is far more concerned than Edith Wharton with pondering the multiple enigmas of character, and he devises a narrative structure that compels us as readers to just such a contemplation. Structure in *The Good Soldier* is both complex, in the sense we saw operating in the poem by Emily Dickinson, and imitative, as we applied the term to the poem by William Carlos Williams. Both aspects of structure as they are manifested in a novel of some 250 pages will need explanation.

Structural complexity in *The Good Soldier* flows from the fact that structure does not inhere chiefly in the single component of plot as it does in *The House of Mirth*, but in an interplay of plot, narrative exposition, and allusive imagery.

The imagery can be adequately followed only through detailed textual analysis, so let it suffice to say here that reminiscences of Dante's *Inferno,* with an emphasis on implacable demons and endless torments, appear early in the novel and become especially dense as the dénouement draws near. As to plot, the bare outline of what happens to the characters, which is not fully decipherable until near the end of the novel, is as follows: A wealthy American couple, the narrator John Dowell and his wife Florence, are obliged to take up permanent residence in Europe because her supposed heart condition, which manifested itself on the first night of their honeymoon voyage from the States, will permit her no further sea travel. As a consequence of the same supposed ailment, their marriage has never been consummated. Three years into their European residence, the Dowells meet at a resort a genteel English couple, Edward and Leonora Ashburnham, and during the next nine years spend a good deal of time with them at various vacation spots across the Continent. Edward is a brick-complexioned, bull-like man, a retired and decorated British army officer, a polo player, and, it would seem, altogether a hale fellow well met. Leonora, the daughter of a respectable but impoverished Irish Catholic family, appears refined, restrained, somehow vaguely troubled. What we eventually discover is that from August 4, 1904, to August 4, 1913, Florence and Edward are lovers. Dowell remains blithely unaware of this erotic arrangement until his wife's suicide on the latter date, but Leonora knows what is going on from the start, as well she might, for Edward has already established a record as a compulsive womanizer with the unfortunate habit of falling desperately in love with each of the women in sequence who agree to be the object of his attentions.

In the final turn of the plot, Edward becomes romantically obsessed with Nancy Rufford, the young girl who is his and his wife's ward. In this case, he will not permit himself to "defile" the girl—egregious appearances to the contrary, he is at all times a man impelled by honor, ever "the good soldier"—and so he cannot bear living near her, though he also cannot live without the sentimental gratification of her devotion to him. In the end, Leonora contrives a way to remove that devotion, or at least to make it seem to have been withdrawn, with the effect of utterly destroying Edward and, inadvertently, Nancy as well.

This account drastically simplifies the sense of the characters—especially of Edward and Leonora—that we get as we read. "It is very difficult to give an all-round impression of any man," Dowell muses, and then, just a few pages on, "For who in this world can give anyone a character? Who in this world knows anything of any other heart— or of his own?"[8] The structure of the novel makes it impossible for us to decide with any confidence whether Edward is a weak and misguided idealist, a contemptible scoundrel, a pitiful victim; whether Leonora is a long-suffering heroine, an avenging angel, a destroying bitch, or, as Dowell claims at the end, just one of those terribly normal people needed for the propagation of the species. The fact that all judgments are mediated by Dowell calls their dependability into radical question. Though he does not appear to misrepresent what happens factually, in regard to evaluation he is the most unreliable of narrators—because of his purblind naïveté, his total estrangement from the life of physical passion, his profound ambivalence toward Leonora, and his bizarre identification (could it be homoerotic?) with Edward.

All these uncertainties of moral knowledge are beautifully embodied in the structure of the novel. My rapid summary of the plot translates it into a linear movement, but in fact Dowell's narration circles back in four large sweeps around the same events, picking up disorientingly new information about them each time. Our attention is called to this formal scheme by the recurrence of the date August 4 (a combination of coincidence and Florence's melodramatic fondness for performing fatal actions on her birthday). On August 4, 1900, she gives herself to a certain Jimmy, a dubious young man who is her uncle's traveling companion. On August 4, 1901, she elopes with Dowell. Three years later, on the same date, as we have noted, she becomes Ashburnham's mistress, having tired of the odious Jimmy, and then nine years later on August 4, she puts an end to her life. Dowell, who calls his own narrative a "maze," never realizes what is going on at the time of any of these events and only later gradually pieces things together. The form of his narrative, in order to be imitative in one respect, must violate mimetic plausibility in another. That is, the Dowell of 1914 who tells the story finally has all the facts at his disposal, but in the telling he suppresses many essential pieces of knowledge till the second or third or fourth time around, offering his mental daze as an excuse, in order to reproduce for his audience the movement from ignorance and illusion to partial understanding.

Two incidents should sufficiently illustrate the cognitive function of this spiraling narrative structure. The electricity of the affair between Florence and Edward first begins to flow when she touches his wrist while the two couples are on an expedition to the castle at M— that contains a pencil draft of Luther's Protest. Florence has just made a pretty little speech saying that thanks to this document we are all Protestants and decent people. Leonora, anguished, wrenches away from the scene, telling Dowell she simply can't stand it. He is momentarily alarmed that something may be going on between his wife and Ashburnham, and then Leonora reveals to him in a clear, hard voice that she is Catholic. The reader at this early point is likely to be taken in as much as Dowell. Before long, we realize the true reason for Leonora's anguish, and late in the novel, Dowell reflects that what she should have told him that day in the castle was that his wife was a whore. Nevertheless, the Catholicism is not entirely a red herring. It

conveniently feeds into certain phobias and fantasies of
Dowell's, but it also has an important bearing on the estrangement between Leonora and Edward, the difference in faith
between them dictating incompatible conceptions of love,
marriage, sex, sin, conscience, and virtue.

In the case of Florence's death, the revised perceptions
of narrative data are more rapidly sequenced. On the evening
of August 4, 1913, Dowell meets an unpleasant Englishman
named Bagshawe in the lounge of a German health resort. As
the two are talking, Florence comes running in from the
garden, white-faced, sees Bagshawe with her husband, and
immediately disappears. Bagshawe at once recognizes her
and archly confides to Dowell that the last time he saw her
was at five o'clock in the morning at his house in Ledbury,
coming out of the bedroom of a scurrilous fellow named
Jimmy. A little later, Dowell finds her stretched out on her
bed, dead, clutching in her right hand "a little phial that
rightly should have contained nitrate of amyl," the heart
medication she always carried with her. Dowell's first take on
her death, then, which almost carries us along with him (a
crack of doubt emerging only in the ambiguity of "rightly
should have contained"), is as follows: Florence, seeing the
man who she knows will expose her, experiences violent
shock, rushes off to her room for her medication, and
succumbs to her heart ailment, which proves after all not to
have been faked. A few pages later—more than a year later in
narrated time—Leonora tells Dowell she thinks it was stupid
of Florence to have committed suicide, and this characterization of her death is news to him. Then Leonora informs him
that Edward that night had been off in the garden, making his
first romantic approach to Nancy Rufford. Leonora, uneasy at
what might be happening, had asked Florence to go after
them as a kind of chaperone. Approaching the couple in the
dark unseen amid the shrubbery in her black dress, Florence
is forced to witness her own displacement as the object of
Edward's romantic feelings; then she rushes back to the hotel

in a fit of despair, and swallows the prussic acid contained in the phial. Dowell in turn, on persuasive reflection, revises Leonora's version of the suicide. Florence was distraught, all right, by the discovery that her lover of nine years was about to abandon her, but it was the sight of Bagshawe that was the last straw, for vanity was so much the mainspring of her character that she could not tolerate, on top of abandonment, the exposure of the false image of herself she had constructed for her gullible husband. The initial reason, then, for her death, radically revised with the new information provided by Leonora, becomes the explanation for her decision to destroy herself. There is no fathoming of motives, no end to pondering the deviousness of character; and the narrative structure of *The Good Soldier* deeply implicates the reader in this perception, this restless process.

Because the permutations of structure are multifarious, because what makes it compelling is the way it is distinctively fashioned for each individual work, the examples we have considered can do no more than suggest the range of its possibilities. Understandably, I have chosen illustrations in which structure plays a particularly prominent role, though it is only fair to add that there are many long narrative and dramatic works in which formal design is not conspicuous, in which for long stretches what seems more evident is simply one thing coming after another in the text. In some narratives, there is not much else there structurally; in others, the structural plan may get lost in the accumulation of surface details, so that it plays little role in our experience as readers, or at least, in our conscious experience. Nevertheless, because all literature is artifice, exploiting the artifice of design is bound to appeal to a vast variety of writers with different aims and sensibilities working in different genres, and even where there is little conscious exploitation, the momentum of mnemonic force intrinsic to literary imagination often produces coherent design.

The articulation of structure may be undertaken for

purely aesthetic reasons: creating balance and contrast and counterpoint of patterns in words surely has its own allure. But literature is an art bound to the making of meaning by the very nature of its verbal medium, and so in a very large number of works, literary structure turns out to be the shape of meaning—the ordering of sounds, images, motifs, ideas, imagined events and personages, into constellations that make the vision of the writer, the character of the objects of representation, visible to the eye of the imagination, palpable in the pulse of experience, as we read.

CHAPTER SIX

Perspective

No formal aspect of literature has received as much attention over the past two decades as have the mechanisms of narrative. As a result of all this attention, we now understand more precisely what are the various options, and the combinations and permutations of options, for telling a story. To be sure, the proliferation of narrative theory has brought with it a sometimes bewildering proliferation of competing views and terminologies. It is not my intention here to become involved in the intricacies of these debates, and with three modest exceptions, I will avoid the many inkhorn terms coined by the narratologists, most of which seem to me gratuitous and some of which are based on downright conceptual confusions. The aim of this chapter, moreover, is not to offer a taxonomy of the formal system of narrative, and so the reader will find none of the tables, charts, and diagrams that abound in the work of contemporary narrative theorists. Instead, in consonance with the adherence to the experience of reading that guides this entire study, I shall try to suggest how the play of narrative perspective richly complicates our perception of what happens in a work of literature—or to view the question, as it ultimately must be viewed, referentially, how the play of perspective gives depth and subtlety to the representation of reality in narrative.

I have chosen "perspective" as my general rubric because it is a term intelligible from ordinary usage that is capacious enough to embrace a variety of narrative sins. Perspective is the particular angle from which we are invited by the nature of the narration to imagine the narrated personages, places, and events. It corresponds more or less to the old-fashioned Anglo-American "narrative point of view," but seems to me preferable as a general term both because it has no specific associations with Henry James and his followers and because it is a little more abstract, even more conveniently vague. I am adopting it precisely because it is an umbrella term that covers both the narrator's approach to his materials and the character's point of view—the two functions Seymour Chatman has usefully distinguished as "slant" and "filter."[1] Some recent students of narrative have rejected both point of view and perspective because of the visual metaphor they imply, but an abstruse alternative like "focalization" neither entirely escapes the visual metaphor nor advances thinking much. Visualizing is by no means the only faculty involved in how we mentally reconstruct a narrative from the conventional signals on the printed page, but it plays a sufficiently frequent—even sufficiently primary—role that we need not be embarrassed about invoking a metaphor from the realm of sight to explain how a story is told in order to be perceived in a certain way.

Do nonnarrative works of literature exhibit perspective? Not in my understanding of the term, because perspective is introduced by some sort of narrator who reports events and thus serves as an intermediary between reader and story. Like Gérard Genette, I reject as an absurdity the claim certain critics have made that there can be narration without a narrator: "In the most understated narrative, someone is talking to me, inviting me to listen as he tells it, and that invitation—whether trust or coercion—constitutes an unde-niable attitude of narration and hence of narrator."[2] Dramatic works do not have perspective because there is no narrating go-between. We see the fictional personages as they are represented for us on the stage by the actors from our fixed vantage point in our seats in the audience, or from the imaginary equivalent of that vantage point when we read the play. Film, by contrast, continuously exhibits perspective in its use of camera angle, framing, focus, montage, and other means of visual narration. And even in film, perspective is not entirely limited to vision because both voice-over narration and sound-track music act as do style, tone, and the providing or withholding of information in literary narratives—to pro-duce an "attitude of narration," which is to say, a perspective.

Lyric poetry, which often enough incorporates quasi-narrative elements, is a more complicated case than drama, but I think the kind of statement it makes, the kind of transaction that is effected between the speaker and the reader of the poem, precludes perspective in the sense I have proposed. Thus, Keats' sonnet, "On First Looking Into Chapman's Homer" is full of verbs, from its opening lines onward, that seem to indicate, semantically and grammati-cally, the report of certain past actions: "Much have I travell'd in the realms of gold, / And many goodly states and kingdoms seen. . . ." But these actions are of scant interest as a sequence of events and no proper narrative perspective is, or can be, imposed on them. The speaker's traveling, seeing, being told, breathing, and hearing, are nothing like, say, Raskolnikov's wandering around the streets of St. Petersburg, before and after murdering the old pawnbroker and her sister. Indeed, there is a margin of ambiguity as to whether these verbs are to be construed literally, the speaker of the poem laying claim to a wealth of actual travel experience never enjoyed by John Keats, or whether they are all metaphors for what he has experienced in reading. Although the latter alternative seems more likely, what is instructive is that it does not make an enormous difference whether we construe the verbs literally or figuratively. Such irresolution is not easily conceivable in a truly narrative text. There may be works in which we are invited to contemplate an allegorical level of signification but this does not undermine the integrity of the narrated events as literal events standing in a definite sequence: Dante does go down into the inferno to contemplate the sundry circles of the damned, whatever else his experience may signify, just as definitely as Zola's hero Étienne Lantier descends into the mine shaft where he is trapped in *Germinal.*

The act of communication, on the other hand, in a lyric poem is not that of a narrator conveying a story to a reader but of a speaker revealing something of himself as he addresses the reader with a statement of attitude, feeling, perception that is presumably of interest to both. In this direct movement from lyric speaker to reader, the quasi-narrative materials are ultimately *exemplary* of the speaker's feelings and understandings, not the real subject of communication, and that is why it is not crucial in the case of Keats' sonnet whether we construe the narrative assertions literally or figuratively. (There are, of course, some short poems that are genuinely narrative, very few literary divisions being absolute.) In such a transaction, tone—the verbal token of the implied relationship between speaker and audience—is an essential element, and tone is also an important nonvisual aspect of narrative perspective. There is, then, some overlap, which is hardly surprising, between narrative and lyric enunciation. Both, after all, powerfully involve the conveying of attitude through stylistic and other verbal means. In lyric, however, the object of the attitudes is not a set of narrated events and characters but an emotion, a concept, an insight, a judgment, a vision (or any combination of the foregoing) in the mind of the speaker.

The last four lines of "On First Looking Into Chapman's

Homer" offer an interesting borderline example of a teasing hint of narrative perspective in lyric because they are a kind of embedded narrative in the poem. The speaker tells us that, coming upon Chapman's translation, he felt like the discoverer of a new planet,

> Or like stout Cortez when with eagle eyes
> He star'd at the Pacific—and all his men
> Look'd at each other with a wild surmise—
> Silent, upon a peak in Darien.

The four lines vividly tell a story and impose on its concise details the attitudinal definition of a narrative perspective. The story would be different if Cortez told it himself, if it were seen by one of his men, or if it were conveyed in the documentary language of a historical chronicle. Instead, what Keats gives us is the epic heightening of—predictable— epithets ("stout Cortez," "with eagle eyes"), the dramatic revelation of that moment of "wild surmise," and the climactic report of the figures, seen in a kind of tableau, struck with awed silence on the Caribbean mountaintop as they look out on the expanse of the Pacific. All this reads like narrative perspective, but it is pseudonarrative, for the whole scene is a simile by means of which the speaker conveys his own state of exaltation on first reading Chapman's Homer. The perspective of these four lines, then, which ostensibly leads to a particular vision of Cortez and his men upon a peak in Darien, in fact is meant to focus our perception of the referent of the simile—the speaker's feeling of awed excitement in discovering Homer's grandeur through Chapman's translation.

When we turn to narrative literature proper, perspective crosses a historical watershed with the emergence in the seventeenth and eighteenth centuries of the new genre—the first to evolve entirely after the invention of printing and so to reflect a new reading situation—that we call the novel. An essential defining feature of the novel is the variety, the subtlety, the unpredictability, and the quicksilver mobility of its uses of perspective. Let me hasten to say that there is very little in literary history which appears wholly unanticipated. The literatures of the ancient Near East and classical antiquity are artful and often exquisitely self-conscious, and even the self-reflexivity of the contemporary Western novel has its forerunner in the performance of the bard within the epic poem in the *Odyssey*. One sometimes encounters, then, interesting shifts in perspective in ancient and medieval narrative, strategic switches from narratorial overview to a character's angle of vision, or bravura effects in which we are invited to envisage a scene in spectacular panorama from some defined vantage point within the narrated world like the top of a tower or a mountain peak. For the most part, however, prenovelistic narrative is characterized by a high degree of uniformity of perspective maintained by an authoritative overviewing narrator. The shifts that are made to the point of view of one or more of the characters—leaving aside the phenomenon of lengthy, embedded first-person narration, quite common, for example, in epic—are usually quite brief, being in one way or another formally bracketed by the uniform perspective of the overviewing narrator. They are, one might say, momentary concessions to the point of view of the characters rather than novelistic moves toward making figural[3] consciousness an important arena of narration. A couple of examples from ancient narrative should make this point clear.

Most readers' impression of biblical narrative is that everything is told from the perspective of an impassive authoritative narrator. However, several recent literary studies of biblical narrative have persuasively argued that in fact the point of view frequently switches at strategic moments to one of the characters. Such transitions in modern narrative are typically unmarked. Conveniently enough for the purposes of narrative analysis, in the biblical stories the transitions are often formally indicated by a Hebrew term philologists call the presentative, *hineh* (in the King James Version translated as either "lo" or "behold"; often, alas, left untranslated in modern English versions of the Bible).[4] *Hineh* can be used simply as a means of pointing verbally to a person or object within sight of the speaker, as, for example, when Isaac on his way up the mount of sacrifice with his father says to Abraham, "Behold [*hineh*] the fire and the wood, but where is the lamb for a burnt offering?" (Genesis 22:7). The biblical narrator, however, often uses the term to mark the crossover between his perspective and that of a character, the "behold" becoming in effect part of the unspoken inner speech of the personage, especially at moments when something unexpected or untoward is seen. Thus, at Judges 4:22, after Jael has killed the Canaanite general Sisera with hammer and tent peg, she invites the Israelite commander Barak into her tent, saying, " 'Come, and I will show thee the man whom thou seekest.' And when he came into her tent, behold [*wehineh*] Sisera lay dead, and the tent peg was in his temples." The syntax after the presentative "behold," confirms that we are following the sequence of Barak's perception: first "Sisera," then "lay," then "dead," then the specific ghastly agency of death, the tent peg penetrating Sisera's temples. What should be observed is that the shift to figural consciousness is dictated entirely by the dramatic purposes of the moment. Barak scarcely expects to find his enemy here at all. As we move through the chain of the Hebrew general's startled discoveries, Sisera is not only there in the tent but sprawled out—in fact, dead—a tent peg driven through his head by the extraordinary woman who had welcomed him into her dwelling. Beyond this momentary revelation, in the Hebrew confined to a bare five words after "behold," Barak's subjectivity is not at issue in the narrative, as it would almost certainly be in a novelistic narrative.

I don't mean to suggest that the biblical writers are never interested in the inner world of their characters. Sometimes, indeed, it is even revealed through little segments of interior monologue. But for the most part, the ancient writers assume that the proper locus of narration is in the overviewing perspective of the narrator, and that the dynamic workings of consciousness on the data of experience are not a primary narrative arena. The cameo appearances, then, of a character's perspective are very much felt as insets.

In Genesis 29, when Jacob, having fled alone and on foot all the way from Canaan to Mesopotamia, arrives in the region of Padan-Aram where his uncle Laban lives, we get the following report:

> And he looked, and behold [*wehineh*] a well in the field, and, lo [*wehineh*], there were three flocks of sheep lying by it; for out of that well they watered the flocks: and a great stone was upon the well's mouth. And thither were all the flocks gathered: and they rolled the stone from the well's mouth, and watered the sheep, and put the stone again upon the well's mouth in its place.
>
> (Genesis 29:2–3)

The transition back from Jacob's point of view to the narrator's is a little ambiguous, but the instructive thing is that the ambiguity hardly matters, as it might in a modern narrative. The perception of the well and the flocks is clearly that of the foot-weary traveler coming at last to a possible bourne, and the seeing of the stone on the well (the Hebrew literally, and more dramatically, says "The stone was great upon the well's mouth") is probably his, too. The report about the local practice—the verbs should be in the iterative tense—of the shepherds gathering to roll off the stone is not information Jacob could possess and so must come from the narrator. Is the little clause, "for out of that well they watered the flocks"

a similar piece of information supplied by the narrator or an
inference of the character's, perceptually continuous with the
two *hineh* clauses that precede it? In a novel, such an
ambiguity might easily involve the secret, even antagonistic,
interplay between two voices, the narrator's and the character's, that is a hallmark of fictional narration in the nineteenth
and twentieth centuries. Here, however, because the real
point of the shift to figural consciousness is the dramatization
of a climactic moment of discovery by the character, and not
a piece of moral or psychological characterization from within,
it does not make much difference whether Jacob's perspective
is restricted to the seeing of the well, the flocks, and perhaps
the stone, or whether it includes an inference about watering
the flocks. In any case, the character's point of view is no
more than momentarily admitted within the governing perspective of the narrator.

Let us consider briefly one last ancient example, this
time from Latin literature, in which the visual aspect of
perspective is more elaborately defined. Book V of the *Aeneid*
begins with a report of Aeneas' flight by sea from Carthage
and from his disastrous dalliance with Dido that has ended,
unbeknownst to him, in her suicide:

> Meanwhile far out at sea Aeneas kept
> Steadily on his course, cutting the waves
> The north wind had darkened. He looked back
> And saw the city lit by the flames
> Burning up Dido. What caused that great fire
> Nobody knew; but what they all knew
> Was what grim pains love suffers when dishonoured
> And what a woman mad with love can do:
> This made the Trojans heavy with forebodings.
>
> As the ships sailed on the high seas
> With no land in sight anywhere
> But sea on all sides, on all sides the sky,

A dark cloud stood above Aeneas' head;
It brought storm, it shut out the light
And all the waves shuddered in the shadow.
The helmsman Palinurus from the poop
Called out: "Why is the whole sky lost in cloud?
What, Father Neptune, are you doing to us?"[5]

These fourteen lines (in the Latin original) offer vivid evidence of the attuned sensitivity of ancient writers to the expressive possibilities of shifts in perspective. The visual realization of the scene has an almost cinematic effect. First, in overview, we see the Trojan ships, led by Aeneas, plowing through the rough, black-looking water; then we get Aeneas' view of the glow of fire on the receding African shore. A couple of hours later in narrated time, beyond the sight of land, "sea on all sides, on all sides the sky" (*maria undique et undique caelum*), sounds like the intimation of the bewildered perception of the crewmen, looking anxiously back and forth across the darkening windblown expanses all around them as the storm impends. (The ABBA structure of Virgil's chiasm reinforces this sense of trapped circularity.) The passage also includes two clear instances of what Dorrit Cohn calls "psycho-narration," that is, the narratorial report not of an external action or event but of the feelings, thoughts, states of knowledge or ignorance, of the characters. The narrator conveys to us Aeneas' ignorance of the reason for the distant glow he can make out from the deck as well as a collective, two-stage reflection of the other Trojans—their brooding over the dire consequences of frustrated love and their vague apprehension of impending disaster. The fear of something ominous, of course, surfaces at the end of the excerpt in Palinurus' cry of dismay at the lowering thunderheads.

For all this concern, however, with what the characters see and feel, the passage, like the ones we looked at from the Bible, is not a real shift from the perspective of the normative narrator that informs the work as a whole. In the midst of Aeneas' looking back in incomprehension to the shore, the same authoritative narrator who provided the initial quick panorama of the ships at sea intervenes to remind us of what neither the hero nor his men know, that the far-off light is from "the flames burning up Dido." And if the emptiness of sea and sky all around the ships suggests the wave-tossed perception of the Trojans, the painterly precision of the "dark cloud . . . above Aeneas' head" returns us to the authority of a narratorial overview.

This is not to suggest that Virgilian narration, or that of the Bible, or of the *Song of Roland*, or of Chaucer, or of Ariosto is in any way more "primitive" than novelistic narrative, only that its deployment of perspective is governed by different assumptions. The authority and hence the relative fixity of perspective of traditional narrative are grounded in a sense that the narrator (and the writer behind him) has certain truths to convey that can speak to the very heart of a culture, revealing its origins, its purposes, its collective character. By contrast, the novel, as Walter Benjamin has poignantly put it, has its birthplace in "the solitary individual, who is . . . himself uncounseled, and cannot counsel others."[6] It is not only that the novel typically deals with a more radically peculiar and assertive species of individual than one encounters in traditional narrative but that it seeks to represent such individuals out of a sense of "profound perplexity" (the phrase is again Benjamin's) as to the meaning and purpose of their lives. Trying to fathom this perplexity, novelists introduce a drastic shift of balance in narrative perspective. Boundaries between perspectives begin to blur, and, in various ways, as the novel becomes the predominant European genre in the nineteenth century, the unstable kinetic movement of inner experience is made a major locus of narration.

Although the focus of this study is not historical, the novel, at least in certain respects, does represent a new modulation of the language of literature, and so some remarks are in order, before we follow more closely the uses of novelistic perspective, about its emergence in the seventeenth and eighteenth centuries. One influential view of the early novel has placed great emphasis on its embrace of pseudodocumentary forms—collections of letters, confessions, supposed histories based on eyewitness written accounts. I would add that equal in importance to this adoption of nonliterary forms of writing for the purposes of fiction is the new centrality accorded to various kinds of first-person narration. This centrality is felt in the retrospective first-person narratives of the picaresque tradition that begins with the anonymous Spanish *Lazarillo de Tormes* (1556) and continues through Lesage's *Gil Blas* (1715–1735) to a host of later works. Long-range retrospection also informs fictional memoirs like *Robinson Crusoe* (1719–1720) and *Moll Flanders* (1722). In France, there is a tendency to use retrospective first-person narration to recover more vividly the emotional immediacy of particular past experiences, as in Prévost's *Manon Lescaut* (1731) and Diderot's *The Nun* (1760). This tendency anticipates or, by the later eighteenth century, is influenced by, the epistolary novel, in which each segment of first-person narration—that is, each letter—reports events that have occurred within hours, sometimes even within minutes, of the purported act of narration. By the nineteenth century, third-person narration would by and large displace these varieties of first-person narration, but an inner connection persists between the two forms that is an essential trait of the new narrative perspective of the novel. That is, in many passages in the novels of Jane Austen, Stendhal, Flaubert, Dostoyevsky, Tolstoy, and others, the third person is a kind of transposition of first-person narration: the grammar reflects the standpoint of the overviewing narrator, but the perspective is the character's, or rather, a fluctuating interweave of the character's and the narrator's.

Narrative fluidity, then, playing the narrative game according to rules that seem improvised from moment to moment, is a signal generic feature of the novel. Such fluidity is as manifest in Fielding, with his extravagantly authoritative narrator, as it is in the sundry first-person narratives of the early novel. Fielding's narrator, after all, flaunts his absolute freedom to speed up the narration or slow it down; to switch back and forth from the report of action to essayistic reflection; to be by turns ironic and straightforward, playful and serious, mock-epic and shrewdly colloquial; to present the speech of the characters as actual dialogue, in summary, or in an odd intermediate form which transposes their actual words into the third person and which I would call "narrated dialogue." This last device strikes me as especially symptomatic of novelistic fluidity, being a nice equivalent in the treatment of outward speech to *style indirect libre* or "narrated mono-logue" (the latter term is again Dorrit Cohn's), which is the conveying of the character's inward speech as the character undergoes experience from the temporal and grammatical standpoint of the third-person narrator. It is instructive that narrated dialogue can occur equally in a magisterial third-person narration like Fielding's or in a highly subjective first-person narration like that of the Chevalier des Grieux—which is actually embedded in the first-person frame-narration of the Gentleman of Quality—in *Manon Lescaut*. Here, for example, is des Grieux, after having been brusquely abandoned by his beloved Manon for the first time, meeting her again two years later, and once again dazzled by the "enchantment" of her beauty:

> I remained ill at ease before her, and not being able to conjecture what might be the purpose of this visit, I waited, eyes lowered and trembling, for her to explain herself. Her embarrassment was, for a few minutes, equal to mine, but seeing that my silence persisted, she placed

> her hand before her eyes to hide her tears. She said to me,
> in a timid tone, that she admitted that her infidelity
> deserved my hatred; but that, if it was true that I had ever
> had any tender feeling for her, there was a good deal of
> harshness in allowing two years to go by without bothering
> to inform myself of her fate, and still more in seeing her in
> the condition in which she was in my presence without
> saying a word to her. The confusion of my soul, listening to
> her, could not be expressed.[7]

One may observe in the passage abundant evidence of that
effort to recover the emotional immediacy of past experience
in first-person narration that I noted above: the indication of
the moments of embarrassed silence between the estranged
lovers, the lowered eyes and the trembling, Manon's gesture
of hiding her tears, and her timid tone of voice. But especially
since straight dialogue is freely used in this novel, why is
Manon's speech to des Grieux conveyed as narrated dialogue?
Because of the very license of narrative fluidity of the genre,
there are rarely clear-cut answers to such questions. Novelists
very often seem to switch methods of presentation and
perspective out of nothing more than an intuitive sense of the
rightness of handling things in a particular way at a given
moment of the narrative. Perhaps Prévost transposed the
dialogue into the third person here because narrated dialogue,
after all, points toward summary and so may be a way of
speeding up the pace a little. Perhaps the writer sensed that
the filter of des Grieux's narration was necessary at this point
for the report of Manon's words because what is at issue, as
the last sentence suggests, is his feelings as he listens to these
astonishing words of remonstration from the woman who has
betrayed him, and not the woman herself as an autonomous
figure. Prévost sets his first-person narrator a task that is
preeminently novelistic: to attempt to express what cannot be
expressed because it exceeds all familiar norms, flows from
the ambivalent intensity of a unique relationship and a unique

moment of experience. It is, as Walter Benjamin puts it, to represent the "incommensurable" in human life, an aim that would scarcely have occurred to a classical narrator. The inner confusion of the character resists adequate expression, but some intimation or approximation of it can be achieved by the way he minutely indicates the atmosphere and the body language of the encounter and by his folding Manon's voice into his own, so that we begin to feel her verbal playing on his heart strings through the vibration of his inner response to her words.

In the great age of the novel, such representational aims tend to be transposed, as I have noted, into the third person. There are, to be sure, conspicuously authoritative narrators of nineteenth-century novels who variously cast themselves as cozy companions, showmen, historians, scientific anatomists of society. But through the middle and late decades of the century, pride of place in novelistic narration is gradually taken over by an extraordinarily complex form of what I call "experiential realism": the character's pulse beats and perceptions and shifting emotions are caught in the full tide of living from moment to moment, while at the same time the narrator who renders this immediacy retains the freedom to ironize, analyze, and judge what is going on in the character. Experiential realism remains vividly in evidence in twentieth-century fiction, pushed to one possible extreme in the different techniques of interior monologue perfected by the modern masters in the 1920s, but also persisting in modes of third-person narration continuous with the practice of the nineteenth-century realists.

Let me conclude these observations on perspective as a historically evolving element in the novel by stressing that the orientation of third-person narration that I have called experiential realism is not a wholly new invention of the nineteenth century. Local intimations of it can be detected in some of the earliest novels. Thus, Madame de Lafayette's *The Princesse de Clèves* (1678), France's candidate for "the first novel," uses a narrator who starts off with the distant overview of a historical chronicler and who throughout relies a good deal on flat summary and formulaic notation. Nevertheless, *The Princesse de Clèves*, almost as though its author were impelled by the representational momentum of what would prove to be a new genre, abounds in discriminated moments that are imaginatively realized from the point of view of one of the characters. Here, for example, is the newlywed Mme. de Clèves at a court ball, laying eyes for the first time on the Duke de Nemours, the man who will fall passionately in love with her:

> When she arrived, her beauty and her jewels were admired. The ball began and, as she was dancing with M. de Guise, there was a rather large hubbub in the direction of the entrance to the hall, as of people making way for someone coming in. Mme. de Clèves finished the dance and, while she was searching with her eyes for someone she had in mind to take as partner, the King called her to take the person who had arrived. She turned and saw a man who she thought at once must be M. de Nemours, making his way over some chairs in order to reach the dance floor. This prince was so fashioned that it was difficult not to be surprised by the first sight of him, especially that evening, when the care he had taken to adorn himself heightened the brilliance of his presence, but it was also difficult to see Mme. de Clèves for the first time without responding in great amazement.[8]

After the narrator's succinct authoritative report of Mme. de Clèves' arrival and of the effect struck by her dazzling appearance, we switch to her point of view, something readily observable in the beautifully precise vagueness of the language in the next few lines. Given the general norm of lucid presentation in this novel, one might have expected a sentence like: With a grand ado of people making way on all sides, the magnificent M. de Nemours, in his finest dress, came striding into the ballroom. Instead, we get an agentless verb, *il se fit un assez grand bruit*, "there was a rather large hubbub"; the exact location of the noise is a little uncertain— it comes *vers la porte*, "in the direction of the entrance"; and there is an element of inference in the naming of its cause, "as of people making way for someone coming in." Again, from the circumscribed position of figural perception, Mme. de Clèves does not see M. de Nemours but rather a man who she concludes can be none other than the famous duke (*qu'elle crut d'abord ne pouvoir être que M. de Nemours*). And her startled gaze catches the duke in a little action that would normally be excluded by the generalizing narrative decorum of this novel: clambering over chairs in the crowded ballroom to reach the area where she stands. All this, set into a manifestly "omniscient" narration, makes the character's step-by-step experience of discovery the momentary subject of narrative report. When the narrator reaches M. de Nemours' remarkable appearance, she reverts from the character's point of view to the declaration in the superlative of information presumed to be common to members of court society. It is hard to be sure whether the duke's having taken particular trouble with his dress that evening is provided from the narrator's stock of certain knowledge or whether this is an inference Mme. de Clèves makes as she quickly takes in his splendid attire. A later novelist would probably have opted more decisively for the latter alternative, using it to intimate the complexities of future relations between these two: an extraordinarily handsome man, thinks the young woman, but to judge by what he is wearing, rather self-conscious about making a big impression with his looks.

Ballroom scenes figure frequently in later novels largely because formal balls continue to be an important social rite of courtship and self-exhibition. More interestingly, novels evince a recurrent fondness for positioning characters in certain revelatory spatial orientations like the one here. A characteristic orientation of this sort is sitting at a window, a dramatized "post of observation," looking out on a scene (that also occurs in *The Princesse de Clèves*). Another is the instance we have just considered, the entrance of a character into a room, a house, a garden, a public concourse. If the point of view is that of someone already within the space to be entered, as in the passage from *The Princesse de Clèves*, the emphasis is on the revelation of the newcomer. If the point of view is that of the character making the entrance (the more common choice), the emphasis is on the discovery by the character of a new realm of experience—the space to be entered—and such discovery is virtually the generic subject of the novel. Let us consider in detail a much more elaborate entrance scene from one of the masterpieces of experiential realism, Tolstoy's *Anna Karenina* (1878). As it happens, this later entrance, written exactly two hundred years after Madame de Lafayette's, is also to a ball, although I think it unlikely that there is any allusion to the French novel. (This would be another instance of generic intertextuality without allusion.) The scene goes on for several pages, leading to the ingenue Kitty's encounter with Anna, whom she is startled but enchanted to find dressed in black rather than in lilac as she had imagined. It will suffice for our purposes to quote the first three and a half paragraphs of Chapter 22 in Part One.

> The ball was only just beginning as Kitty and her mother walked up the grand staircase, flooded with light and lined with flowers and footmen in powder and red livery. From the rooms came a constant, steady hum, as from a beehive, and the rustle of movement; and while on the landing, between the plants, they gave last touches to their hair and dresses before the mirror, they heard from the ballroom the careful, distinct notes of the fiddles of the orchestra beginning the first waltz. A little old man in

civilian clothes, arranging his gray curls before another mirror, and smelling of perfume, stumbled against them on the stairs and stood aside, evidently admiring Kitty, whom he did not know. A beardless youth, one of those society youths whom the old Prince Shcherbatsky called "young bucks," in an exceedingly open vest, straightening his white tie as he went, bowed to them and, after running by, came back to ask Kitty for a quadrille. As the first quadrille had already been given to Vronsky, she had to promise this youth the second. An officer, buttoning his glove, stood aside in the doorway and, stroking his mustache, admired the rosy Kitty.

Although her dress, her coiffure, and all the preparations for the ball had cost Kitty great trouble and consideration, at this moment she walked into the ballroom in her elaborate tulle dress over a pink slip as easily and naturally as though all the rosettes and lace, all the minute details of her attire, had not cost her or her family a moment's attention, as though she had been born in that tulle and lace, with her hair done up high on her head and a rose and two leaves on the top of it.

When, just before entering the ballroom, the princess, her mother, tried to straighten the ribbon of her sash, Kitty had drawn back a little. She felt that everything must be naturally right and graceful, and nothing could need adjusting.

It was one of Kitty's best days. Her dress was not uncomfortable anywhere; her lace berthe did not droop anywhere; her rosettes were not crushed or torn off; her pink slippers with high, curved heels did not pinch but delighted her feet; and the thick rolls of fair chignon stayed up on her head as if they were her own hair. All three buttons fastened without tearing on the long glove that covered her hand without concealing its lines. The black velvet of her locket nestled with special softness around her neck. That velvet ribbon was delicious; at home, looking at her neck in the mirror, Kitty had felt that it was eloquent. About everything else there might be a doubt,

but the velvet was delicious. Kitty smiled here too, at the
ball, when she glanced at it in the mirror. Her bare
shoulders and arms gave her a sense of chill marble, a
feeling she particularly liked. Her eyes sparkled, and her
rosy lips could not keep from smiling from her awareness
of her own attractiveness.[9]

Everything here is of course mediated by the narrator, and
we will need to attend to the particular ways in which that
mediation is carried out, but it is also clear that figural
perspective predominates from the moment Kitty and her
mother are introduced at the beginning of the first sentence.
To begin with, it is the shared perspective of the two women
coming up the grand staircase together, taking in the light and
the flowers and the red-liveried footmen, hearing the hubbub
and the first strains of music from the rooms above that they
are about to enter. The pause at the mirror on the landing
when Kitty becomes an object of admiration is a thematically
appropriate juncture for her point of view to be separated out
from her mother's, and the rest of the passage is articulated
entirely around Kitty's chain of perceptions. The first paragraph is figural narration, as we can see from the spatial
location of the narrative report vis-à-vis the sounds from the
ballroom, and as we may conclude from the little sensory
detail of detecting the smell of perfume on the old man as he
stumbles against the women, and also from the inferentiality
of "evidently admiring Kitty" and from the prim adverbial
judgment of the beardless youth's sartorial daring, "an exceedingly open vest." There is as yet no report of mental
processes, and no intimation of the character's unspoken
inner language.

   The second paragraph moves fluently—fluent transition,
as I have argued, being a hallmark of novelistic narration—
from the preceding figural narration to analysis of the character: although the preparations had cost Kitty great trouble,

she now feels perfectly at ease in her splendid attire. The brief third paragraph brackets a simple report of action (Kitty's drawing back when her mother tries to straighten the ribbon of her sash) with a bit of psycho-narration that explains the action: "She felt that everything must be naturally right . . ." The next paragraph, though it contains possible strands of psycho-narration ("Kitty had felt that it was eloquent"), moves into narrated monologue—the words, conveyed by the narrator, that Kitty would be speaking to herself. As is usually the case with narrated monologue, the clues to its presence are for the most part not unambiguous linguistic signals but are given by the substance of the utterances, what is insisted on by them, the hints of a more colloquial intonation in them. "It was one of Kitty's best days." This does not make much sense as an "objective" narrative datum conveyed to us on the authority of the narrator, but it is perfect as a third-person transposition of Kitty's saying to herself, "This is one of my best days." The sheer sensuality of Kitty's experience of what she is wearing ("That velvet was delicious. . . . About everything else there might be a doubt, but the velvet was delicious") sounds very much like the character's inner language. (The use of the deictic "that" before velvet is, in fact, one of the few dependable linguistic signals of narrated monologue. That is, it is a pointing word that points to an object from an attitudinal—in other cases, spatial or temporal—standpoint belonging to the character, not the narrator.) Is the piquant predicate that is attached to the pink slippers, "delighted her feet," the character's phrase or rather the narrator's, and hence a bit of psycho-narration? There is no way of determining, and it hardly makes much difference. In any case, a fine intimation of the excited young girl at her first big ball in colloquy with herself subtly and strongly pervades the last of our four paragraphs.

The passage, then, moves through four different narrative treatments of scene and character, coincidentally corresponding to the paragraph breaks: figural narration, analysis, psycho-narration, and narrated monologue. The movement is so seamless that most readers will be aware of the transitions only subliminally. Yet the delicate, beautifully flexible dance of perspective is a principal source of the pleasure of reading and the chief vehicle of our intimate knowledge of the character. It is what the reading of novels is all about. At a time when several schools of criticism have come to regard mimesis as a sham or an impossibility, it must be said here that the persuasive representation of reality in an artistic medium answers a deep human need and provides profound and abiding delight in itself. Why otherwise would a reader care about the mother and daughter standing on the landing on the way up to the ballroom? It is a little moment of narrated time that could be easily deleted without in the least affecting what happens in *Anna Karenina*. But the deft definition through figural narration of the look and feel of the place and moment, with the exciting sounds of the ball drifting down from above and the stir of preparation all around, speaks to us as social animals, gives us back our own experience, or that of our ancestors, only brighter and sharper and more coherent.

In the novel, these representational techniques are used above all to provide intimate insight into character, an end Tolstoy realizes in this passage with astonishing assurance. As I had occasion to observe earlier about Stendhal in the chapter on character, it is hard to imagine how Tolstoy—a man at times outrageous in his actual relations with women—*knows* all this about his nubile young woman, but at least to this male reader, the rendering of Kitty's state of mind and body as she prepares to enter the ball is utterly convincing. Perhaps that knowledge is triggered in part by the sheer momentum of identification in concrete particularity by which the writer associates his narrator with the inward point of view of the character, mentally checking the disposition of all the elements of her splendid attire from pink slip to tulle dress, reveling in the delicious softness of the black velvet locket nestling round her neck, feeling her bare arms and shoulders as chill marble in the triumphant sensation (of course, illusory) of having transformed herself through all this exquisite cosmetic care into an object of art. (Soon after, when Kitty sees Anna at the ball, the more mature woman's shoulders and bosom will look to her "as though carved of old ivory.") In all this, the underlying fact of third-person narration is not a mechanical detail but a dimension of our perception of the character. The narrator of *Anna Karenina* is not the sort that flaunts his presence, but that presence, even in the abundant moments of association with the character's point of view, is not inconsequential. There is, as we noted, some brief analysis of the character and hence incipient judgment of her here. And in the narrated monologue proper, though there is a good deal of oblique reference to the words Kitty uses inwardly, the actual enunciation of words belongs to the narrator, which means that in the midst of affectionate, sensuously particular identification with the character, there is also an indefinable hint of playful detachment, ironic distance, perhaps even superiority. Experiential realism in the novel thus permits us to know characters as they might know themselves and at the same time as they might be known by an especially curious, patiently perceptive god.

All that I have said still leaves us with a rather incomplete account of the experience of reading the passage, and in particular of what goes on in the first paragraph. If perspective is the way the story is told and the way we are invited to see the characters and events, its effects are never independent of the nature of the narrated materials themselves and the formal or formal-thematic configurations in which they are placed. To put this more simply, how a story is told always interacts with what is told in the story. That interaction is particularly striking in our first paragraph, which is a buzzing crossroads of recurrent polarities and motifs. The two human subjects, Kitty and her mother, are paired in gender and opposed in age, and the contrast between youth and age is immediately underscored by the introduction of the gray-haired old man, who is played off against the foppish young buck. This contrast is particularly apt for this moment in the novel because the grand ball is, after all, a rite of initiation for Kitty, and the main part of the chapter will center on the still adolescent Kitty's encounter with Anna, a lovely, socially poised woman in her thirties. The contrast in age between the two women will in turn be elaborated by a whole set of contrasts in appearance—between blond Kitty and black-haired Anna, between Kitty with her chignon, her elaborate tulle dress, and Anna in her own hair and a black dress that is "only the frame" to show her off, "simple, natural, elegant."

Everybody at the beginning of the chapter is preening. The perfumed old man, in a grotesque parody of femininity, is "arranging his gray curls," just as Kitty and her mother are arranging their hair. The beardless youth is glimpsed "straightening his white tie." The officer is "buttoning his glove" and "stroking his mustache" as he admires Kitty, thus joining a vaguely erotic ogle with the narcissism of self-caress. Kitty's satisfaction in the perfect fastening of the three buttons on her long glove "that covered her hand without concealing its lines" then rhymes piquantly with the image of the officer buttoning his glove. What begins to emerge from the persuasively verisimilar sequence of details observed is a thematically coherent vision of society as a great hothouse of narcissism. The preoccupation with one's appearance and the seduction of self-admiration easily lead to excess and become the objects of satire, as in the little old man and the mustached officer, though these traits seem condonable and even winningly appropriate in a girl like Kitty just entering the social whirl. The emblem of Narcissus is the mirror, and mirrors define the space of our passage, are the outward symbol of Kitty's delighted self-inspection and her silent speech. Mother and daughter stop before one mirror, the little old man at another. In the one brief fragment of memory here, Kitty recalls preparing for the ball at home and her own image in the mirror there with the black velvet at her throat. The trajectory from home to ballroom is from mirror to mirror. Now, at the dance itself, she glances again at her reflected image and smiles at what she sees.

Tolstoy no doubt exhibits a higher degree of formal organization that do many novelists. There is something architectonic about his imagination, not only in the large planned symmetries and antitheses—like the contrasts between the two families, the Oblonskys and the Karenins, and the two cities, Moscow and St. Petersburg—but also in individual scenes, where the patterns often seem intuitively improvised. But his practice as a novelist merely makes more conspicuous what is detectable at least intermittently in most novels—the local pressure of elements of structure influencing our interpretation and even our visual reconstruction of scene, character, and action, whatever the narrative perspective. The details picked up by the narrator's eye, even when it acts like a hand-held camera moving with the character and seeing as the character does, are never random. When we see one mirror and at once another, we are attuned to looking for a third and a fourth; and are likely to infer some meaning in that insistent motif, are likely to understand or even "see" other images and acts in the immediate context (the buttoning of gloves, the attention to tulle) in relation to those mirrors. Such patterning of narrative, of course, is by no means the special prerogative of the novel. Biblical and classical literature abounds in brilliant examples of its use. What is distinctively novelistic is the subtle weaving of pattern into the narrative texture of verisimilitude.

The experiential realist catches in the rhythms and language of narration the sequential mental movements of the experiencing subject, the sight and sound and smell of things as they are experienced, the character's sense of place, her memories, her self-scrutiny, even the sensuous directness of the proprioception of the body. But since all literature is not only representation but also a giving form to and a making sense of experience, the rendering of the character's perceptions and reflections is structured by symmetry, antithesis, and recurrence, by means of which the novelist gathers the narrated materials into the satisfying shape of artifice and conveys a vision of the overarching meanings of his story. Even at its most convincingly realistic moments, literature remains the art that signifies.

The joining of structure and fluidity is a defining feature of novelistic narration. The novel might be described as the narrative form in which from moment to moment any one—or any combination—of a variety of perspectives can be used. Let us look at a final example, both to observe the artful playing out of perspective that it exhibits and to try to imagine what might have been the technical alternatives, with what consequences, to telling the story in this particular way. Toward the end of Joseph Conrad's *The Secret Agent* (1907), Mrs. Verloc, whose retarded younger brother has been blown to bits while unwittingly carrying a bomb for her anarchist husband, has a sudden visual apprehension of the boy's violent death triggered by the words "Greenwich Park" pronounced by Mr. Verloc. A moment later, in a narrative tour de force, Conrad will switch from her point of view to his as she seizes the carving knife to stab her husband. (He observes her approach while lying on the sofa in a state of stupefaction, watching in slow motion the knife that is actually descending quite rapidly, and so he is incapable of initiating the movements of self-defense that his torpid mind begins to plan.) Let us consider one crucial moment in the representation of her inner paroxysm which leads to the seizing of the knife:

Greenwich Park. A park! That's where the boy was killed.
A park—smashed branches, torn leaves, gravel, bits of
brotherly flesh and bone, all spouting up together in the
manner of a firework. She remembered now what she had
heard, and she remembered it pictorially. They had to
gather him up with the shovel. Trembling all over with
irrepressible shudders, she saw before her the very im-
plement with its ghastly load scraped up from the ground.
Mrs. Verloc closed her eyes desperately, throwing upon
that vision the night of her eyelids, where after a rainlike
fall of mangled limbs the decapitated head of Stevie
lingered suspended alone, and fading out slowly like the
last star of a pyrotechnic display. Mrs. Verloc opened her
eyes.[10]

The passage is an interweave of narrated monologue and an
elaborately metaphorical variety of psycho-narration, with the
latter predominating. The beginning of the excerpt is vivid
narrated monologue: "A park! That's where the boy was
killed," followed by a string of nouns without predicate, such
fragmentary syntax being a characteristic sign of some form of
interior monologue. But even here, the narrator does not
hesitate to intervene briefly, the macabre irony of the adjective in "brotherly flesh and bone" being more plausibly
attributable to him than to Mrs. Verloc and the literary
diction of *in the manner of* a firework" (instead of simply
"like") reflecting his style and not her inner speech. Immediately following this is a psycho-narrative report ("She
remembered . . .") that not only informs us what is going on
in Mrs. Verloc but also of the way in which it is going on
("pictorially"), which provides an explicit warrant for the
narrator's mode of presentation in both the previous sentences
and the ones that follow. "They had to gather him up with the
shovel" is the last bit of narrated monologue here. The rest of
the passage combines a report of the character's externally
observable actions ("Trembling all over with irrepressible

shudders. . . ," "Mrs. Verloc closed her eyes desperately") with the spectacular and horrific images she sees with her mind's eye. It is a nightmarish vision, but one aesthetically rendered, the disembodied head of the mangled brother envisaged as the last fading star of a pyrotechnic display.

The passage, then, joins two modes of presentation and two clearly distinguishable perspectives, the character's and the narrator's. What results is a powerful, immediate sense of Mrs. Verloc's horror and rage together with a perception of her from the outside racked by convulsive movements, looking quite pathetic. How else might a novelist have handled this moment, working with exactly the same narrative data? Let me sketch out just a few hypothetical alternatives (the possibilities are always in principle manifold) so that we may contemplate the tactical uses and the potential of flexibility of shifting novelistic perspectives.

When Mr. Verloc pronounced the words "Greenwich Park," he observed a sudden pallor in his wife's face. Her shoulders trembled oddly, as though from a fever. Still not responding to what he had said, she closed her eyes for a few moments, then opened them, staring blankly. She had definitely not been looking well these last days, he reflected. Perhaps she was coming down with something, or it might be that anemia they get with their monthlies.

This unlikely strategy of rendering Mrs. Verloc at this moment from her husband's point of view has the limited advantage of underscoring the irony of his complacent imperceptiveness in the novel (when she heads for him with the knife, he first imagines she is approaching him with amorous intentions). The big disadvantage is that it leaves her opaque, and, given her previous role as a meek and compliant wife, we urgently need to know about the horrendous surge of outrage within her over her brother's death so that the murder she commits will seem sufficiently motivated.

But even if this leaves Mrs. Verloc's point of view and the narrator's as the only workable options, the perspectival possibilities are abundant. Let us look at three.

> The mention of the name Greenwich Park brought to Mrs. Verloc's consciousness in a sudden rush the image of the park itself and of her hideously dismembered brother blown to pieces by the bomb. She was seized with violent trembling, and, as if to ward off that nightmarish vision, she closed her eyes desperately, but the attempt proving futile, she opened them again after a few moments of anguished silence.

The author of this version is obviously a much more conventional novelist than Joseph Conrad. He is interested in conveying the contents of the character's consciousness but not in dramatically realizing the dynamic process of consciousness. He makes no use at all of narrated monologue, and the kind of psycho-narration he provides us tends toward the summary of inner states, with a neatly perspicuous arrangement of cause and effect. There is no hint of the arresting concreteness that metaphoric elaboration imparts to Conrad's treatment of consciousness, nor is there any aspiration to extract, as Conrad does, a kind of ghastly beauty from the representation of suffering ("throwing upon that vision the night of her eyelids"). This striking difference should be carefully registered because as analytic readers we need to keep in mind that a particular mode of representation like psycho-narration or narrated monologue may be handled in extraordinarily different ways, and so we always have to ask ourselves not simply what is the technique but how is it used. The distanced, orderly, summarizing report of Mrs. Verloc's mental images is not only a good deal less interesting in itself than what Conrad actually does, but also, more important, it serves the larger narrative needs of the novel much less well.

In the version from her husband's point of view, Mrs. Verloc, as we have noted, is most unfortunately opaque. Here, her mind is transparent to the narrator's summarizing overview, but because of the narrator's distance the extreme and violent psychological shift within her is barely perceptible. At this juncture, for this character, the summary has the effect of blurring the radical nature of what she is undergoing. The effect we are likely to pick up is something like this: Oh, yes, the poor woman is horribly distraught in recollecting her brother's violent death. This does not do the same job as "the rainlike fall of mangled limbs" and all the rest in persuading us of the extraordinary motivation that will in a moment drive her to the carving knife.

But we should beware of embracing the notion that concreteness, the illusion of immediacy, "dramatic power," showing instead of telling, are intrinsically superior narrative values. Every good novelist creates a distinctive world in which the tonalities of style and the modes of presentation determine the range of appropriate perspectives, and every juncture of a given plot makes certain options more effective than others. In a novelistic world different from Conrad's— say, one fashioned by George Eliot or the early Thomas Mann—or with a kind of character different from Mrs. Verloc, it is quite conceivable that a distanced summary of consciousness could be the best way to handle a particular scene. And immediacy itself has its limitations. Consider, for example, this rendering of our moment from *The Secret Agent:*

A park! That's where the boy was killed. A park—smashed branches, torn leaves, gravel, bits of flesh and bone, all spouting up together. Fireworks. When was it, Guy Fawkes Day on the strand then, crowds all around, he holding my hand, Oh! he said, Oh! squeezing, squeezing tightly. Red rain of skyfire, red rain of flesh. Scraped from the ground with a shovel, ashes to ashes, dust to dust. No,

mustn't look, mustn't see—Stevie's head starlight star-
bright fading all alone in the dark.

I have taken my hint here from the actual opening words of
Conrad's passage, which in their fragmentary form are already
close to stream of consciousness. The essential difference is
that in this version the formal, framing narrator disappears
entirely, the character becoming the narrator through a
verbal equivalent of her thought processes which would in
fact be partly verbal, partly preverbal or nonverbal. This
Joycean mode of presentation clearly has the advantage of
immediacy over Conrad's method, with its abundant narratorial interventions, and I suppose one might claim that the
rendering of Mrs. Verloc's moment of anguish as continuous
interior monologue has a certain imaginative interest. This
version is actually a more extreme aestheticization of the
character's experience than Conrad's because it is hard for a
novelist to do this sort of thing without turning the contents of
consciousness into a prose poem, as Joyce repeatedly does in
Ulysses and as Virginia Woolf, in quite another way, often
does in her major novels beginning with *Mrs. Dalloway*. My
guess is that such aestheticizing would tip the balance too
much for Conrad, who also wants us to see his character in
moral and relational terms. In any case, the stream of
consciousness has the general effect of setting the dynamics of
consciousness entirely in the foreground. We are invited to
attend to the sheer associative freedom of consciousness, its
odd little leaps of memory, the scraps of song and written
texts that cling to it like flotsam and jetsam. All this, I fear,
would make the consciousness of poor Winnie Verloc loom
too large for Conrad's purposes. He wants to show us how she
is overwhelmed by horrified rage, but he also wants us to see
her as a limited, pathetic creature. Even more important, he
wants us to envisage her standing in a particular dramatic
situation at a crucial nexus of plot, her husband supine on the

sofa, she about to reach for the carving knife. For these purposes, it is helpful to have the perspective of the narrator observing her "from above," describing to us how she remembers pictorially, evoking the image of her body racked with shudders, her eyes desperately closed. Perhaps there are excitements for the reader in the poetic disorientation of the fragmentary interior-monologue style, but at least for this juncture in this novel, much would also be lost in that mode of presentation.

Conrad stands instructively on the threshold between the nineteenth-century tradition of narratorial high profile and the modernist fascination with figural consciousness. If the version we have just considered rewrites the passage in the novelistic idiom of the 1920s partly anticipated by Conrad, we might usefully consider, as a final possibility, how the passage would sound if it had been written more strictly in accordance with the Victorian antecedents with which Conrad also maintained a strong connection.

> The mention of the name Greenwich Park brought to Mrs. Verloc's consciousness in a sudden rush the image of the park itself and of her hideously dismembered brother. She remembered now what she had heard and she remembered pictorially, seeing, despite herself, the rain of flesh, the decapitated head, the bloodied shovel with which they scraped up Stevie's ghastly vestiges. Mrs. Verloc was not an especially imaginative person. Among women of the people, however, even the simplest mental apparatus, the most limited faculties of inward vision, can attain a poet's power of vividness when stimulated by great emotional shock. Humanity for the most part may be composed of sluggish, purblind, mutely compliant creatures of habit, but even these may be galvanized by anguish into terrific perception and even more terrific action. So it was that Mrs. Verloc closed and opened her eyes on that nightmarish scene, then grimly contemplated the supine figure of her husband.

I have borrowed the first sentence from our second version, the one that was built on a summarizing form of psycho-narration, because it seemed a tonally appropriate lead-in to what follows. The main clause of the second sentence is retained verbatim from Conrad because its defining overview of the character's mental process points toward the possibility of other kinds of overview. With the next sentence, our narrator moves away from figural consciousness into a series of generalizations: about the kind of person Mrs. Verloc is, about the psychology of imagination of women of the people, about the nature and range of responses of humanity at large, both in habitual circumstances and under stress. Then we return to Mrs. Verloc, who now appears as a particular instance of the general principle. The narrator has in effect given us a neatly packaged, "scientific" explanation of her impulse to commit murder before she performs the act. This stance of the narrator as an impeccable authority on human nature, society, psychology, and much else, whose word is to be taken on trust, was often favored by novelists in the early and middle decades of the nineteenth century. There is, for example, a great deal of it in Balzac and in Dickens. Lest it seem perverse to apply so antiquated a procedure to a scene from Conrad, let me observe that *The Secret Agent* has a good many such Dickensian touches. Here, for example, is part of one of the earliest characterizations in the novel of Mr. Verloc:

> But there was also about him an indescribable air which no mechanic could have acquired in the practice of his handicraft however dishonestly exercised: the air common to men who live on the vices, the follies, or the baser fears of mankind; the air of moral nihilism common to keepers of gambling hells and disorderly houses; to private detectives and inquiry agents; to drink sellers and, I should say, to the sellers of invigorating electric belts and to the inventors of patent medicines. But of the last I am not sure, not having carried my investigations so far into the depths.[11]

If Conrad could use so ostentatious a narrator, generalizing from character to social types, introducing himself in the first person as "investigator" or (elsewhere) historian, flaunting coy ironies, why does he exclude that perspective from the climactic scene between Mrs. Verloc and her husband? If our first two versions left Winnie too opaque and our third one made her too imposingly transparent, this last rendering gives her too much clarity of context—indeed, partly displaces character with context. Conrad wants us to see Mrs. Verloc driven to murder in her terrific individuality, not as a pat illustration of a general principle. For this end his narrative movement of approach to consciousness and withdrawal from it, without recourse to authoritative pronouncements on underlying laws, is exactly right.

By the turn of the twentieth century, a good many serious novelists were beginning to see character and motive as expressions of an imponderable individuality that could not be readily referred to systems of general explanation, whether moral, social, biological, or even psychological. The narrator as authoritative historian is eroded—though his presence has by no means disappeared entirely in the contemporary novel—because many writers could no longer believe in the myth of authority on which much of the technical practice of nineteenth-century fiction was founded. Conrad is intriguing as a transitional figure between two eras of the novel, clinging to elements of the authoritative narrator but typically handling his material with a taut interweave of narratorial and figural perspectives that makes his version of our scene more beautifully apt than any of the alternatives spun out here by his four alter egos.

The ultimate aim of all these considerations is to demonstrate that there is no hierarchy of narrative perspectives, never one best way to tell a story, though often, after the fact, we can see that for the particular story a great writer has told and the particular world he or she has created as the arena of the story, the perspective actually used works better than any alternative we can imagine. Perspective is as essential to literary narrative as the use of words or the ordering of significant sequences of action into a plot. The artful deployment of perspective is thus variously observable in all genres and eras of literary narrative, from epic to fabliau to novel, from ancient to medieval to modern. But for the reasons I have tried to indicate, it is above all in the novel that the full spectrum of perspectival possibilities is explored, in which sometimes the combinations and permutations of perspective become the virtual subject of the fiction. Our examples have dealt with certain generically representative options, but they are by no means a comprehensive catalog of novelistic perspectives. There are novels written in the second person, novels that alternate between first and third persons, novels that switch from lyric to clinical to documentary narrators from one section to the next, novels that rapidly and bewilderingly intercut half a dozen or more different, even conflicting, perspectives. But what it is well to bear in mind as readers is that even when we look beyond such spectacular experiments of literary modernism and its heirs to the classics of realism, the fluctuating play of perspective very often gives experiential depth and conceptual complexity to the represented figures and actions. An awareness of that play as we read can heighten our pleasure, sharpen our perception, help us to see what the novel can do that other forms of representation cannot.

CHAPTER SEVEN

Multiple Readings
and the
Bog of Indeterminacy

In the course of this study, I have variously argued that a discriminating awareness of the distinctive resources of literary expression—style, allusion, structure, perspective, and much else—can amplify the pleasure and the precision of the reading experience. But let me hasten to add that, having earlier objected to the mechanical nature of the conception of literature assumed by Structuralism and some of its heirs, I do not propose still another mechanical model. The formal aspects of the literary text may deserve the nicest attention, but reading is not a matter of nuts and bolts, and an account of formal categories cannot serve as a simple checklist, like the directions for assembling a bicycle. A work of literature, as I shall try to explain, consists of too many disparate elements engaged in constant, shifting interplay for reading ever to be a linear assemblage of parts by even the most patient analyst. Most literary works, moreover, turn on an experiential dimension that is not finally reducible to the formal vehicles through which it is conveyed. We had occasion to consider this issue in regard to character in the realist novel, but similar arguments could be made for what is represented in lyric poetry, epic, tragedy, and comedy.

Much has been made by literary theorists over the last two decades of the indeterminacy of the literary text. The idea would be unexceptionable were it not for the extremes to which it has been pushed (a question we will deal with later) and were it not for the pretense that it is a new idea. A wide variety of critics directly or obliquely inspired by Jacques Derrida have promoted the courageous newness of their new work by creating the impression that criticism before them was an unbroken chain of "authoritative" readings. There are, I would suggest, qualities of tentativeness and openness in many traditional critics that one could scarcely guess from the versions of them proposed by the recent iconoclasts. Most major critics have had too much respect for the elusiveness as well as for the complexity of the literary text to imagine that there could be anything like a definitive reading of a great work of fiction or poetry. To cite two divergent examples from American criticism in the middle decades of this century: Lionel Trilling's discussions of novels by Jane Austen and Dickens, and of Wordsworth's poetry, are delicate explorations of the moral, psychological, and political implications of the texts, the strength of the criticism inhering precisely in its exploratory character. The contemporaneous New Critics do seem ultimately to have assumed that poetry possesses a kind of transcendent unity, but their own emphasis on paradox and ambiguity—which has been duly "deconstructed" by Paul de Man—often indicates a perfectly conscious awareness that they are rendering an account of precarious tensions in the text, rhetorically encompassing its multiplicity but not etching it in bronze. Harold Bloom's notion of strong readings and weak readings is more pertinent to criticism as it has been practiced and to the nature of the literary text than the idea of radical indeterminacy that claims to displace a tradition of spuriously authoritative readings. For our purposes, I would like to modify his language of power and emphasize perception instead of oedipal struggle by speaking of precise and imprecise readings. There are many precise readings of a given text (even, paradoxically, conflicting ones), depending on what aspects of the text you are looking at, what questions you are asking, what issues beyond the text you mean to address. There are also demonstrably imprecise readings—not just "weak" readings but actually wrong ones—though this is a possibility that many of the indeterminists seem unwilling to grant. Let us first consider the fundamental fact of multiple readings and what it is about the literary text that generates them.

A feature of *Robinson Crusoe* that is clearly registered by most readers of Defoe's novel through the sheer amount of space devoted to it is Crusoe's extraordinary preoccupation with fortifications. At the beginning of his narrative of life on the island, Crusoe offers a circumstantial account of how he first secures the dwelling place on the island where he has been shipwrecked. He sets up his tent in front of a hollow place worn into the face of a rock, and then builds around it a double row of strong stakes sharpened at the top in a semicircle twenty yards in diameter. The stakes are interwoven with pieces of ship's cable, and reinforced with still another row of stakes leaning on the outer ones from within. Access to the tent from outside is achieved by means of a ladder, which Crusoe pulls in after him once he has climbed in. Feeling thus "compleatly fenc'd in, and fortify'd . . . from all the World," Crusoe is by no means content, but now proceeds to burrow behind him, working his way into the rock at the cost of even more painstaking labor until he has succeeded in hewing out a cave behind his tent that can serve him as a cellar. But there is no discernible limit to his thirst for physical security. A little later in the same section we learn that he has built up his palisade from the outside with chunks of turf so that it is now properly a wall and not merely a fence. Still later, after discovering the print of a man's naked foot, when Crusoe's old anxieties about being devoured by savages are aroused by this evidence of another human presence, he flings himself into a paroxysm of fortification. He thickens his original wall to a full ten feet with compacted earth, and at the same time drives piles between the double row of trees he had planted in a semicircle beyond his wall a dozen years earlier, thus turning them into an outer wall. Beyond this, he sets into the ground "near twenty thousand" (!) saplings of osier-like wood. In this fashion, he consummates the double goal of impenetrable enclosure and absolute concealment:

> Thus in two Years Time I had a thick Grove, and in five or six Years Time I had a Wood before my Dwelling, growing so monstrous thick and strong, that it was indeed perfectly impassable; and no Men of what kind soever, would ever imagine that there was any Thing beyond it, much less a Habitation.[1]

What is all this doing in *Robinson Crusoe*? There are, to begin with, two obvious functional explanations that are necessary to state, though they will not take us very far. It is a necessity of the plot that Crusoe have a secure refuge when cannibals and then pirates arrive on the island. One might also argue that it is a necessity, or at least a convenience, of narration that Crusoe have something to do on the island beyond hunting and foraging, so that Defoe can have something to tell us about. But neither the function of plot nor that of narration explains why such energy of invention, such profusion of detail, is lavished on the fortifications by the writer. In my own experience as a reader, the fortification passages, far from being excrescences, are an essential part of what is peculiarly fascinating about *Robinson Crusoe*, and the testimony of criticism suggests that many readers share this response. The testimony of criticism also suggests that there are different ways for accounting quite cogently for the power of the fortification scenes, with none precluding the others.

For a critic who assumes—plausibly enough—that the writer in the act of literary imagination taps certain primordial fears and desires in his own unconscious experience and engages readers by touching similar fears and desires in them, the ever thickening walls around the scooped-out cave would be a successfully enacted return to the womb—perfect envelopment, perfect concealment, no harm can befall you. Since, moreover, psychoanalysis allows for the strong possibility that any given fantasy may be overdetermined, a Freudian critic might also observe that the cave is a place of storage for Crusoe, and thus the fortifications are intimately bound with the pronounced psychological theme in the novel of anal retention: the hero is constantly accumulating more goods of every sort, constantly putting them away for some future contingency, and constantly multiplying the ramparts and bulwarks with which he seals off himself and his stored treasures from the intruding eye and the rapacious hand. An anthropologically inclined critic might note that Crusoe's construction of barrier after barrier is an enactment of the process of civilization as it is often represented by folklore, in which the founding human figure partitions himself off from feral surroundings, and, as is attested in the widest variety of folktales and archaic iconography, marks the civilizing moment of separation by juxtaposing the hewn tree, token of civilization (Crusoe's inner walls), and the green tree, token of natural origins (Crusoe's outer wall).[2]

Works of literature, however archetypal, also reflect particular moments in cultural or, indeed, economic, history, and *Robinson Crusoe* surely shows signs of its production by a member of the British mercantile class in the early eighteenth century, at a moment of confident expansion of the British Empire. Historically minded critics, Marxist and others, have abundantly commented on the nice correspondence between Crusoe's activities on the island and the dynamic of early capitalism. Defoe's castaway lives, with a vengeance, by a work ethic, for which the erection of fortifications serves as an important channel, and the multiple bulwarks beautifully concretize the ideal of the sacredness of private property to which Crusoe directs so much of his effort. Like a good capitalist, Crusoe watches his possessions multiply from the stock he has rescued from the shipwreck—tools, grain, dried fruit and meat, all manner of provision—and his proliferating palisades guarantee that all this will be his alone, touching us as readers two and a half centuries later because we still live in societies where private property is deemed inviolate. Coordinate with this informing capitalist idea is the recapitulation of colonialism in *Robinson Crusoe*. This is a process that becomes explicit when Crusoe discovers Friday, imposes his language and religion on the native, and makes him a loyal subordinate. The fortification, however, is a necessary first step in the process, for the colonizer must set up an impregnable base in the wilderness, turning his superior technology to advantage, before he can safely lay claim to the territory and subdue whatever of its population he may encounter.

The mesmerizing power of fortifications in Defoe's novel is far from exhaustively accounted for by such historical and archetypal explanations. Homer O. Brown, with an eye both to the writer's biography and to the way the novel engages issues of identity, reminds us that Defoe's narrators in general are obsessed with concealing themselves and that Defoe himself was haunted by the fear of imprisonment (among many occupations, he was a spy). Brown goes on to observe that Crusoe's fear of exposure is bound up with a seemingly contradictory fear, of what might happen if he stayed holed up and did not venture out into the open, something which in fact he is repeatedly driven to do. "Both fears are basically fears of engulfment: one, the fear of being lost in the recesses of one's own nature (the earth), fear of solipsism and anonymity; alternately, fear of being captured, 'eaten' by the other."[3]

Elizabeth Deeds Ermarth, avowing an indebtedness to Brown's reading, shrewdly brackets *Robinson Crusoe* with Richardson's *Pamela* as landmarks in the formative stage of English realism, pointing out that Pamela's obsession with protecting private space—the locked doors, the alcoves, the bedrooms, and, innermost, the maidenhead—is cognate with Crusoe's obsession. And since Ermarth defines realism as a new kinetic relation in narrative form between consciousness and time, she construes the motif of enclosure in these two early, only incipiently realist works as a "metaphor for life unmediated by time and consciousness." The great realist novels of the nineteenth century will find ways to create continuity between the individual and the community, between the discrete narrated moment and the flux of accumulated temporal experience, but these two early novels give us an ontology of individual consciousness grounded in radical isolation: "the enclosure or barricaded space denies the possibility of continuity and creates problems of access . . . suggests in spatial terms the presence of differences inaccessible to mediation."[4]

In another direction, Everett Zimmerman, perhaps inspired by the common insight of contemporary criticism into the ultimately self-reflexive nature of even the most realistic works, observes that "Crusoe's dogged collection of the unneeded corresponds to Defoe's cataloging of the irrelevant. . . . The enumerating, the organizing of oneself in verbal possessions, is the comfort, perhaps cold, of writer and character: the quantity of material collected by the one has its analogue in the language compiled by the other."[5] Zimmerman immediately links this instinct of collection with "the impulse to barricade oneself," and though he does not spell out the connection, it is clear that in order to collect, one needs barriers to protect the collection. (It is less evident what would be the equivalent in the writer's situation to Crusoe's palisades. The limits of sentence structure? The covers of the bound book?)

None of these readings gives much weight to the novel's urgent concern with personal salvation in explicitly Christian terms, an emphasis that has received much intelligent attention in the recent criticism of Defoe. Paul Alkon, for example, notes that Crusoe's experience of shipwreck marks "a movement away from historical time toward the encounter with private and sacred time on his island."[6]

If withdrawal from the world to the island is a necessary step for Crusoe's salvation, the circumvallation of his isolate abode is a withdrawal within a withdrawal. More specifically, it is a literal enactment, or a kind of typological realization, of the imagery of the biblical psalms that Crusoe reads, in which the providential God is repeatedly figured as a bulwark, a rampart, a high tower, a mighty fortress. Within the safety of his multiple barricades (see, for example, Psalm 48), Crusoe can con his battered Bible and feel that divine providence manifestly shelters him.

Other readings are possible, and, indeed, the rule of thumb for literary texts is that as a matter of principle other readings are always possible. But our sampling should suffice to illustrate the general inevitability of multiple readings. Each of the interpretations I have sketched out possesses a certain plausibility, though it goes without saying that no reader (including this one) will find them all equally plausible. The perplexing thing, in any case, is that one would be hard put to demonstrate that any one of these nine readings was actually wrong, or, on the contrary, that any one was so triumphantly right that it excluded the possibility of all the others. Such a situation might be anticipated in a work of literature that is obviously enigmatic or "difficult," like Kafka's *The Castle* or Mallarmé's *Hérodiade*, but *Robinson Crusoe*, after all, is on some level perfectly easy to understand —schoolchildren have read it for generations. The fact that literary texts by their nature generate multiple readings is not a function of their enigmatic character, though an enigmatic text is likely to encourage the proliferation of readings. We must say, rather, that all literary texts are composed of such heterogeneous elements and present, even in seeming simplicity, so many different faces to the world, that as they are scrutinized by different readers with different agendas, they are bound to yield reading after reading.

Defoe's novel appears to be a straightforward, linear narrative about a man who is cast up on an uninhabited island, goes to great lengths to build himself a secure dwelling, lives there amidst hardship and occasional danger for many years, and finally returns to his native England. But there are infinitely more things to look at in the book than this drastic summary suggests, more things than the awareness of any single reader is likely to contain. What *do* you look at in *Robinson Crusoe*? You could look at the account of Crusoe's origins and in particular his relationship with his father (something not done in any of the critical positions in my little catalog), and thus read all of the protagonist's actions as elements in an individual psychological portrait. You could look at the tone and perspective of the first-person narration. You could consider the kinds of syntactical structures Crusoe as narrator favors, his uses of metaphorical language, the nature of his habits of description. You could concentrate, as only our last reading does, on the repeated references to Christian faith and the allusions to the Bible. Noting the emphasis Defoe himself places on Crusoe's affiliations with the English mercantile class, you could read his sundry actions, including the fortifications, as class reflexes, or even as symbolic enactments of the project of mercantilism. Considering that the protagonist is impelled by adversity to recreate whatever he can of civilization in a desert place, you could scan the novel for all those details that seem to say something about the processes of civilization or that define the polarities of nature and culture. And, then, since the novel offers us a welter of details, many of them perhaps without great importance in themselves, every reader is faced with the question of which details to isolate as particularly significant, and which details to connect with each other as patterns of signification. Thus, Crusoe at the beginning imagines he is being swallowed up by the sea; on the island, he has recurrent fears of cannibals; in his trip across the Alps on the way home, he is surrounded by wolves. A reader attending to other features of the book may see no connection among these three details (the first a metaphor, the second an obsession, the third a fact of plot), or may feel they are not very important, but Homer O. Brown, on the trail of engulf-ment, links the three and invites us to view them as a key to a threatened sense of self at the heart of the novel.

The restless multiplicity of meanings and implications is engendered not merely by the numerical abundance of aspects that constitute the literary text but, more crucially, by the fact that many of these aspects belong to qualitatively different categories; because they are heterogeneous in rela-tion to each other, the ways a reader will link them are inherently unpredictable. A bare listing of some of the principal aspects of the text will suggest this heterogeneity: structure, style, diction, imagery, syntax, perspective, tone, allusion, repetition, convention, genre, segmentation, typog-raphy, characterization, motif, theme, extraliterary reference. Benjamin Hrushovski introduces order into this welter of possibilities by proposing that the literary text gives rise "to constructs on three interlaced and interdependent dimen-sions: (a) speakers, voices, and positions; (b) meanings, refer-ences, and frames of reference; (c) the organized text."[7] The last of these three categories embraces everything that Roman Jakobson conceives as the "poetic function"[8]—rhythm and other kinds of sound patterning, parallelism and apposition, formal divisions, and so forth. Of the critical readings we surveyed, that of Everett Zimmerman comes closest to looking at the organized text; more attention to the various aspects of text formation would no doubt produce still other readings. Hrushovski's middle category is where objects, ideas, human types, and experiences known from the world outside the text become the stuff of the text's fictional world—in the case of *Robinson Crusoe*, the Protestant doctrine of personal salvation, the King James Version of the Bible, English middle-class habits of prudence and hard work, the accumulation of possessions, carpentry tools and bags of seed, cannibals and pirates and wolves. It should be evident that the decisions of individual readers about meaningful configurations among all the items in the category of reference and meaning open up dizzying possibilities of proliferating readings. But when one adds that such decisions then must be interarticulated with a reader's perception of how the materials of reference and meaning are related to the role of the narrator and the organization of the text, the permutations of perception of the self-same text become virtually infinite.

The overall picture, however, is still more complicated. For this account of the text as a kinetic system of interacting heterogeneous elements leaves out the equally powerful permutational force of the different freight that each reader brings to the text. I have called this the reader's "agenda," succumbing to what may be too fashionable a term, for what is involved includes agenda but also often goes beyond it. An ideological critic, like our Marxist who sees in *Robinson Crusoe* a fable of the capitalist enterprise, manifestly has an agenda, which is in one way or another to uncover in this and other texts that history of exploitation which is the concentration of wealth in the hands of the entrepreneurial class. A general critical thesis and a context for comparison can also serve as an agenda. Thus, Elizabeth Deeds Ermarth is led to her reading of enclosure in *Crusoe* by her general definition of realism as a mediation between self and world and by her decision as a matter of literary history to bracket Defoe's novel with *Pamela*. Another critic working out a different thesis—say, about the centrality of the cataloging of material details in realist fiction—with different terms of comparison—perhaps, *Moby-Dick* or Balzac's *Lost Illusions*—would no doubt propose still another way of accounting for the inordinate attention to fortifications in *Crusoe*.

A reader's bias of selection, however, in sorting out and construing the mass of heterogeneous aspects of the text, is generally determined by more than a conscious intellectual project, owing something in varying degrees to his or her personal history, psychology, sensibility, education, belief system, and even mood. To this we must add, at least for all texts not produced by living writers, the intervention of history as a highly refractive medium. More than two and a half centuries stand between us and *Robinson Crusoe*. In literary history, that period encompasses a grand evolution of the novel that many critics trace back to Defoe, in one way necessarily altering the early text by fixing it as a point of origin. There have also been numerous imitations, parodies, polemic or admiring recreations of Defoe's novel, in which the gender, the number, the attitudes and aspirations, of the castaway have been emphatically changed. In the history of ideas, Marx, Freud, Jung, Wittgenstein, Saussure, Lévi-Strauss have made their appearance and become part of our context as readers, offering us a wealth of new questions to ask of the text and new ways to look at its strategies and details. Momentous geopolitical shifts have occurred: in the post-colonial era of the 1980s the wrongness of racism and colonialism is taken to be self-evident in most intellectual circles, but that would hardly have been the case a century ago, and so readers in our own time are likely to approach Defoe's novel with a suspicion of its implicit ideological premises that would not have been shared by many readers of the 1880s or earlier.

All that accumulates in the passage of time not only distorts texts but also sometimes illuminates them. On the

one hand, we are often confronted as readers with the
problem of sheer forgetting. The precise meanings of terms
and the implications of concepts current two or three centuries ago frequently elude us, and it is a traditional task of
literary scholarship to try to recover this lost verbal and
conceptual material. Even more seriously, conventions and
techniques, the operation of whole systems of literary communication, are sometimes forgotten or badly misperceived
in the succession of cultural eras, as happened to the fine
narrative art of the Hebrew Bible when Jews and Christians
variously directed their reading instead to legal, theological,
typological, and morally edifying ends. On the other hand, a
later literary text or system of thought or turn of history may
provide revelatory insight into an earlier text. There is no way
of knowing whether Kafka's gripping story "The Burrow" was
ultimately inspired by *Robinson Crusoe*, but in its more
extreme, more acutely anxious working-out of the fantasy of
protective enclosure in the form of an animal fable, it offers a
suggestive new context for reading Crusoe's novel. One need
not claim any absolute validity for the theories of Freud and
Marx to argue that certain of their ideas may heighten our
understanding of what compels attention in *Robinson Crusoe*.
Freud's grounding of the self in infantile fantasy and Marx's
explanation of history through economic motive are arguably
far too one-sided, but Defoe, with an imagination shadowed
by archaic anxieties and pervaded by the values of his class,
may have intuitively shaped his fictional materials in patterns
to which the thinking of both Freud and Marx is pertinent.

    At times, it seems almost a matter of luck whether the
historical location of readers will skew their relation to a given
text or provide them better access to it than their predecessors. Consider the fate of the Samson story over the centuries.
For most of the Christian era, it was read typologically as an
adumbration of the Christ story. Samson's mother, like Mary,
is vouchsafed by an angel an annunciation of the birth of a son

who is to play a role as savior of Israel. Samson's binding, blinding, and imprisonment by the Philistines foreshadow the arrest, torment, and mocking of Jesus by the Romans in the Passion narratives. Samson's self-inflicted death in bringing down the temple of Dagon looks forward to the crucifixion, an end willingly accepted by the Son of Man, and the triumph in death over the Philistines obliquely intimates the divine victory after seeming defeat represented by the resurrection.

There is a good deal of ingenuity in all this, but it is, to say the least, a peculiar way to read the ancient Hebrew story of a brawny wild-man hero who is a compulsive sexual adventurer, a trickster, a man bent on personal vengeance and personal gratification, who conjures not with spiritual mysteries but with riddles that seem to point toward the alluring and threatening enigma of female sexuality (sweeter than honey, stronger than a lion). Milton's *Samson Agonistes* is proof that a writer of genius, even in the full tide of typology, could be a brilliant reader of at least some aspects of the biblical tale, but the notion of Samson as a Christ figure remains far from the demonstrable emphases and even the wake of unconscious associations of the original story. Readers in our own century, on the other hand, enjoy a certain serendipity in coming to the text in Judges 13–16 with an awareness of *The Interpretation of Dreams* or later works by Freud. That is to say, the connection between castration and hair cutting, blinding, and loss of other parts of the head like teeth and nose, had not been clearly perceived until Freud's notion of "upward displacement" of sexual materials as a mechanism of inner censorship. One need not reduce the Samson story to a simple fantasy of castration anxiety in order to say that the Freudian idea offers a sharp new focus on some of the key elements of the narrative: the causal link between the shaving of the head and the loss of supernatural powers, the role of the seductive woman as instrument in the unmanning of the hero, the Philistines' decision to blind Samson rather than to kill him, the leapfrogging relation throughout the story between erotic adventure in alien territory and the exercise of devastating manly force. For all the reasons we reviewed above in regard to the multifaceted character of literary texts, the line of psychoanalytic interpretation I have just sketched out by no means accounts for everything that goes on in this intriguing story, but I would argue that some consideration of unconscious associations and unconscious image-making processes provides real illumination on this narrative sequence that, more than any other in the Hebrew Bible, is rooted in the folklore and folk imagination of the ancient Israelites.

For those who are persuaded, as I am, that the Freudian reading of Samson, whatever its limitations, brings us closer to the imaginative power of the story than the Christian typological reading does, it should be evident that there must be some grounds for discriminating between plausible interpretations and preposterous ones. We are able to make such a distinction above all because a work of literature is a highly articulated verbal construct, not a Rorschach blot onto which everyone can project his own fantasies, as one school of contemporary psychoanalytic criticism and at least a few of the more doctrinaire deconstructionists like to pretend. Although Samson's birth, like Jesus', is announced by an angel (because the early Christian writers were tying in to an annunciation type scene used a number of times in the Hebrew Bible), there is nothing Christlike about the hero in the words he speaks, the actions he performs, the settings in which he chooses to place himself. Since the story, after all, is made up of dialogue, narratorial report, plot episodes, motifs, repetitions of words and phrases, and parallelisms of incident, a reading that does visible violence to most of these formal articulations deserves to be judged a bad reading. A reader of *Robinson Crusoe* who saw the fortifications as an expression of the human love of beautiful artifice, Crusoe as architect erecting a lovely edifice in the rawness of the wilderness, would be wrong for the demonstrable reason that no aesthetic value is ever attached to the palisades in the text of the novel—on the contrary, the narrator's constant emphasis is that they are strictly utilitarian, an ever-thickening means of warding off real or imagined dangers. Beyond the evidence of the text, a reading may be disqualified on the ground of self-contradiction. Thus a linguistically-minded critic could not reasonably claim that Crusoe's enclosures represent the barrier of language humankind sets up between itself and the natural world not merely because there is nothing language-like in the novel's actual representation of the palisades but also because language, as a complex system of differences which make possible reference to entities outside the system, could scarcely be figured in an opaque barricade of stakes identical in length and appearance.

These last two hypothetical readings may seem too silly to invoke as possibilities, but in fact many of those who like to think of themselves as the vanguard of contemporary criticism appear unwilling to conceive a middle ground between the insistence on one authoritative reading and the allowing of all readings. Since much of this criticism is ideologically motivated, the ideological agenda itself is taken as sufficient warrant for any reading that will realize the ends of the ideology, however tenuous the connection with the actual details of the text under discussion. It may be instructive to look at an example of this exploitation of radical indeterminacy in the critical exposition of a literary text in order to understand why the principle of many readings does not mean any reading.

A vivid case in point is the interpretation of the story of Ruth in Mieke Bal's *Lethal Love: Feminist Literary Readings of Biblical Love Stories*. The subtitle by no means covers all the perspectives that Mieke Bal, a prolific Dutch literary scholar, brings to bear on her subject, for as she herself makes clear, the procedures she uses are feminist, psychoanalytic, semiotic, narratological, and, at least in some ways, decon-structive as well. She is certainly not a foolish reader, and, indeed, the book, intermittently, offers suggestive insights into a number of the stories, some of its proposals, inciden-tally, on the Samson cycle being especially intriguing. Bal explicitly touches on the issue of indeterminacy at several points, and spells out her understanding of it in a brief Afterword. "The point of literary analysis," she contends, "is that there is no truth," and she wants to make it perfectly clear that she has not sought to recover the "original meaning" of the stories because there is no such animal. "My readings present an alternative to other readings, not a 'correct,' let alone the 'only possible' interpretation of what the texts 'really say.' " All this is unexceptionable, certainly in the light of what we have observed about the interaction of different elements in the literary text compounded by the multiple interaction with the text of different readers and their sundry contexts. Bal goes on, however, to lay out her own notion of multiple readings in terms that may give one pause:

> Texts trigger readings; that is what they are, the occasion of a reaction. The feeling that there is a text in support of one's view makes texts such efficient ideological weapons. Every reading is different from, and in contact with, the text. . . . If one can easily disagree with my readings, if only because one does not share my interests, at least I will have raised possibilities that can make people think in their turn.[9]

It is of course true that texts trigger reactions, for they are there to be read, but to state flatly that a text is "the occasion of a reaction" is to fail to distinguish between works of literature and cloud formations, pollen, bee stings, changes of temperature. It is tautologically true that "Every reading is different from, and in contact with, the text," but that formulation does not register the possibility of wholly tenuous or downright absurd contact. A critic who attributed all of Hamlet's hesitations to the idea that the prince was actually a lesbian masquerading as a male would be "in contact with the text," because the focus of the discussion, after all, would still be Shakespeare's play and not the Manhattan telephone directory or the odes of Pindar; but one might question whether such contact would be of much use to other readers, even to raise possibilities that might make them think on their own. Finally Bal's language tends to suggest that most, or perhaps all, readings are ideologically determined, like her own. In her last sentence, despite the slight syntactical confusion of the successive if-clauses, one gathers that the chief reason she imagines for disagreement with her readings is a reader's not sharing her ideological interests. Let us turn to her treatment of Ruth and see if we may detect other grounds for rejection.

There are more intricacies to Mieke Bal's argument on Ruth than need detain us here, not to speak of certain notions that are merely inscrutable, like her claim that the story ultimately dissolves chronology or that it consists of a series of *mises-en-abyme*, or embedded reflections of its own structure. Her treatment of Boaz and his relationship with Ruth should suffice for our purposes. She begins with four lines from a poem by Victor Hugo, "Booz endormi" ("Boaz Asleep") in which the prosperous Judean farmer is represented with a long silvery beard. It is of course Hugo's privilege as poet to imagine Boaz any way he chooses, but for some unspecified reason Bal decides to regard the reading of this "metatext" (her favored term for Hugo's midrashic allusion) as an indispensable clue to what transpires in the story. Hugo's Boaz is old, and thus Bal's is as well, though the text itself gives not the slightest hint of his being either aged or white-bearded, beyond the bare fact that he is obviously Ruth's senior (in his thirties or forties?—one can only guess), addressing her as "my daughter." In any case, his energetic sallies into the fields during the harvesting, his alertness to the presence of a newcomer and to the activities of his retainers, hardly suggest senescence. In Hugo's treatment, one may infer that the aged Boaz is troubled by the threat of impotence, another notion for which the text offers no evidence, but which Bal, teasing out an argument about the relation between the sexes, makes central to her reading: with Hugo, she imagines that the plot turns on "Boaz's fear of old age, of losing his sexual potency and attractiveness." The sole textual warrant for this supposed drama of failing virility is the following verse, which Boaz speaks to Ruth after she comes to him as he lies sleeping on the threshing floor: "Blessed be thou of the Lord, my daughter: for thou hast shown more kindness [better: loyalty, steadfastness] in the latter end than at the beginning, inasmuch as thou followest not the young men, whether poor or rich" (3:10). The term for young men, *baḥurim*, in general refers to unmarried men already of the age for army service, twenty. Boaz is probably emphasizing status at least as much as age, they being the town's young single males, he an established householder. He is certainly praising Ruth for turning to him instead of to another man. It is at least possible to infer a pained consciousness of aging in Boaz's choice of this single term, but in the absence of the faintest indication of such a condition anywhere else in the story, this reading is tied to the text only by a thin fragile thread.

The thread is strained to the breaking point when Bal tries to buttress her argument for a reversal of sexual roles in the story ("Boaz . . . accepts being reflected, by the *mise-en-abyme*, in a female role"[10]) with lexical evidence. The words of the text afford us at least a narrow strip of solid ground in the quagmire of indeterminacy because the words a writer uses, despite the margin of ambiguity of some of them, have definite meanings, and no critic is free to invent meanings in order to sustain a reading. Bal's procedure is to state philological conjecture as established linguistic fact or to improvise meanings on unspecified grounds. Thus, she makes much of the irony in the fact that "Boaz's name means the powerful/potent."[11] Some scholars have in fact speculated that the name could have that meaning, but the derivation is problematic because *oz* is the word for strength and the initial consonant *b* does not in the least look like a prefix. The progenitor of the line of Boaz, mentioned in 4:18, is Pharez. Bal, noting that the name means "break," claims Pharez is "breaker of the rules" and "represents also the '*brèche vers une latence*' [breach toward a latency] of the cure."[12] Here, she has the meaning of the name more or less right, but the literary etymology is actually spelled out on the occasion of Pharez's birth in Genesis 38:29, and it has nothing to do with breaking rules: he is called Break or Burst because he burst out of the womb before his twin brother, who was about to be born first. If the narrator himself presents the name as a link in the great Genesis theme of sibling rivalry and the triumph of the younger over the elder, it is, at the very least, fanciful to push the meaning into rule-breaking, whether in psycho-analytic process or social institution. The linguistic evidence is telling. The Hebrew root of the name Pharez suggests bursting forth or rushing out, not violation or transgression of boundaries. It is chosen for its nice appropriateness to the biblical theme of reversing primogeniture, which is repeatedly rendered not as a breaking of rules but as the result of a struggle between formidable adversaries, the exertion of superior or unexpected force.

Things become far more problematic when Bal tells us about the meaning of ordinary verbs and nouns in the story. A key for her to the reversal of sex roles is the fact that Ruth is repeatedly the subject of the verb "to cleave" (Hebrew, *dabaq*), which, we are informed, "is exclusively used with a male subject, in reference to the matrimonial bond."[13] The sole evidence for this claim in the entire Hebrew Bible is the verse about conjugal unity after the creation of the first woman, in Genesis 2:24. But the verb *dabaq* is not in the least gender-bound. It refers regularly to any two substances, persons, spiritual entities sticking together, and it is freely used in cultic, medical, military, political, and personal contexts of all kinds. When Ruth uncovers Boaz's feet as he sleeps on the threshing floor, we are asked to imagine that she may be doing a good deal more than cooling his toes, for "the Hebrew word is ambiguous and also means 'testicles.' "[14] If there is such an ambiguity, it is certainly not evident in any of the recorded uses of the term in the Hebrew Bible. The particular grammatical form, in fact, of the root for "feet" used here is symmetrical with the form derived from "head" that is used in the story of Jacob's slumber at Bethel, and the two terms would seem to indicate the head and foot of the bed, or of the sleeper.

Beyond such misrepresentation of the meaning of terms, Bal forges the links of her reading with demonstrably false claims about social institutions, national entities, and even about what happens in the story. As the dénouement to her plot of reversed gender roles, the final scene is a "trial at the city gate, at the entrance to the female domain."[15] It is actually not a trial, but, more important, the gate of the city throughout the Hebrew Bible is the place where the *men* of the city sit to carry out the business of law, and by no stretch of the imagination, however archetypal, could it be construed in the ancient Near East as the entrance to the female domain. Moab, Ruth's homeland, is identified as "the country of promiscuity,"[16] a notion that will be news to any reader of the Book of Ruth, and that is scarcely intimated anywhere else in the Bible, which gives Moab bad press but does not single it out for promiscuity. Ruth, aligned by the genealogy at the end of Chapter 4 with Boaz's ancestress Tamar, must be, when she comes to Boaz in the night, "the veiled woman, unacknowledgeable, who is denied the status of inter-subjective subject by her sexual partner."[17] But quite unlike the veiled Tamar, who couples with her father-in-law by pretending to be a prostitute, Ruth clearly reveals her identity to Boaz, who far from denying her "the status of inter-subjective subject," treats her with respect and kindness both in this scene and in the harvesting scene that precedes it. Finally, the contention that patriarchal gender roles are subverted by the text is confirmed by a claim that the story ends with a "*lapsus* in the classical sense." That is, 4:17 states, "There is a son born to Naomi," when we would expect that expression to be reserved for the father. "Here again [i.e., as purportedly in "to cleave"] a word is 'inadvertently' attributed to a woman."[18] In this case, Bal is right about the term ("born" in the passive voice is generally attached to the father) but wrong about the textual data. Naomi is the woman who, as she says, has gone out from Bethlehem full and come back empty. It is she, not her dead husband Elimelech or Boaz, who urgently needs fulfillment in progeny. It is she who takes the newborn and places him in her bosom in a gesture of nurture and adoption. And since the words, "There is a son born to Naomi," come from the townswomen, the phrase is not in the least a "lapsus" but, given the facts of the narrative, the only thematically conceivable attribution that could be made. The author, quite deliberately, wants to stress not paternity but maternity at the end of the story.

Let us return for a moment to the question of ideology and reading. It is clear that Mieke Bal's ideological concerns as a feminist have led her to the reading she offers, as she herself avows. But one does not have to be an ideological adversary, as she comes close to proposing, in order to reject her reading. In fact, a sympathetic engagement with the condition of women in a male-ordered society might be worked out in Ruth in altogether different terms from those Bal proposes, as I intimated in my comment on the final attribution of the child to Naomi. We may enthusiastically concur in the proposition that there is never one "correct" reading of a literary text; but when a reader assigns arbitrary meanings to key words or names in the text, when he or she proposes implications of social institutions invoked in the text that they never had in their historical setting, and when details provided by the narrator or by the characters in their dialogue are ignored or misrepresented, we are entitled to conclude that the reading in question is wrong. A story or poem or play may mean many things, but in the words it uses and in the multifaceted information it provides us, it also gives us some grounds for identifying many things it cannot mean.

In fact, the capacity of literary texts, as intricately structured vehicles of communication, to stimulate many readings and exclude many others, is essential to what I called at the outset of this study the high fun of literature. It is "high" because, unlike, say, the fun of coming down a water slide or watching a clown get splattered in the face with a cream pie, it engages a good many of our most complicated faculties of perception—our nuanced knowledge of language, people, social institutions, politics, history, morality; our ability to grasp analogies, parallelisms, antitheses, significant repetitions, ellipses, ironies, double meanings, even crypto-grams. It is "fun" because of our response as readers to the beauty, the wit, the profuse inventiveness of the text's language (as we saw in the chapter on style) and of its constructed world (as we saw in the chapter on character). To translate this aesthetic response into cognitive terms, the high fun of reading is also the pleasure we take in the exercise of all those faculties of perception, our enlistment by the text as players in one of the most elaborate and various games that human culture has devised. The open-endedness of the text plays a key role in this pleasure because the reader is the recipient of a kind of communication that, unlike graffiti or bumper stickers or telegrams, offers a rich multiplicity of messages in which the mind may delight.

All this notwithstanding, I confess that my choice of terms is a little provocative. Is it fun to read *Oedipus Rex* or *Crime and Punishment*? In one important sense, I would say, yes. We may be haunted by these representations of hideous suffering, perhaps even react physiologically by reading with pounding temples and aching muscles. Nevertheless, the experience of the most empathetic reader remains altogether different in kind from that of a man who unwittingly kills his father and sleeps with his mother, or that of a wretched ex-student in a stifling tenement room maddened by his own blood-guilt. In even the darkest works of literature, suffering and despair are, in the sense of the term that antedates Freud, sublimated by their transformation into cadence and image and significant pattern. A great poem about the most horrendous subject, like Paul Celan's astounding "Death Fugue" on the mass murder of European Jewry, both lays bare the horror of its subject and lifts it into significant form that sets the trauma into multiple contexts of reference (in Celan's poem, Bach, German history, Jewish history, Goethe's *Faust*, the Song of Songs), as all literature does.

The Fool in *King Lear* is a small but instructive illustration of the link between the pleasure of reading (or watching) and the polyphonal character of literary expression. It is of course possible to talk about Shakespeare's use of fools in terms of Renaissance convention and literary history, but I would suggest that the particular kind of wild and scathing wit he unleashes through the Fool in *Lear* is also a realization of the peculiar logic of multifariousness that generally characterizes the literary imagination. On many different levels, good literature is the continual, apt discovery of the unexpected, and the presence of this zany juggler of seeming nonsequiturs at the heart of one of Western literature's greatest representations of existential anguish is, repeatedly, just such a discovery. Let me cite one small example. In Act I, Scene IV, when Lear has begun to feel the bite of cruelty in his two daughters' harshness toward him, Goneril enters as the Fool is discoursing to the self-deposed king, who comments on her frowning appearance:

> *Fool.* Thou wast a pretty fellow when thou hadst no need to care for her frowning; now thou art an O without a figure. I am better than thou art now; I am a fool, thou art nothing. [*To Gon.*] Yes, forsooth, I will hold my tongue; so your face bids me, though you say nothing. Mum, mum,
>
> > "He that keeps nor crust nor crumb,
> > Weary of all, shall want some."
>
> [*Pointing to Lear.*] That's a sheal'd peascod.
>
> (210–219)

Here and elsewhere the Fool's daring in his chastisement of the king is breathtaking. The scourge he wields in his words makes him seem almost like an externalization of self-knowledge repressed in Lear himself. The explosive relationship between the two bears witness to the power of literature to set into revelatory interplay such basic aspects of experience as self and other, consciousness and the unconscious, reason and unreason, intention and remorse. The chief internal reference in the Fool's speech here is obvious and has been abundantly observed by critics. The family tragedy begins when Cordelia responds with "Nothing" to Lear's request for a declaration of love, to which he objects, "Nothing will come of nothing." Now he himself is reduced to nothing, an idea the Fool vividly translates into mere ciphering—"an O without a figure." This piece of metaphoric arithmetic points toward the numerical reduction of Lear's retainers (100, 10, 0), and to his unthroned condition, no longer a figure that can give numerical value to a zero by standing before it. We may think again of the O without a figure when Lear, stripping naked on the storm-swept heath, sees in Poor Tom (a doubling of the Fool function) an image of "unaccommodated man . . . a bare forked animal." We may also contrast the grim silent speech of Goneril's frowning face with Cordelia's silent speech at the beginning, which her bombast-deafened father is unable to construe properly for what it is, love.

The incisive wit of the Fool's language, complicated by the multifarious connections it makes with other moments in the play, encourages us not to restrict the statement to a single register of meaning. Zero versus integer, nothing versus something, is an image of the hierarchy of power reversed (the mere Fool is more than the ex-king); an emblem of the pitiful human condition under the terrible aspect of eternity; an intimation of castration, as we shall see in a moment; a suggestion of the ambiguous tension between all the play's forms of speech—soaring poetry, mincing versified lies, pungent prose, nonsense—and silence ("you say nothing").

The Fool's language also calls attention, as is often the case in literary texts, to the linguistic medium and the formal mechanisms through which literature organizes language. The movement of his words has a certain look of free association while at the same time adhering to explicitly formal requirements. Having mentioned Goneril's silence, the Fool chants, "Mum, mum," the homey monosyllabic indication for keeping your mouth shut. This in turn sets up the rhyme for the doggerel couplet. Is the point of this piece of banal folk wisdom about saving one's resources its sheer pointlessness, its flaunted violation of reason, or does it allude indirectly to Lear's not having saved any power for himself? Does it refer in any way to the just-mentioned holding of one's tongue, perhaps as Cordelia has done and her sisters have not? The erratic leaping of the language does not allow us to settle in comfortably with a confident linear construal of what is going on.

The most abrupt jump in this passage occurs at the very end. After the lines about keeping crust and crumb, the Fool points at Lear and says, perplexingly, "That's a sheal'd peascod." Perhaps there is an associative trigger here in the contiguity of the larder items, crust and crumb, with the peascod. "Sheal'd" means empty. Using this metaphor for Lear, the Fool is no doubt reverting to the question of nothingness. The new image, however, rather explicitly suggests impotence, not only in the physical shape to which it refers but in its sound, for "peascod" (the older term that would later be replaced in usage by "peapod") sounds very much like a spoonerism for codpiece, which, if empty, would be a striking emblem of the king unmanned. In the clotted monosyllabic sequence of sheal'd-peas-cod, the words exhibit a disquieting inclination to tumble over one another and spill into nonsense. Might "sheal'd" be heard or construed as "shield," yielding an asyntactical chain of three nouns instead of a decipherable modifier followed by a compound noun? Language is laden with thematically portentous meanings and at the same time threatens to break down into meaninglessness, exposing its own material condition as a mere congeries of arbitrary sounds. In some respects, this is the double dance that the literary use of language always performs, often enough actually pointing, as do the Fool's words, toward the doubleness.

Let me suggest, with this example from *Lear* in mind, that it is very often possible to detect in literary texts a capacity to multiply and destabilize meanings through aesthetically pleasing patterns which we could call the Fool Principle. In drama, because voices, positions, and attitudes are generally split off into different characters, the Fool Principle is likely to be externalized in one or more of the personages, as happens in Shakespeare. In poetry and fiction, virtually any aspect or combination of aspects of the text— syntax, diction, imagery, repetition, the focusing on some odd detail—may turn up performing this function. The range of possibilities is dizzying, and might profitably be the subject of a study in its own right, but for our purposes, to illustrate the link between multifariousness and pleasure in the reading experience, a single last example will serve. In Nabokov's poignant comic novel *Pnin*, the hero himself might seem to be a prime candidate for the Fool Principle, figuring as one of the most spectacularly maladroit characters of modern fiction—myopic, habitually baffled by the American world into which he stumbles as a Russian emigré, hopelessly floundering with the mysteries of English idiom and pronunciation, repeatedly wounded by those who are more calculating and more selfishly assertive than he. What may be more instructive, especially for the purposes of illustrating a general literary dynamic, is to observe how the Fool Principle operates in the narrator's prose and in the sundry objects of attention Pnin encounters. At the end of the sixth section of Chapter Two, after Pnin has concluded a predictably unsatisfactory meeting with his ex-wife (she asks for more money and, as they part, expresses contempt for the brown suit he is wearing), he goes shuffling across the Waindell College campus, lost in troubled thought, until he is interrupted by an unexpected request:

> A squirrel under a tree had seen Pnin on the path. In one sinuous tendril-like movement, the intelligent animal climbed up to the brim of a drinking fountain and, as Pnin approached, thrust its oval face toward him with a rather coarse sputtering sound, its cheeks puffed out. Pnin understood and after some fumbling he found what had to be pressed for the necessary results. Eyeing him with contempt, the thirsty rodent forthwith began to sample the stocky sparkling pillar of water, and went on drinking for a considerable time. "She has fever, perhaps," thought Pnin, weeping quietly and freely, and all the time pressing the contraption down while trying not to meet the unpleasant eye fixed upon him. Its thirst quenched, the squirrel departed without the least sign of gratitude.[19]

Since fictional character, as we had occasion to observe earlier, deepens our understanding and our sense of engaged acquaintance through repeated revelation and revelatory repetition, the most obvious pleasure afforded by the passage is that it is so splendidly Pninian. The compulsively compassionate Pnin not only complies with the squirrel's request but, with no more warrant than the animal's thirst, concludes, "She has fever, perhaps" (English: "Maybe it's feverish"). The foreigner's mistake of using a (female) gendered pronoun instead of the neuter one has the effect of reinforcing the analogy we are likely to perceive in any case between Pnin's encounter with the squirrel and the immediately preceding encounter with his ex-wife: in both instances, he responds to an insistent demand for material aid and gets no thanks for his kindness. Analogy being a two-way street, we may be invited to superimpose this decidedly unpleasant squirrel—note the sequence of epithets: "squirrel," "intelligent animal," "thirsty rodent," and finally "squirrel" again—demanding its water (a bit improbably) in pantomime on the image of the haughty ex-wife demanding more child support.

Within its own circumference, the squirrel passage exhibits niceties of design and invention. The creature climbs to the brim of the drinking fountain in "one sinuous tendril-like movement," a finely precise adverbial phrase for the motion in question that simultaneously connects the squirrel with the tree under which it was first sitting ("tendril-like") and the path on which Pnin is walking ("sinuous"—from the Latin *sinus*, "bend"—being a familiar epithet for paths). The more striking mimetic device is Nabokov's use of the technique of defamiliarization of which he was past master. Nearsighted Pnin, native of a realm where no doubt drinking fountains are ordered differently, does not discriminate any actual lever or handle but "after some fumbling he found what had to be pressed for the necessary results." The ensuing jet of potable liquid, as though a surprising revelation to man and rodent alike, is represented as a kind of new object in the scene: "the stocky sparkling pillar of water." A reader may find pleasure in the inventiveness of the language, which is, after all, a freshness of perception as well. But here and throughout the novel, the resourceful defamiliarizing makes us feel that Pnin is a person continually surprised by the world, continually unable to get a grip on it with the prearranged tools of language, certainly not the English language. Like the Fool's "sheal'd peascod," words at once are startlingly expressive and dissolve into the arbitrariness of the formal systems in which they take part.

No passage, of course, can be isolated from the complex tissue of the work from which it is excised, and Pnin's squirrel exhibits the same sort of multifariousness of connections as the Fool's O without a figure. Squirrels, real, painted, and stuffed, past and present, abound in Nabokov's novel. Pnin, not consciously remembering the squirrel that presided over the nursery of his Russian childhood, sends his son Victor "a picture postcard representing the Gray Squirrel" which informs the boy that "squirrel" is derived from a Greek term that means "shadow-tail." Later, Pnin confesses to an emigré friend that whenever he is X-rayed, the doctors detect what they call "a shadow behind the heart," to which the friend rejoins, "Good title for a bad novel." In the tour-de-force rendering of a minor heart seizure early in Chapter One, the fainting Pnin slides back into a memory of the bed he slept in as a boy, by which there stood a painted screen "with pyrographic designs representing a bridle path felted with fallen leaves, a lily pond, an old man hunched up on a bench, and a squirrel holding a reddish object in its front paws."[20] When he comes out of his long swoon, which occurs as he sits on a stone bench, the first thing he sees is "A gray squirrel sitting on comfortable haunches on the ground before him . . . sampling a peach stone."[21] This is a vivid instance of Nabokov's famous—or for some readers, notorious—ingenuity. The painted squirrel on the screen in Petersburg steps out onto a park path in North America four decades later, revealing the hand of the artificer who has made a verisimilar fictional world that actually traces an elegant arabesque of cunning design. The ingenuity can scarcely be gainsaid, but it may be more useful to emphasize instead the effect of semantic multiplicity in the repetition of the motif. There is, for example, something spooky in the idea that the painted screen should turn retroactively into a prophetic representation, down to the image of an old man hunched up on a bench. Elsewhere, Pnin, through a somersault of etymology, connects squirrel fur with Cinderella's slippers, leading us to muse as to whether in some grotesque and touching way he might not be a kind of male Cinderella, suffering from the cruelty of a world of stepsisters, eternally awaiting the advent of a fairy god-mother. At the water fountain, the squirrel reminds us of the harsh ex-wife, Liza. In the seizure passage, it is associated with childhood, memory, and death. In its overlap as "shadow-tail" with the "shadow behind the heart," it is fate, and perhaps also an intimation of artistic representation, a shadow image of the thing itself, appearing in the novel first as a painted design and then as a living animal and later as a picture on a postcard.

In all this, the literary high fun of the squirrel is not that it serves as the half-hidden key to an elaborate code (for which, of course, Nabokov had a well-known fondness) but, on the contrary, because it sets our minds spiraling with swarming prospects of meaning and connection. The ultimate paradox of the language of literature is that it is at once centripetal and centrifugal. In a great many works of litera-ture, it seems as though everything is powerfully pulled toward an imaginative center. One token of that pull is what I called earlier the mnemonic force of the literary text: things are not forgotten as we read, even if their effect is sub-liminal—a phrase, a key word, a rhetorical pattern, an image, a fictional gesture or event interlaces with all that resembles it at other points in the text, generating an order of cohesion not encountered in extraliterary language. Even works that manifestly defy order conform to this rule, as the zany, sexually-punning digressiveness of *Tristram Shandy* produces an imaginatively consistent world that, unlike our own, is ontologically constituted by such digressiveness in the most cohesive way (in this extreme instance, the Fool Principle may be seen in the underlying articulation of the text, its rhetoric and narrative technique). At the same time, the language of literature is centrifugal because, except in the dullest schematic works, it is never possible to specify definitively what the center of the text is or what it means. This impossibility is dictated by the very multifariousness of the text that we have been contemplating: too many heterogeneous elements come together, and in their coming together, too many disparate realms of experience are invoked, to be contained in a single interpretive definition. *Lear*'s "nothings" send out widening circles of implication, like a pebble thrown in a pond, though there are also limits on where the circles may touch: "nothing" in *Lear*, for example, cannot suggest the divine Nothingness of the Kabbalah not only because Shakespeare was ignorant of it but also because the specific associations attached to the idea by the language of the play make any such theosophic link absurd.

To state this paradox in other terms, the lovely tension between structure and openness is one of the distinctive, abiding pleasures of the experience of reading imaginative literature. If the text were only openness, we could say whatever we wanted about it, and we would end up, tediously, talking only about ourselves, as certain contemporary critics are inclined to do. If the text were only defined and definable structure, every work of literature would soon reach a saturation point in the readings it could sustain. This, indeed, is what a good many critics seem to have concluded in the past two decades—as in the slogan "How many more interpretations of *Middlemarch* can anyone write?" Such despair has variously led to the rejection of interpretation, to ignoring all textual restraints to interpretation, and to the directing of criticism to issues at one or two removes from any literary text. There are, of course, certain identifications, certain descriptive observations, about particular texts that, once made, need not be made again. Once a critic has noted the prominence in *Middlemarch* of imagery drawn from optics, the "discovery" is no longer there for another critic to claim. What remains, however, is the essential, unending business of what to make of the observation, whether and how to connect it with George Eliot's biography, her self-awareness as a woman, her thematic concerns, her descriptive technique, her diction, nineteenth-century science, the tradition of the novel before her, and much, much else.

Reading is a privileged pleasure because each of us enjoys it, quite complexly, in ways not replicable by anyone else. But there is enough structured common ground in the text itself so that we can talk to each other, even sometimes persuade each other, about what we read; and that many-voiced conversation, with which, thankfully, we shall never have done, is one of the most gratifying responses to literary creation, second only to reading itself.

Notes

INTRODUCTION: *The Disappearance of Reading*

1. Luc Ferry and Alain Renaut, *La pensée 68* (Paris, 1985).

CHAPTER ONE: *The Difference of Literature*

1. Terry Eagleton, *Literary Theory* (Minneapolis, 1983), p. 11.
2. The translation is the King James Version, but I have silently emended several small inaccuracies.
3. Wolfgang Iser, in *The Act of Reading* (Baltimore, 1978), provides a valuable theoretical model for the interaction between literary text and reader. I am in sympathy with his aims, though I have some reservations about both his terminology and his conceptual framework, and will use neither in what follows.
4. Roger Fowler, *Linguistic Criticism* (Oxford, 1986), p. 26.
5. Fowler, p. 50.
6. For a particularly interesting discussion of the world built by the text, see Benjamin Hrushovski, "Fictionality and Fields of Reference," *Poetics Today* 5:2 (1984), 222–251. Using semiotic terms, Hrushovski refers to the world as the "internal field of reference." He also offers a concise argument against what he calls "the semiotic reduction" that levels the difference between literary and nonliterary texts. See especially pp. 239–242.

7. A. R. Ammons, "A Poem Is a Walk," *Epoch* 18 (1968), p. 115.

8. *The Poetry of Robert Frost,* edited by E. C. Lathem (New York, 1979), p. 250.

9. On the linguistic concept of cohesion, see M. A. K. Halliday and Ruquiya Hasan, *Cohesion in English* (London, 1976).

CHAPTER TWO: *Character and the Connection with Reality*

1. Denis Donoghue, "The Limits of Language," *The New Republic,* July 7, 1986, pp. 40–45.

2. I have discussed this issue in *Don Quixote* at length in *Partial Magic: The Novel as a Self-Conscious Genre* (Berkeley and Los Angeles, 1975), Chapter 1.

3. For an incisive critique of this general trend, see Hugh Bredin, "The Displacement of Character in Narrative Theory," *British Journal of Aesthetics,* Autumn 1982.

4. Hélène Cixous, "The Character of 'Character,' " *New Literary History* 5 (1974).

5. Tzvetan Todorov, *The Poetics of Prose,* trans. Richard Howard (Ithaca, 1977), p. 82. In fairness to Todorov, it should be said that by the 1980s he renounced many of these early extremist views.

6. A. D. Nuttall, *A New Mimesis: Shakespeare and the Representation of Reality* (London, 1983), p. 53.

7. Baruch Hochman, *Character in Literature* (Ithaca, 1985), p. 50.

8. E. M. Forster, *Aspects of the Novel* (New York, 1927), p. 78.

9. Hochman, p. 46.

10. Nuttall, p. 75.

11. Balzac, *Splendeurs et misères des courtisanes,* ed. Pierre Barberis (Paris, 1973), pp. 431– 436 (my translation).

12. W. J. Harvey, *Character in the Novel* (Ithaca, 1968), p. 187.

13. I have introduced small emendations into the King James Version for the sake of accuracy.

CHAPTER THREE: *Style*

1. Denis Donoghue, *Ferocious Alphabets* (Boston, 1981), p. 51.

2. James Boswell, *Life of Johnson* (New York, 1953), p. 876 (23 September, 1777).

3. Boswell, p. 319 (26 July 1763).

4. Johnson, "Preface to Shakespeare," in *The Oxford Authors: Samuel Johnson,* ed. Donald Greene (New York, 1984), pp. 421–422.

5. Dorothy Van Ghent, *The English Novel: Form and Function* (New York, 1953), p. 130.

6. Barbara Cartland, *Royal Punishment* (New York, 1985), p. 164.

CHAPTER FOUR: *Allusion*

1. Ziva Ben-Porat, "The Poetics of Literary Allusion," *PTL* I:1 (January 1976), 107–108.

2. For an intelligent general statement on "intertextuality" that illustrates some of the weaknesses of its semiotic bias, see Laurent Jenny, "The Strategy of Form," in *French Literary Theory Today*, ed. Tzvetan Todorov (Cambridge, 1982), pp. 34–63. In the mechanistic metaphor endemic to Structuralist thinking, allusion becomes "intertextual processing," an activity said to occur even when nothing more than general conventions or nonliterary forms of speech are invoked in a literary text.

3. John Hollander, *Melodious Guile* (New Haven, 1988), p. 56.

4. Virginia Woolf, *Mrs. Dalloway* (New York, 1925), p. 13.

5. *Mrs. Dalloway*, p. 23.

6. Alfred Appel, Jr., provides a witty and wonderfully informative guide to literary allusions and other obscure references in *The Annotated Lolita* (New York, 1970). For his comments on Poe, see pp. 330–333.

7. Again, I have corrected the more egregious misconstruals of the King James Version.

CHAPTER FIVE: *Structure*

1. Tzvetan Todorov, "Poétique," in *Qu'est-ce que le structuralisme?*, ed. O. Ducrot (Paris, 1968), p. 102.

2. William Carlos Williams, *The Collected Later Poems* (Norfolk, 1963), p. 11.

3. John Crowe Ransom, *Selected Poems* (New York, 1978), p. 9.

4. *The Poems of Emily Dickinson*, ed. T. H. Johnson (Cambridge, Mass., 1955), vol. 1, p. 272.

5. I have analyzed this story in detail in *The Art of Biblical Narrative* (New York, 1981), pp. 107–113.

6. This distinction corresponds approximately to Joseph Frank's seminal notion of spatial form first articulated in his "Spatial Form in Modern Literature," *The Widening Gyre* (New Brunswick, 1963), pp. 3–62.

7. William Faulkner, *The Sound and the Fury* (New York, 1929), p. 331.

8. Ford Madox Ford, *The Good Soldier* (New York, 1951), pp. 151, 155.

CHAPTER SIX: *Perspective*

1. Seymour Chatman, "Characters and Narrators," *Poetics Today* 7:2 (1986), 189–204.

2. Gérard Genette, *Nouveau discours du récit* (Paris, 1983), p. 68.

3. Since it is a real convenience to have an adjective that means "pertaining to the characters, or fictional figures," I borrow the term "figural" from Dorrit Cohn's admirable study, *Transparent Minds: Narrative Modes for Presenting Consciousness in Fiction* (Princeton, 1978). Later in the chapter I enlist two other terms of hers, "narrated monologue" and "psycho-narration," explaining their meaning in the body of the text.

4. The point about *hineh* as a shifter into figural point of view has been made by J. P. Fokkelman, *Narrative Art in Genesis* (Assen and Amsterdam, 1975), pp. 50–51.

5. Virgil, *The Aeneid*, trans. C. H. Sisson (Manchester, 1986), p. 111.

6. Walter Benjamin, *Illuminations*, trans. Harry Zohn (New York, 1968), p. 87.

7. Antoine-François Prévost, *Histoire du chevalier des Grieux et de Manon Lescaut* (Paris, 1967), p. 59 (my translation).

8. Madame de Lafayette, *La Princesse de Clèves* (Paris, 1966), p. 53 (my translation).

9. Leo Tolstoy, *Anna Karenina*, trans. Constance Garnett, revised by Leonard J. Kent and Nina Berberova (New York, 1965), pp. 82–83.

10. Joseph Conrad, *The Secret Agent* (Garden City, New York, 1953), p. 214.

11. *The Secret Agent*, pp. 24–25.

CHAPTER SEVEN: *Multiple Readings and the Bog of Indeterminacy*

1. Daniel Defoe, *Robinson Crusoe*, ed. Michael Shinagel (New York, 1975), p. 127.

2. For an intriguing account of the motif of the two trees in folklore, see David Bynum, *The Daemon in the Wood* (Cambridge, Mass., 1978).

3. Homer O. Brown, "The Displaced Self in the Novels of Daniel Defoe," *E.L.H.* 38:4 (December 1971), p. 569.

4. Elizabeth Deeds Ermarth, *Realism and Consensus in the English Novel* (Princeton, 1983), p. 123.

5. Everett Zimmerman, *Defoe and the Novel* (Berkeley and Los Angeles, 1975), p. 30.

6. Paul Alkon, *Defoe and Fictional Time* (Athens, Georgia, 1979), p. 64.

7. Benjamin Hrushovski, unpublished prospectus for *Poetics of Poetry*, a work in progress.

8. Roman Jakobson, "Linguistics and Poetics," in *Style in Language*, ed. T. E. Sebeck (Boston, 1960).

9. Mieke Bal, *Lethal Love: Feminist Literary Readings of Biblical Love Stories* (Bloomington and Indianapolis, 1987), p. 132.

10. Bal, p. 87.

11. Bal, p. 75.

12. Bal, p. 86.

13. Bal, p. 72.

14. Bal, p. 70.

15. Bal, p. 83.

16. Bal, p. 81.

17. Bal, p. 86.

18. Bal, p. 83.

19. Vladimir Nabokov, *Pnin* (Garden City, New York, 1957), p. 58.

20. Nabokov, p. 23.

21. Nabokov, pp. 24–25.

Index

About the Author

Robert Alter is Professor of Hebrew and Comparative Literature at the University of California at Berkeley. His work as
a critic has concentrated on the novel, with volumes devoted
to Fielding and Stendhal and a broad study of the novel from
Cervantes to Nabokov, and has also included a foray into the
literary analysis of the Bible. His essays and reviews have
appeared in *Commentary*, *The New Republic*, *The New York
Times Book Review*, *The Times Literary Supplement*, and
other journals.